A Guide to the Practice of
Church Music

A Guide to the Practice of
Church Music

Marion J. Hatchett

 CHURCH PUBLISHING
New York

Preface

At the request of the Standing Commission on Church Music this author prepared A MANUAL FOR CLERGY AND CHURCH MUSICIANS. His manuscript was reviewed and edited and accepted by the Commission as the consensus of its members. It became available in published form in January 1981. By the time that the manual came into print THE BOOK OF OCCASIONAL SERVICES had been approved by General Convention and published. Since that time THE HYMNAL 1982 has been approved by Convention and published, and various supplemental music resources and the first eight volumes of the Church Hymnal Corporation's HYMNAL STUDIES series have become available. The publication of THE HYMNAL 1982 and of supplementary resources necessitated extensive revision of the original text. The publication of THE BOOK OF OCCASIONAL SERVICES called for substantial expansion of the text and for the provision of a number of additional check lists for planning the services provided in that book.

In addition to revisions and additions called for by the availability of these new works, the text and the check lists for planning services have been substantially revised for the purpose of clarification. Check lists have been added for "Rite III" Eucharist, Marriage, and Burial. Two new Appendixes have been added: APPENDIX I: Descants, Fauxbourdons, Varied Harmonizations, Varied Accompaniments, Suggested Alternative Treatments of Hymns, and Hymns Scored for Other Instruments in THE HYMNAL 1982, and APPENDIX II: Metrical Index of Tunes in THE HYMNAL 1982 with the First Lines of the Texts. It is hoped that these revisions and additions will make the book more useful than its predecessor and that the new format will prove more convenient.

Marion J. Hatchett

Contents

Appendix I: Descants, Fauxbourdons, Varied Harmonizations, Varied Accompaniments, Suggested Alternative Treatments of Hymns, and Hymns Scored for Other Instruments in THE HYMNAL 1982

Appendix II: Metrical Index of Tunes in THE HYMNAL 1982 with the First Lines of the Texts

Appendix III: Check Lists for Planning Services

Abbreviations

The following are abbreviations used in the text for publications of The Church Hymnal Corporation referred to with great frequency in the text:

Acc. Ed. Vol. 1	The Hymnal 1982 Service Music Accompaniment Edition Volume 1
Acc. Ed. Vol. 2	The Hymnal 1982 Hymns Accompaniment Edition Volume 2
BCP	The Book of Common Prayer
BOS	The Book of Occasional Services, Second Edition
GPAVT	Gradual Psalms, Alleluia Verses and Tracts
HEAE	The Holy Eucharist: Altar Edition (the bound edition or the loose-leaf edition with its supplement, Proper Liturgies for Special Days)
HYMNAL STUDIES FIVE	Hymnal Studies Five: A Liturgical Index to The Hymnal 1982
HYMNAL STUDIES SEVEN	Hymnal Studies Seven: An Organist's Guide to Resources for The Hymnal 1982
MMC	Music for Ministers and Congregation

Introduction

Role of Music in the Church

From the early days of the Church, music has been integral to the worship of God. Music gives solemnity, beauty, joy, and enthusiasm to the worship of the community. It imparts a sense of unity and sets an appropriate tone for a particular celebration. It is an effective evangelistic tool. It nourishes and strengthens faith and assists worshipers in expressing and sharing their faith. It heightens texts so that they speak more fully and more cogently. It highlights the basic structure of the rites. It expresses and communicates feelings and meanings which cannot be put into words. As Messiaen expressed it, "The joy of music is that it can go beyond words — which are too precise. Music can express what there is in the soul."* Music however must not dominate the liturgy; all elements of liturgy must work in harmony. Music, and the other arts, including speech, serve together in the liturgical action.

Music is not necessarily helpful in a service. It can, in fact, be destructive of a rite. This is the case when music is used for its own sake or only as a demonstration of the virtuosity of the performers, when it is beyond the abilities of the performers, when it interferes with the basic movement of the rite, when it gives undue prominence to secondary elements in a rite, or when the mood is out of keeping with the day or occasion.

Music should serve to set a tone, to convey texts, to highlight basic structures, to unify the congregation, to express the highest possible excellence. An appreciation of the proper relation of music and of other arts to the liturgy must be sought and developed if the Church is to resume a major role as patron of the arts.

The Canon: Of the Music of the Church

It is imperative for clergy, musicians — in fact, for all liturgical planners — to "read, mark, learn, and inwardly digest" the present canon of the music of the Church.

Title II, Canon 6, Of the Music of the Church, Section I, reads:

---

*NEWSWEEK, *November 23, 1970, page 139*

It shall be the duty of every Minister to see that music is used as an offering for the glory of God and a help to the people in their worship in accordance with The Book of Common Prayer and as authorized by the Rubrics or by the General Convention of this Church. To this end the Minister shall have final authority in the administration of matters pertaining to music. In fulfilling this responsibility the Minister shall seek assistance from persons skilled in music. Together they shall see that music is appropriate to the context in which it is used.

These last two sentences date from the General Convention of 1976, replacing these lines:

To this end he [the Minister] shall be the final authority in the administration of matters pertaining to music, with such assistance as he may see fit to employ from persons skilled in music. It shall be his duty to suppress all light and unseemly music and all irreverence in the rendition thereof.

Provisions for Music in the Prayer Book

The emphasis on music is heightened in the new edition of THE BOOK OF COMMON PRAYER. Much that had been assumed is now verbalized. Music has a larger place in many of the rites. Specific directions appear for its use in many situations not dealt with in general directions or in the rubrics of previous editions of THE BOOK OF COMMON PRAYER.

In the section "Concerning the Service of the Church" (pp. 13–14) four paragraphs deal with general directions concerning music:

Hymns referred to in the rubrics of this Book are to be understood as those authorized by this Church. The words of anthems are to be from Holy Scripture, or from this Book, or from texts congruent with them.

On occasion, and as appropriate, instrumental music may be substituted for a hymn or anthem.

Where rubrics indicate that a part of a service is to be "said," it must be understood to include "or sung," and vice versa.

When it is desired to use music composed for them, previously authorized liturgical texts may be used in place of the corresponding texts in this Book.

It is important to note that these paragraphs take the place of a rubric included in the 1892 and 1928 editions:

Hymns set forth and allowed by the authority of this Church, and Anthems in the words of Holy Scripture or of The Book of Common Prayer, may be sung before and after any Office in this Book, and also before and after sermons.

The texts of anthems are no longer limited to words of Holy Scripture or THE BOOK OF COMMON PRAYER; "texts congruent with them" may also be used. The general permission to utilize hymns or anthems before and after any rite or sermon has been withdrawn. Such uses are often antithetical to the text of the rites (for example, a hymn prior to the Opening Preces of Morning Prayer ["Lord, open our lips"] or after the Dismissal at the Eucharist ["Go in peace. . . . ."]). Hymnody should not interrupt the movement from the Readings to the sermon or from the sermon to the Creed or Prayers. In its rubrics for individual rites or in the directions appended to the rites, this new edition of the Prayer Book designates points for appropriate use of hymns or anthems.

The word "hymn" as used in the rubrics of the Prayer Book refers to a congregational song whose text is currently authorized. "Hymn" is used consistently in the rubrics of the Daily Offices, the pastoral Offices, the episcopal services, and the Holy Eucharist: Rite One and Rite Two. In An Order for Celebrating the Holy Eucharist (pp. 400–401), however, the more inclusive word "song" appears. The text of a "song" need not have current authorization. The word "anthem" in the rubrics refers to music sung by the choir rather than by the congregation.

This is the first edition of THE BOOK OF COMMON PRAYER to mention the use of instrumental music in the rites. It explicitly suggests instrumental music as an alternative to a hymn, psalm, or anthem at the entrance and exit of a wedding party (pp. 423 and 432) and during the procession and after the dedication of a musical instrument in the rite for the Consecration of a Church (pp. 567 and 572). "On occasion, and as appropriate" instrumental music may be substituted for a hymn or anthem in other rites.

THE BOOK OF COMMON PRAYER gives general permission either to say or sing any text. There is no historic basis for the late Victorian idea that it is only proper to say certain texts and to sing others. In the Eastern Church and in the medieval "high mass" the entire text heard by the people was sung. Merbecke's BOOKE OF COMMON PRAIER NOTED (1550) provided music or musical directions for almost the whole text of the Eucharistic rite, including the Prayer for the Church and the Eucharistic Prayer. The acoustics of the building, the ability of the various participants, the taste of the congregation, and the relative importance of the day or occasion, rather than any canons of proper procedure, should determine what is said and what sung.

The last of the general musical directions gives explicit permission, when using music composed for them, to use previously authorized liturgical texts in place of the corresponding texts of the current BOOK OF COMMON PRAYER. Since 1789 the American texts of the Te Deum laudamus and the Benedicite, omnia opera Domini have been different from those in the English Prayer Books. On occasion it may be desirable to use music composed for the English versions of these canticles. It may also, at times, be advantageous to use earlier versions of various other forms, especially when the earlier version is in the hands of the congregation or when the music cannot be adapted easily to the revised text.

Uses of Silence

Prior editions of THE BOOK OF COMMON PRAYER specifically directed silence at only one point, in the ordination of a priest. The new edition suggests silence at many other points including: after the Readings, before General Confessions, immediately before the Collect of the rite, during the Breaking of the Bread. Silence is creative and has its own validity. Silences allow for recollection (as before Confessions or Collects) or for reflection (as after the Readings and during the Breaking of the Bread). Additional silences would often be appropriate, for example, before and/or after the sermon and prior to the Eucharistic Prayer or the postcommunion prayer. Actions do not always need musical accompaniment. THE BOOK OF COMMON PRAYER explicitly directs that the Bread be broken in silence. The organist must resist the temptation to fill every silence with sound. An improvisation is often unneeded between prelude and entrance hymn or between Offertory anthem and Sursum Corda; a period of silence is often much more effective. Until a congregation becomes accustomed to silence and does not interpret it as a missed cue, periods of silence should be noted in the service sheet. The liturgical planners in a congregation should assume an active role in teaching the meaning and uses of silence.

Part One:

Musical Ministries

In all services, the entire Christian assembly participates in such a way that the members of each order within the Church, lay persons, bishops, priests, and deacons, fulfill the functions proper to their respective orders, as set forth in the rubrical directions for each service.

This principle, set forth in the section, "Concerning the Service of the Church" (p. 13), of THE BOOK OF COMMON PRAYER, is true for the music as well as for the other aspects of the worship of the Church. The Church's tradition, and the rubrics of the new edition indicate that certain functions belong to lay persons, others to bishops, others to priests, and others to deacons. Furthermore, by tradition (and frequently by rubric) certain musical portions of the rites are reserved for the people. Other musical elements of the rite are properly performed by choirs, by cantors, or by instrumentalists. (See Acc. Ed. Vol. 1, pages 11–17.)

The Musical Ministry of the People

The Songs of the People

The rubrics of THE BOOK OF COMMON PRAYER are true to tradition in reserving for the people the responses to the Opening Acclamation, the Salutation, the acclamations at the beginnings and endings of Lessons, responses in the Prayers of the People, the response to the Peace, responses in the introductory dialogue of the Eucharistic Prayer, and the response to the Dismissal. The Amen, wherever it occurs, belongs to the people. The Kyrie and the Trisagion are songs of the people. The Sanctus and Benedictus qui venit, the Memorial Acclamation, and the Lord's Prayer are songs which the people sing along with the celebrant. The word *hymn* is used in the rubrics to indicate a metrical song of the people. In other rites, as well as in the Eucharist, certain portions are reserved for the people as, for example, the responses to the Opening Preces and the Suffrages in the Daily Office. The Apostles' Creed and the Lord's Prayer are songs which the people and celebrant sing together. It is highly inappropriate for these portions of the rite to be preempted by a choir. These portions belong to the people; unless the congregation can sing them easily, they should say them. Music too complicated for the congregation should not be used for these portions of the rites. A church music director desiring to perform a more complicated setting of one of these texts (for example, the *Sanctus*) should do so either at a time within the service appropriate for an anthem or at a concert. In early Anglicanism the more elaborate settings of the Sanctus were used, not within the Eucharistic Prayer, but rather as an introit for the rite. Often the Sanctus within the Prayer was said or sung to a simple setting, so important was congregational participation in the historic songs of the people. (Compare the elaborate music for the celebrant's portion of the Eucharistic Prayer from the ancient Mozarabic rite provided in the Altar Book for use with Prayer D with the simple setting of the people's Holy, holy, holy / Holy, holy, holy Lord [*Sanctus*] at S 123.)

In addition to those portions of the rites reserved to the people, traditionally the congregation sings hymns or canticles as a part of the entrance rite; the response in the Gradual Psalm (or the Psalm itself); the Alleluia, Psalm or Sequence hymn prior to the announcement of the Gospel; the Nicene Creed; the Fraction Anthem; and possibly hymns or psalms during the preparation of the Table, during the Communion of the People, and before or after the postcommunion prayer. In the Daily Office it is traditional for the people to sing the Invitatory Psalm, the Psalmody of the Day, and the Canticles, or to sing antiphons when a cantor or choir sings the aforementioned portions of the rite.

The Function of the Songs of the People

The aim of the songs of the people is that "full, conscious, and active participation ... demanded by the very nature of the liturgy" (*The Constitution on the Sacred Liturgy*, 14).

Though music may add solemnity, effectiveness, beauty, enjoyment, and unity to a celebration, that is not always true. It is not always better to sing than to say; silence is to be preferred at times to sound. It is essential to consider the particular gathering of people, the size of the group, their traditions, their musical abilities, the available musical leadership, the architectural setting, and the relative importance of the day or occasion. Also important are the predominant age group, the degree of experience with a particular service, and the musical interest of the particular gathering. The music must not dominate the rite but instead highlight its basic structure.

The Musical Ministry of the Cantor, Song Leader, or Clerk

The Functions of the Cantor

A fourth century practice still maintained in large portions of the Church today is to have a soloist sing the Gradual Psalm, the Alleluia Verse at the Eucharist, and the Invitatory Psalm (Venite or Jubilate Deo) at the Daily Office. In the Gradual Psalm the cantor sings first a refrain enunciating the theme of the Psalm or setting forth its application to the day or occasion. The choir and congregation then repeat the refrain and sing it at subsequent appropriate intervals throughout the Psalm. (See GPAVT.)

The cantor initiates the Gospel Acclamation by singing the Alleluia(s) which is then repeated by the choir and congregation. The cantor then sings the Verse, after which the choir and congregation repeat the Alleluia(s). (See GPAVT.)

Several of the Fraction Anthems in THE HYMNAL 1982 are designed to be sung in this manner (S 151 and S 167–S 172).

The Invitatory Psalm at the Daily Office may be treated in the same manner as the Gradual Psalm, making use of the Invitatory Antiphons as refrains. (Acc. Ed. Vol. 1, S 289–S 294.)

In addition to the Gradual, the Alleluia, the Fraction Anthem, and the Invitatory Psalm, other psalms (See THE PLAINSONG PSALTER) or hymns with refrains may be very effective if sung by a cantor, with congregational refrains, at the entrance of the ministers, during the Offertory procession or during the Communion of the People. Sometimes a cantor can effectively initiate the Memorial Acclamation, the Fraction Anthem, or even the the Holy, holy, holy / Holy, holy, holy Lord (Sanctus) and Blessed is he (Benedictus qui venit). With shorter texts, such as Lord, have mercy upon us / Lord, have mercy (Kyrie), Kyrie eleison, Holy God (Trisagion), the Memorial Acclamation, or the Fraction Anthem, it is often effective for the cantor to sing the whole text or a section of it after which the celebrant, the choir, and the people repeat it. In fact there are explicit directions to sing one setting of the Lord, have mercy (Kyrie) in exactly this manner (S 95). (See also S 85, S 88, and S 94.)

By singing new music as a solo on several occasions, the cantor can be very helpful in teaching new music to the congregation. Also, the cantor might lead a rehearsal before the service, or, on occasion, within the rite at a time for announcements or some other appropriate time.

In some situations it is both more desirable and practicable to use a cantor for those portions of the rites normally sung by choirs than to attempt the development of a choir. In situations where the instrument and/or the skills of the instrumentalist are limited, the cantor can often provide the necessary leadership. (See Acc. Ed. Vol. 1, pages 11–12 and 16–17, on the functions of the cantor and the use of Antiphons or Refrains.)

The Qualifications of the Cantor

Because of the functions of the cantor, it is important that this person have a pleasant voice; a commanding presence; and the ability to read music accurately, to learn music with ease, and to sing with confidence. The cantor must also be able to present ideas clearly and briefly. The procurement of an able cantor would greatly enhance the musical performance in many churches. Even churches with limited budgets should think seriously about hiring a cantor if a talented volunteer is not available. This person could be either male or female.

The Musical Ministry of the Choir

The function of a choir in the rites of the Church is not that of a choral society or a glee club. In the last two groups the music brings the people together, and their principal purpose is to provide an opportunity to practice and perform music which cannot be performed individually. A choral society or glee club performs publicly for the edification and enjoyment of others and for their own gratification. Although these same functions may be served by the church choir, they must be subservient to the role of music within the liturgy of the Church. (See the "General Performance Notes," Acc. Ed. Vol. 1, pages 11–17.)

Types of Choirs

Each congregation should decide whether a choir is desirable for it, and, if so, what type of choir or choirs. In some situations, the formation of a choir would necessitate gathering from the congregation all those who sing with confidence, thereby robbing the congregation of leadership and support needed in their midst.

(1) The Cathedral or Collegiate Choir In some situations a cathedral or collegiate choir is both possible and appropriate. In the traditional cathedral or collegiate situation the choir is the congregation; the chancel serves as the church or chapel for the services. (The nave is the place for occasional visitors, but essentially the choir is the congregation and the congregation is the choir.) In many ways the cathedral or collegiate situation is analogous to a congregation with no choir. The difference lies in that the daily services in the cathedral or collegiate situation include music, and in the ability of the regular congregation to perform music not within the capability of a typical congregation. Historically, it was in the former situations that a divided choir was to be found. Since antiphonal psalmody was basic to the repertoire, the divided choir was functional. Today where the choir and congregation are essentially the same (as in some seminary chapels, monasteries or convents, and in occasional American cathedrals and school chapels), it is certainly appropriate to make use of highly complicated service music which, in other situations, might obscure the liturgy.

(2) The Parish Choir The parish choir and most cathedral and collegiate choirs must take seriously the presence of a congregation which neither practices nor sings together with great frequency. These choirs must recognize their primary function to be that of providing leadership, support, modeling, and teaching for those of more limited musical aptitudes and abilities. Many congregations include a sufficient number of children and adults with musical interests and abilities to comprise a choir. In some parishes the choir of volunteers is sufficiently talented to provide music beyond the talents of the congrega-

tion. In some situations even two people could be the choir. In other situations it is necessary to pay a certain number of trained singers to fill particular needs or to provide the backbone for the larger volunteer group. Just as a church must often pay for the time and talents of clergy, secretaries, sextons and others vital to the proper functioning of the congregation, so it must be willing to pay for the time and talents of persons with musical abilities to provide leadership and enhance the program of the parish choir. Money spent for musicians can make the difference in a congregation's ability to attract or to hold people. It is sometimes the most effective missionary money spent by the congregation.

In a cathedral or parish choir it is sometimes possible, or even desirable, to have a small group of people with extraordinary time and talents devote themselves to performing highly complex music beyond the time and abilities of the entire choir. This select group might take the place of a cantor or choir at appropriate points in the rites.

(3) The Young People's or Children's Choir A children's choir can make its own contributions. It can sing alone and, on occasions, sing with an adult choir as well as provide a training school to feed into the adult choirs. The young people's choir and the children's choir both provide an excellent opportunity for education in the liturgy and music of the Church. Because they have not been negatively acculturated, young people or children are often able to learn music such as plainchant much more easily than adults and then to initiate its use in a congregation. In many places a young people's or children's choir could be the only choir; the combination of cantor and young people's or children's choir might be ideal.

(4) The Ad Hoc Choir In many congregations people who do not have time or interest sufficient for involvement in the regular choir(s) can augment the choir for certain special events or compose a choir for certain functions. Because the members of the regular choir(s) are often busy at the times of weddings and funerals, many churches have compiled lists of persons available to form a choir when desired. Since regular service music and a few well-known hymns generally make up the repertoire for weddings and burials, an ad hoc choir can often contribute effective leadership after only a brief practice just prior to the rite.

The Functions of Choirs

Of primary importance to the church choir is its role as leader, supporter, and teacher of the congregation in the songs of the people and in unison reading, and as model and teacher for the congregation in good liturgical and worship habits. Any choir failing to understand the significance of these roles may be of more detriment than help in the worship of the church. A substantial portion of many choir practices should be devoted to the study of liturgy, unison reading, and the practice of the songs of the people so that the choir may better perform its primary functions. In addition to these, the choir may be able to provide other rite-enhancing elements, beyond the abilities of the congregation.

The choir may also enhance songs of the people and hymns which the congregation sings with confidence by supplying harmony, descants, or fauxbourdons. Caution must be exercised, however, lest such variations discourage the singing of the people. THE HYMNAL 1982 provides descants, fauxbourdons, or varied harmonizations for a number of tunes. (See Appendix I [below].) HYMNAL STUDIES SEVEN, volumes 1 and 2, lists descants, etc., for many of the tunes in THE HYMNAL 1982. Among the available collections containing descants, or fauxbourdons, the following are especially valuable:

THE CHRIST CHURCH DESCANT BOOK (2 vols.). Fyfe, Lois, Cumberland Press.

THE DESCANT HYMN-TUNE BOOK, *Books I & II*. Shaw, Geoffrey, Novello.

FAMILIAR HYMNS WITH DESCANTS. Kettring, Donald, Westminster Press.

FESTIVAL PRAISE. Routley, Eric, Hinshaw Music.

55 HYMN DESCANTS FOR FESTIVE AND GENERAL USE. Proulx, Richard & Young, Michael E., G. I. A. Publications.

48 HYMN DESCANTS FOR FESTIVE AND GENERAL USE. Various Composers, G. I. A. Publications.

41 DESCANTS TO FAMILIAR HYMN TUNES. Winn, Cyril, OUP

HYMNS FOR CHOIRS. Willcocks, David, OUP.

THIRTY-FOUR HYMN DESCANTS. Williams, David McK., H.W. Gray (Belwin-Mills).

THIRTY-SIX DESCANTS. Shaw, Geoffrey, OUP.

20 HYMN-TUNE DESCANTS. Lang, C.S., Novello.

THE HYMNAL 1982 includes several Rounds and Canons (710–715) and suggests that several other tunes might be sung in canon (9, 25, 43, 25C, 254, 534, and 671). See Appendix I (below) for a list of additional tunes which might be treated in this manner.

Often the choir may take the place of the cantor in singing the text of the Gradual Psalm or the Alleluia Verse at the Eucharist or in singing the text of the Invitatory Psalm at the Daily Office. On occasion it is also appropriate for the choir to sing certain portions of the rites often sung by the people; i.e., the Lord, have mercy upon us / Lord, have mercy (*Kyrie*), Kyrie eleison, Holy God (*Trisagion*), Glory be to God / Glory to God (*Gloria in excelsis*) or other Song of Praise at the Eucharist or a canticle at the Daily Office. The rubrics state that an anthem may be used at the place of the Gradual or of the Alleluia Verse at the Eucharist. The functions of these components of the rite must be carefully considered in the choice of anthems. Some of the early Church Fathers referred to the Gradual as the Lesson from the Psalms. The Alleluia is an acclamation at the appearance of Christ present in his Word, symbolized by the Gospel Reading. It is common for the choir to sing the Fraction Anthem (in fact, the Prayer Book uses the word *anthem* rather than *hymn* at this place in the rite) to afford opportunity to the people for concentration on the liturgical action. It is traditional in Anglicanism for an anthem to follow the Collects of the Daily Office.

The Songs of the Choir

From the fifth century the songs traditionally assigned to the choir have been the three processional songs of the Eucharistic rite: the entrance song, the Offertory song, and the Communion song. Other musical portions are integral to the rite, and the texts are normally read when they are not sung. These processional songs serve primarily to accompany actions and are not essential to the actions. Traditional liturgies have assigned the music at the three processions to the choir so that the people might be free to take part in the procession or to watch it in progress.

In classic liturgies the entrance song, which sets the mood for the rite, was assigned to the choir who sang only that portion of a psalm needed for the entrance of the ministers. Hence, the *Gloria Patri* at the end provided a climax and a cue to the celebrant to be ready to start. Throughout most of Anglican history, however, a congregational hymn has replaced this choir anthem. The Trial Liturgies listed a psalm as the first option at this point, but in response to popular request, THE BOOK OF COMMON PRAYER restored the hymn to primacy here. If the people sing the entrance song, it is certainly legitimate or even desirable on occasion for the choir to sing the Glory be to God / Glory to God (*Gloria in excelsis*) or another song of praise in its place. It is probably wise for the congregation to sit during the choir's singing of the song of praise, especially if it is lengthy. Then the people stand again at the Salutation.

The Offertory song serves to accompany the preparation of the Table and the presentation of the bread and wine and money or other offerings. As at the entrance, the needed portion of an appropriate psalm was sung with the ending indicated by the Glory to the Father (*Gloria Patri*). Music used at this point in the rite should serve as a meditative aid to the congregation in its preparation for participation in the Great Thanksgiving. The music should not overshadow the songs of the people within the Eucharistic Prayer.

The Communion song is the third of the processional songs traditionally assigned to the choir. Anthems too lengthy or too dramatic for use at the preparation of the Table are often suitable at this point. Responsorial psalms or hymns or anthems which include refrains work well at this time for they enable the congregation to participate without being bookbound.

In addition to its function within the liturgical rites, the choir may make an offering to God and serve the church through special services with music possibly not suited for use in liturgical rites. Concert masses, oratorios, cantatas, services of lessons and music (especially those associated with the Advent and Christmas Seasons), and paraliturgies (services created for various seasons and occasions) are rich resources for such special musical offerings. Often singers and instrumentalists not available for the regular Sunday and Holy Day Eucharists or for the Daily Office can augment the regular choir.

The Location of the Choir

During the late nineteenth and early twentieth centuries many Anglican parish churches forsook the traditional west end gallery or "singers' pew" position for the parish choir. Because of a misunderstanding of the makeup and function of the cathedral or collegiate choir, many churches in building or remodeling created a chancel placement for the choir (often divided into two sides). The resultant separation of the clergy from the people had harmful effects on the liturgy. Also, the choir was less able to give effective leadership to the people. Happily, with the building of new churches and many remodelings of existing buildings, we now see a return to the traditional Western choir placement in a gallery or in the back of the church or to the traditional Eastern position among the people in the nave (possibly slightly raised above the nave floor). Each position has its own distinct advantages. Some churches, when remodeling, have found it best to reverse the placement of the choir and sanctuary, placing the organ and choir in the old sanctuary facing the people, and using the old choir area as the place for altar and pulpit. Thus the united choir can provide better leadership for the people. In turn, the people are better able to see and feel involved with the actions at the principal liturgical centers.

Facilities for Choir Practice

Although a frequent final rehearsal in the church is helpful, the choir should not be forced to do all their preparation there. A well-arranged choir room can greatly facilitate rehearsals and save an appreciable amount of time. The room should be spacious and well-ventilated. Absolutely essential is a good piano placed so that the director faces the choir. The room should be isolated from other activities and free before services to allow for a brief warmup. Other essential equipment includes: chairs with book racks; book shelves and filing cabinets or other storage facilities for hymnals, Prayer Books, anthems, and other music, and a chalk board, probably with a section lined with music staves. A large wall clock facing the director facilitates the best use of time. A bulletin board and a tape recorder and/or turntable are helpful.

Vestments

In medieval cathedral or collegiate churches the members of the choir wore the clerical vestments appropriate to their order. This vestment was often a quite full form of the ankle-length alb known as the *surplice* ("over the fur," for this full form could be worn in unheated buildings over an overcoat, often in the form of a cassock). After the Reformation the young scholars, taking the place of eliminated minor orders, continued to wear the clerical surplice in choir. Those in parish choirs generally wore no special vestments. About the turn of this century an unattractive abbreviated version of the surplice, known as a *cotta,* appeared in many places, but currently there seems to be something of a return to the more traditional fuller and longer form. Many churches have found a simple robe modeled after the academic gown more practical as it is easier to keep clean and fresh and is also more comfortable. It is not necessary, and probably not even desirable, to wear a headcovering with vestments. In situations where the choir is located behind the people, vestments are often considered more of a nuisance than a help. Some of these churches have returned to the tradition of the unvested parish choir, although other churches still find vestments an aid to morale.

Music

The inflated cost of anthems and larger choral works has in recent years put quite a strain upon many music budgets. In many areas choirs are able to exchange catalogues of their music libraries and then borrow from each other. The new music included in THE HYMNAL 1982 is a tremendous resource for choirs. This music performed as anthems serves to familiarize the people with music which they can eventually sing as songs of the people. Later in this book appear hints on how to add interest for the choir as well as the congregation when using a hymn or canticle as an anthem.

The following collections contain multipurpose, high quality anthems:

ANTHEMS FOR CHOIRS BOOK I. (ed. Francis Jackson) 4 part choirs, OUP.

ANTHEMS FOR CHOIRS BOOK II. (ed. Philip Ledger) unison & 2 part choirs, OUP.

ANTHEMS FOR CHOIRS BOOK III. (ed. Philip Ledger) 3 & 4 part treble choirs, OUP.

ANTHEMS FOR CHOIRS BOOK IV. Compiled by Christopher Morris, mixed choir, OUP.

THE OXFORD BOOK OF TUDOR ANTHEMS. (ed. Christopher Morris), OUP.

CAROLS FOR CHOIRS, 1, 2, 3. (ed. David Willcocks, Reginald Jacques, and John Rutter), OUP.

OXFORD EASY ANTHEM BOOK. OUP.

SIXTEENTH CENTURY ANTHEM BOOK. OUP.

THE CHURCH ANTHEM BOOK. OUP.

THE CHESTER BOOK OF MOTETS. (ed. Anthony G. Petti) 6 volumes, OUP.

THE OXFORD BOOK OF CAROLS. OUP.

MOTET BOOK I, II. Concordia.

SAB Choir Goes Baroque. Concordia.

16 Hymns of Today for use as Simple Anthems. (ed. John Wilson), RSCM.

Bach for Choirs. (ed. Paul Steinitz), RSCM.

Six Easy Three-Part Anthems, SAB. (ed. A. Greening), RSCM.

Twelve Easy Anthems. RSCM.

Five Anthems for Today. RSCM.

Anthems from Addington. RSCM.

Anthems for Unison or Two-Part Singing. RSCM.

Churches must resist the temptation to duplicate music under copyright. Copyright laws make it legitimate to reproduce portions of works of music for classroom purposes and to reproduce certain music no longer available for purchase. However, it is not legitimate to reproduce for performance entire copies of available anthems or other works under copyright. The basic principle seems to be that music may not be reproduced if that reproduction interferes with sales.

Guidelines for Educational Uses of Music* _____

The purpose of the following guidelines is to state the minimum and not the maximum standards of educational fair use under Section 107 of H. R. 2223. The parties agree that the conditions determining the extent of permissible copying for educational purposes may change in the future; that certain types of copying permitted under these guidelines may not be permissible in the future; and conversely that in the future other types of copying not permitted under these guidelines may be permissible under revised guidelines.

Moreover, the following statement of guidelines is not intended to limit the types of copying permitted under the standards of fair use under judicial decision and which are stated in Section 107 of the Copyright Revision Bill. There may be instances in which copying which does not fall within the guidelines stated below may nonetheless be permitted under the criteria of fair use.

A. Permissible Uses

1. Emergency copying to replace purchased copies which for any reason are not available for an imminent performance, provided purchased replacement copies shall be substituted in due course.

2. For academic purposes other than performance, single or multiple copies of excerpts of works may be made, provided that the excerpts do not comprise a part of the whole which would constitute a performable unit such as a section, movement or area, but in no case more than (10%) of the whole work. The number of copies shall not exceed one copy per pupil.

3. Printed copies which have been purchased may be edited or simplified, provided that the fundamental character of the work is not distorted or the lyrics, if any, altered, or lyrics added if none exist.

4. A single copy of recordings of performances by students may be made for evaluation or rehearsal purposes and may be retained by the educational institution or individual teacher.

5. A single copy of a sound recording (such as a tape, disc or cassette) of copyrighted

---

*COPYRIGHT HANDBOOK, *Donald F. Johnston, R.R. Bowker Co.*

music may be made from sound recordings owned by an educational institution or an individual teacher for the purpose of constructing aural exercises or examinations and may be retained by the educational institution or individual teacher. (This pertains only to the copyright of the music itself and not to any copyright which may exist in the sound recording.)

B. Prohibitions

1. Copying to create or replace or substitute for anthologies, compilations or collective works.
2. Copying of or from works intended to be "consumable" in the course of study or of teaching, such as workbooks, exercises, standardized tests and answer sheets and like material.
3. Copying for the purpose of performance, except as in A(1) above.
4. Copying for the purpose of substituting for the purchase of music, except as in A(1) and A(2) above.
5. Copying without inclusion of the copyright notice which appears on the printed copy.

Training of Choirs

Even the smallest choirs with the most inexperienced directors can improve their ability to lead congregations in the liturgy. There are a large number of books, booklets and pamphlets, workshops, seminars and conferences as well as recordings which demonstrate and illustrate concepts of choral techniques, including breathing, good tone, rhythmic singing, blend, balance, interpretation, etc.

Many diocesan liturgical and music commissions sponsor weekend workshops for directors and choir members, and the summer months provide numerous opportunities for workshops and seminars at colleges and universities. The Standing Commission on Church Music often sponsors workshops on the relation of music and the liturgy and each summer the Sewanee and Evergreen Conferences provide large numbers of church musicians with new choral skills and a deeper understanding of the relation of music to the liturgy.

Some important choral training books include:

CHORAL DIRECTING. Wilhelm Ehmann, Minneapolis, Augsburg, 1968.
THE CHURCH CHOIR TRAINER. Henry Coleman, London, OUP, 1964.
BASIC CHOIR TRAINING. Edward Wright, Croydon, RSCM, 1953.
CHORAL CONDUCTING — A SYMPOSIUM. Hurford and Becker, Prentice Hall.

Also helpful are the Adult and Childrens' choirs Training School booklets and the self-help booklets published by the Royal School of Church Music.

The Ministry of Directors and Instrumentalists

Functions of Directors and Instrumentalists

Often one person is both director and instrumentalist, but even if several different persons perform these tasks, the functions still overlap.

The church musician is inevitably cast into a pastoral role. The musician works closely with a substantial segment of the parish and may be the one most likely to function as pastor to those people. It is imperative that the musician and clergy work together and support each other in this aspect of their ministries. The musician must also deal in a pastoral manner with choir, clergy, and congregation. This does not mean that discipline cannot be exercised or that people's horizons cannot be broadened or their abilities stretched, but it does mean that the musician must teach, lead, accompany, and perform in a manner which is loving and pastoral.

The director or instrumentalist is first of all a teacher and a leader; all other roles (aside from that as pastor) are secondary.

(1) A Teacher The director or instrumentalist is a teacher of the people, of the choir, and of the clergy. This person should know thoroughly the contents of THE BOOK OF COMMON PRAYER, THE HYMNAL 1982, THE HOLY EUCHARIST: ALTAR EDITION, MUSIC FOR MINISTERS AND CONGREGATION, CHURCH HYMNAL SERIES VI: GRADUAL PSALMS, and the various volumes in the HYMNAL STUDIES series. This person has not only primary responsibility for teaching the people hymns, canticles and service music but also the opportunity to teach the Prayer Book and to engender good worship habits. The director or instrumentalist can teach the choir in even greater depth and wider compass. This is the person to introduce new music to the clergy and to coach them in singing their parts of the rites.

(2) A Leader The ability to give firm leadership to the congregation is the most important performing skill for a church musician. The instrumentalist is normally the conductor or song leader. In the playover or introduction, the instrumentalist must set the tempo and provide articulation and registration which inspires confidence in the congregation. Few congregations are able to transcend any lack in the skills of the instrumentalist.

As important as right notes are in the playing of hymns, the rhythm is still more important. An instrumentalist can play so fast that a congregation is left breathless or so slowly that they are left exhausted. Within these limits, the acoustics, the structure of the tune, and the content of the text should determine the phrasing. Few commas in the text call for breaks in the music.

While it is not always necessary or wise to play through the entire tune of a hymn (or of a canticle or piece of service music such as the Holy, holy, holy / Holy, holy, holy Lord [*Sanctus*]) before the congregation sings, it is necessary to play enough to allow the congregation to find the place and to establish clearly the tune and the tempo. If the tune is unfamiliar, it might be wise to play the melody line in octaves. Throughout a hymn, free use should be made of detached playing on repeated notes. If a congregation sings sluggishly, even more detached playing may be advisable. At the end of each stanza, enough time should be allowed for the congregation to take a comfortable breath. Equal time should be allowed between each stanza.

The basic tone for leading hymns is the principal chorus. Since the 8′ level is that at which the people sing, stops at pitch levels above 8′ should be added: 4′, 2⅔′, 2′, and mixtures. Additional stops which muddy the texture are to be avoided, and the tremolo is never to be used with congregational singing. The pedals should be allowed to rest on occasional stanzas. Sufficient volume should be used so that timid singers will not fear being heard individually, but the congregation must not be overpowered. Changes in registration for various stanzas should be determined primarily by the text. The same volume and tempo should prevail through the Amen, if one is sung.

Familiar hymns can often become more interesting with judicious variations in the accompaniment. Canonic treatments, fauxbourdons, or descants can be used. (See Appendix I [below] for descants, fauxbourdons, varied harmonizations or accompaniments, lists of tunes that may be treated as canons and of tunes scored for other

30

instruments within the pages of THE HYMNAL 1982 itself.) On rare occasions an instrumental interlude between stanzas is effective; careful consideration should be given to the placement of such interludes within the text. The instrumentalist can work out such variations or can turn to collections of varied accompaniments such as the following:

ACCOMPANIMENTS FOR UNISON HYMN-SINGING. Compiled and edited by Gerald H. Knight, RSCM.

Bairstow, Edward C. ORGAN ACCOMPANIMENTS TO THE UNISON VERSES OF TWENTY-FOUR HYMN-TUNES FROM THE ENGLISH HYMNAL, OUP.

Bender, Jan. THE HYMN OF THE WEEK: ORGAN SETTINGS, Concordia.

Busarow, Donald. ALL PRAISE TO YOU, ETERNAL GOD: ORGAN ACCOMPANIMENTS FOR THIRTY HYMN TUNE CANONS, Augsburg.

FREE ACCOMPANIMENTS TO HYMNS. 4 Volumes, Augsburg.

FREE HARMONIZATIONS OF HYMN TUNES BY FIFTY AMERICAN COMPOSERS. Edited by D. DeWitt Wasson, Hinshaw Music.

Goode, Jack C. THIRTY-FOUR CHANGES ON HYMN TUNES, H. W. Gray.

Hancock, Gerre. ORGAN IMPROVISATION FOR HYMN-SINGING, Hinshaw Music.

HYMN PRELUDES AND FREE ACCOMPANIMENTS, AUGSBURG.

Johnson, David N. FREE HARMONIZATION OF TWELVE HYMN TUNES, Augsburg.

Marshall, Jane. 15 HARMONIZATIONS ON HYMN TUNES, Abingdon.

Noble, T. Tertius. FREE ORGAN ACCOMPANIMENTS TO ONE HUNDRED WELL-KNOWN HYMN TUNES. J. Fischer.

Noble, T. Tertius. FIFTY FREE ORGAN ACCOMPANIMENTS TO WELL-KNOWN HYMN TUNES. J. Fischer.

Oxley, Harrison. LAST VERSE IN UNISON. 2 Volumes, RSCM.

Petrich, Roger. HYMNS FOR THE CHURCH YEAR, Augsburg.

Powell, Robert J. 48 ORGAN DESCANTS ON WELL-KNOWN HYMN TUNES, G. I. A. Publications.

Routley, Eric. FESTIVAL PRAISE COMPANION, Hinshaw Music.

Thiman, Eric H. VARIED ACCOMPANIMENTS TO THIRTY-FOUR WELL-KNOWN HYMN TUNES, OUP.

Thiman, Eric H. VARIED HARMONIZATIONS OF FAVORITE HYMN TUNES, H. W. Gray (Belwin-Mills).

Wyton, Alec. NEW SHOOTS FROM OLD ROUTES: NEW HARMONIZATIONS OF 48 WELL-KNOWN HYMN TUNES, Sacred Music Press.

Young, Michael E. 25 ORIGINAL HARMONIZATIONS FOR TWENTY-FIVE OFT-USED HYMN TUNES, G. I. A. Publications.

The two principal Lutheran hymnals, LUTHERAN BOOK OF WORSHIP (Augsburg) and LUTHERAN WORSHIP (Concordia), are also good sources for varied harmonizations or accompaniments by reputable composers. Two books provide easy three-part accompaniments for well-known hymn tunes:

Cooper, Janette. HYMN TUNES FOR THE RELUCTANT ORGANIST, OUP.

Mealy, Margaret. 34 EASY HYMN ACCOMPANIMENTS, G. I. A. Publications.

Also see HYMNAL STUDIES SEVEN, Volumes 1 and 2, for additional suggestions.

The instrumentalist uses one technique as the leader of the hymns, of "through composed" settings of canticles, and of much service music; plainsong and Anglican chant call for a different technique. Ideally, plainsong should be sung unaccompanied; certainly, however, in the learning stages and in many situations regularly thereafter, accompaniment is necessary to keep the congregation moving and on pitch. The opening intonation is usually a sufficient introduction. The organist should aim for lightness and flexibility and should use the pedals sparingly, if at all. Where available, handbells make an effective accompaniment for plainchant.

(3) An Accompanist   When playing for a congregation, an instrumentalist is cast in a leadership role; when playing for a cantor, other soloist, or a choir, that of accompanist. In this role, the instrument must be subordinate to the voice. This normally calls for a more subdued registration and a willingness to allow the singer to determine the tempo.

(4) Special Contributions   In addition to providing leadership for the congregation and accompaniment for the choir or cantor, the instrumentalist makes special contributions to the services. The prelude and postlude provide the musical framework for the service. Here the instrumentalist has excellent opportunities to teach new tunes to the congregation, to reinforce the themes of the liturgy of the day, and to set the mood for the people entering or leaving. A rubric in THE BOOK OF COMMON PRAYER states, "On occasion, and as appropriate, instrumental music may be substituted for a hymn or anthem" (p. 14). Often instrumental music is to be preferred to hymns or anthems at the time of the Offertory or of the Communion of the People. On occasion an instrumental fanfare might be a good substitute for the Alleluia prior to the announcement of the Gospel or for the Fraction Anthem.

Qualifications and Contracts

Because the Church musician is inevitably put into the position of being a pastor and teacher, ideally this person should be well trained in the Scriptures, the liturgy, theology, and pastoral care in addition to having high competency in music. Efforts are underway to establish standards for Episcopal musicians, and there is some enthusiasm for establishing a diaconal ministry of music program. Only a fraction of the Churches are able to procure musicians with such training. High priority belongs to furthering the education of Church musicians by making it financially possible for them to attend workshops, conferences, and summer schools devoted to liturgy and Church music. Clergy should make their libraries available to musicians and guide them in their studies. In some situations it may be desirable for a portion of the compensation of the musician to be in the form of lessons under more experienced and knowledgeable Church musicians. Where this teaching is not really available or as a supplement, we recommend the use of cassettes produced by and available from Catacomb Cassettes, 3376 Peachtree Road, N.E., Atlanta, GA 30326:

    C-83 How to Sing the Liturgy
    C-113 The Holy Eucharist, Rite Two

C-176   The Proper Prefaces from the Altar Edition of the
        Holy Eucharist
C-177   Music for Ministers and Congregation
C-232   HYMNS III (selections)
C-245   Songs for Celebration
C-348   Sing the Canticles!
C-512   Joyful Noise: Teaching Music in Small Churches

Another valuable resource is the set of three cassettes published by the Church Hymnal Corporation, WHEN IN OUR MUSIC GOD IS GLORIFIED.

The musician should enter into a contract or letter of agreement with the rector. This agreement should state clearly certain things which otherwise could become sources of conflict. Where applicable, these items should appear: salary and fringe benefits; fees for weddings and funerals; time and financing for continuing education; vacation; use of the organ for practice and teaching and for pupils' practice; the availability of the choir room for the organist's use; the heating or cooling of the church and choir room; the selection of music for both the choir and the congregation; the selection of choir personnel; selection of assistants and substitutes; the relationship to the committee on liturgy; the number and nature of services with music; the number and nature of the choir(s); the number and time of rehearsals; the budget for singers, for music, and for supplementary instrumentalists; and the tuning and care of the instruments. Valuable works for clergy and musicians are:

COMPENSATION OF THE CHURCH AND SYNAGOGUE MUSICIAN. American Guild of Organists.

Farr, David. THE WORKING RELATIONSHIP BETWEEN PRINCIPAL PRIEST AND CHIEF MUSICIAN, Commission on Liturgy and Church Music, Diocese of Los Angeles, P.O. Box 2164, Los Angeles, California 90051.

WHEN A CHURCH CALLS A MUSICIAN. The Music Commission of the Diocese of Connecticut.

Purchasing and Maintaining Instruments

The pipe organ continues to be the most desirable and satisfying instrument for the leading of congregational singing, for the accompaniment of choir or cantor, and for the performance of a great portion of the instrumental music written for the Church. Where space and budget are limited, there are still available small organs adequate for the requirements of the liturgy. The organ should stand free within the room, preferably on the east-west axis; it should not be hidden and muffled in a closet or around a corner. See John Fesperman, ORGAN PLANNING: ASKING THE RIGHT QUESTIONS (HYMNAL STUDIES FOUR).

If a true pipe organ cannot be obtained, the next best choice in most situations is a good piano. This provides more adequate leadership than most instruments, it is easier to maintain, and competent pianists are generally easier to procure than other instrumentalists.

Throughout most of Anglican history, there were no inhibitions about using whatever instruments or instrumentalists were locally available. Harpsichord, handbells, timpani, brass (especially trumpets, trombones, or French horns), recorders, and strings (including guitars) can on occasion supplement or take the place of organ or piano. This author has in his possession an old Anglican hymnal with accompaniments for organ, harpsichord, flute or guitar.*

In many ways the least satisfactory and, in the end, the most expensive substitute for an organ or a piano is an electronic instrument. Few of these instruments, if any, provide a principal chorus, so basic and necessary for the music of the liturgy. The lifetime of these instruments is that of any normal electric appliance, whereas a real pipe organ, though more expensive initially, can be expected to last through many decades. In fact, pipe organs have been known to last through centuries, given reasonable care.

The most satisfaction and the greatest value for the dollars invested in musical instruments come with regular maintenance by a competent tuner. In many situations a long term contract is the best solution.

Carpets, cushions, curtains, and acoustical tile are detrimental to congregational participation and other musical performance; they must be used very sparingly, if at all.

The Musical Ministry of the Clergy

Many clergy have had little opportunity to study Church music. Later, some find that the music of the Church makes greater demands upon them than they had anticipated or that the anticipated help of a knowledgeable Church musician is not available. Clergy should familiarize themselves with the contents of Accompaniment Edition (2 vols.), not neglecting to study the Preface, the General Performance Notes, the various Indexes, and the Appendix (S 289–S 449). They should familiarize themselves with the musical provisions of THE HOLY EUCHARIST: ALTAR EDITION and its supplement, PROPER LITURGIES FOR SPECIAL DAYS. They should study the volumes in the HYMNAL STUDIES series. They should also avail themselves of the various conferences, workshops, and summer schools in liturgy and music and of the coaching of competent local musicians. A cassette recording of the music of THE HOLY EUCHARIST: ALTAR EDITION, available from The Episcopal Radio-TV Foundation, affords potential help to many clergy. (See above, p. 32.)

The Deacon

In the Eucharistic rite, the deacon has, since the fourth century, sung the Gospel, the Prayers of the People, and the Dismissal. The Palm Sunday Procession is initiated by the deacon who also traditionally sings the Exsultet of the Great Vigil of Easter. Music for each of these appears in THE HOLY EUCHARIST: ALTAR EDITION or its supplement, PROPER LITURGIES FOR SPECIAL DAYS. Even if none of the celebrant's parts are sung, it is still fitting for the deacon to sing any or all of the deacon's portions of the rites.

The Celebrant

The Eastern Churches still maintain the old tradition of singing all of the celebrant's portion. Various factors caused the breakdown of this custom in the West in the late medieval period. Merbecke essentially attempted to revive it in the BOOKE OF COMMON

*THE HYMNS, ANTHEMS AND TUNES WITH THE ODE USED AT THE MAGDALEN CHAPEL, *London: Henry Thorowgood, n.d.*

PRAIER NOTED (1550). THE HOLY EUCHARIST: ALTAR EDITION provides music for all of the celebrant's portions of the rite except the Absolution and the Post-Sanctus of the Eucharistic Prayer. THE HYMNAL 1982 provides two settings for the complete text of Eucharistic Prayer C (S 369 & S 370). Settings for the Post-Sanctus of the other Eucharistic Prayers of Rite II are available from Mason Martens, 175 West 72nd Street, New York City NY 10023.

The Rector

The rector has special responsibilities for the music program, for ultimately the rector is responsible for hiring and firing, for entering into contracts or letters of agreement with church musicians. The rector, as chair of the vestry, has some oversight of the music budget. As chair of the liturgy committee and as chief liturgical officer of the parish, the rector is in a position to exercise a tremendous influence on the music program. When there is competent professional or volunteer leadership, the rector is wise to delegate much of this authority but is still ultimately responsible for the liturgy and music of the church. (See Title II, Canon 6, "Of the Music of the Church," p. 15, above). Some parishes have found it helpful to have a "choir warden" with seat and voice on the vestry to function as a liaison between the choir and rector and the choir and vestry.

In hiring a church musician the rector should be concerned for the pastoral instincts and abilities of the applicant, for the church musician is inevitably cast into a pastoral role. Will the musician give top priority to the hymns and service music of the people and provide for them leadership which will encourage that "full, conscious, and active participation . . . demanded by the very nature of the liturgy"*? Is the applicant adept at teaching enthusiastically new hymns and service music to enrich, enlarge, and upgrade the liturgical repertoire of the congregation? Does this person have sufficient grasp of liturgical and theological principles to contribute to the education of the congregation and to have a voice in the planning of the rites? Can the applicant contribute to the liturgical life of the people? Given satisfaction on these counts, the rector should proceed to test other areas. Will the applicant be able to work with the choir in providing leadership for the congregation and in helping them to learn new music? Will the applicant be able to direct the choir in anthems and other music beyond the capability of the congregation? Will the applicant be able to make offerings of instrumental music?

The Musical Ministry of the Committee on Liturgy

A resolution of the General Convention 1979 called for every parish to have a committee on liturgy. This committee should include: the clergy; the church musician; representatives of the vestry, the altar guild, the layreaders, the Christian education program, and the ushers; and other persons representative of various ages, educational backgrounds, and approaches to worship. There should not be a separate music committee.

---

*CONSTITUTION ON THE SACRED LITURGY, 14.

Functions of a Committee on Liturgy

The primary function of the committee on liturgy is to listen to the congregation, to evaluate the rites, and to provide feedback for the clergy, musicians, layreaders, ushers, altar guild, and servers. (This should not take the place of a regular Monday morning evaluation by the clergy and musician, with videotapes of the service where possible.) Periodically the committee on liturgy should brainstorm in the search for new ideas, new approaches.

Whether the committee on liturgy should plan the principal services in detail from week to week is open to question, but it should certainly have involvement in major decisions and changes. Not only will the opinions of the group be helpful, but also this group, having been consulted, will be in a position to communicate to others the rationale for programs and/or changes.

Whether it is done by the entire committee on liturgy, by a selected group from the committee, or simply by the clergy and musician, the planning of the rites week by week should be the responsibility of more than one person. This planning should begin with a study of the lectionary for the day and should occur several weeks in advance even though certain details may have to be changed or modified later. Otherwise, music cannot be procured, and various options possible with advance thought are not feasible. Before summer vacations clergy and musician should complete planning for the fall through Christmas. Then in the fall they should finish planning for Lent and Easter. Some of the best planning for the rites of a particular day on next year's calendar occurs the morning after this year's rites. The clergy and musician should keep notebooks with plans and cautions for serious consideration in the Monday morning evaluation sessions.

A basic function of a committee on liturgy is interpretation to the congregation. Lay persons on the committee can often be much more effective than the clergy or musician.

Bibliography for a Committee on Liturgy

The members of the committee on liturgy should be encouraged to study the history and rationale of the liturgy. Some helpful books are:

Borsch, Frederick H. INTRODUCING THE LESSONS OF THE CHURCH YEAR: A GUIDE FOR LAY READERS AND CONGREGATIONS, New York: Seabury Press, 1978.

Bushong, Ann Brooke. A GUIDE TO THE LECTIONARY, New York: Seabury Press, 1978.

CHRISTIAN INITIATION: A THEOLOGICAL AND PASTORAL COMMENTARY ON THE PROPOSED RITES, Associated Parishes.

ENVIRONMENT AND ART, National Bishops' Committee on the Liturgy.

HANDBOOK FOR LITURGY COMMITTEES, Liturgical Conference.

Hatchett, Marion J. COMMENTARY ON THE AMERICAN PRAYER BOOK, New York: Seabury Press, 1980.

Hatchett, Marion J. A MANUAL OF CEREMONIAL FOR THE NEW PRAYER BOOK, Sewanee: St. Luke's Journal of Theology, 1977.

Hatchett, Marion J. SANCTIFYING LIFE, TIME AND SPACE, New York: Seabury Press, 1976.

Hovda, Robert. STRONG, LOVING AND WISE: PRESIDING IN LITURGY, Liturgical Conference.

HYMNAL STUDIES. Church Hymnal Corporation.

1. Perspectives on the New Edition
2. Introducing The Hymnal 1982 (for Preface and Foreword)
3. Teaching Music in Small Churches (Marilyn Keiser)
4. Organ Planning: Asking the Right Questions (John Fesperman)
5. A Liturgical Index to The Hymnal 1982 (Marion J. Hatchett)
6. A Commentary on New Hymns (Raymond F. Glover)
7. An Organist's Guide to Resources for The Hymnal 1982 (Dennis Schmidt)
8. A Scriptural Index to The Hymnal 1982 (Marion J. Hatchett)

Middleton, Arthur Pierce. NEW WINE IN OLD SKINS: LITURGICAL
CHANGE AND THE SETTING OF WORSHIP. Wilton, Connecticut: Morehouse-Barlow, 1988.

MINISTRY I: HOLY BAPTISM, Associated Parishes.

MINISTRY II: LAITY, BISHOPS, PRIESTS, AND DEACONS, Associated
Parishes.

Mitchell, Leonel L. PRAYING SHAPES BELIEVING: A THEOLOGICAL
COMMENTARY ON THE BOOK OF COMMON PRAYER, Minneapolis:
Winston Press, 1985.

MUSIC IN CATHOLIC WORSHIP, National Bishops' Committee on the
Liturgy.

PARISH EUCHARIST, Associated Parishes.

Porter, H. Boone. KEEPING THE CHURCH YEAR, New York: Seabury
Press, 1978.

Price, Charles P. INTRODUCING THE PROPOSED BOOK: PRAYER
BOOK STUDIES 29 REVISED, New York: The Church Hymnal Corporation.

Price, Charles P. and Weill, Louis. LITURGY FOR LIVING: THE
CHURCH'S TEACHING SERIES 5, New York: Seabury Press, 1979.

Stevick, Daniel B. BAPTISMAL MOMENTS: BAPTISMAL MEANINGS,
Church Hymnal Corporation, 1987.

Stevick, Daniel B. CRAFTING OF LITURGY, Church Hymnal Corporation, 1989.

Stuhlman, Byron D. PRAYER BOOK RUBRICS EXPANDED, Church
Hymnal Corporation, 1987.

Stuhlman, Byron D. EUCHARISTIC CELEBRATION 1789–1979, Church
Hymnal Corporation, 1988.

Sydnor, William. THE REAL PRAYER BOOK: 1549 TO THE PRESENT,
Wilton, Connecticut: Morehouse-Barlow, 1978.

Sydnor, William. YOUR VOICE, GOD'S WORD: READING THE BIBLE
IN CHURCH, Wilton, Connecticut: Morehouse-Barlow, 1988.

THE GREAT VIGIL OF EASTER, Associated Parishes.

THE HOLY EUCHARIST: RITE TWO — A COMMENTARY, Associated
Parishes.

THE OCCASIONAL PAPERS OF THE STANDING LITURGICAL COMMIS-
SION: COLLECTION NUMBER ONE, Church Hymnal Corporation,
1987.

THE PARISH WORSHIP COMMITTEE. Associated Parishes.

Part Two:

Hymns, Psalms, Service Music,
Anthems, Instrumental Voluntaries

Hymns

Hymns are the "take home package" of the congregation. People's theology is almost surely more heavily influenced by the hymns which they sing than by the sermons which they hear or the prayers which they pray. This is but one illustration of the power of music and of the importance of making right choices in planning services.

Evaluating Hymns

Hymns must be evaluated in terms of both text and tune and the particular wedding of text and tune.

Though hymns have the nature of poetry, they are a unique medium. Very few items from the corpus of great poetry are usable as hymnody. Because they are linked with music, hymns must be written in units suited to musical phrasing. A hymn is poor if the music makes nonsense of the text. Consider this example where musical lines and textual lines are at odds:

> Anoint them prophets! Make their ears attent
>   To thy divinest speech; their hearts awake
> To human need; their lips make eloquent
>   For righteousness that shall all evil break.
>   (HYMNAL 1940, 220, st. 2)

Contrast the revised version of this stanza in THE HYMNAL 1982 (359):

> Anoint them prophets! Teach them thine intent:
>   to human need their quickened hearts awake;
> fill them with power, their lips make eloquent
>   for righteousness that shall all evil break.

On the other hand, when linked with its music, such simple lyrics as those of "Were you there when they crucified my Lord?" make a great hymn.

However, some of the hymns in any hymnal are probably more appropriate for private devotional use than for corporate worship. Some in fact, because of their subjectivity work very much against the spirit of corporate worship. Certainly services should neither begin nor end with hymns of a highly subjective nature. Certain other hymns are more appropriate for use in pageants or carol services than in the regular corporate worship services.

Texts expressing in objective terms the praise of God or the proclamation of the Gospel or providing an appropriate corporate response to the Word or Sacrament best serve the liturgy and best teach the people.

A good hymn tune should be simple and easy for the congregation to sing. Those so simple that a congregation can pick them up on first hearing (for example, many of the "gospel songs") soon become tiresome and cloying. A hymn tune should be simple enough and yet have enough character so that, once learned, it stays with the congregation. It should be written for performance by a congregation rather than by a choir. The melodic range should be suitable for congregational singing. (The normal congregational range is from middle C to the second D above.) Ideally the musical accents should agree with the word accents. A good hymn tune has distinction and beauty in the melody; it is not dependent on harmony for its main effect (note how the interest in the tune of 42, "Now the day is over," depends upon the harmony). In a well composed harmonization there will be some melodic interest in all the parts. A tune should have sufficient interest in its rhythm and melodic outline to maintain interest through several stanzas. A tune with strong current associations with a secular text should be shelved for a period of time. In some congregations certain tunes must be avoided because they have strongly unpleasant associations from other religious traditions. (For example, in some areas of the country 693, "Just as I am, without one plea," is too closely associated for many people with emotional, manipulative altar-calls, or 685, "Rock of ages, cleft for me," with maudlin funerals.)

The tune should express a mood corresponding with that of the words. (Contrast, for example, the intensity of the text "O for a closer walk with God" with the sprightliness of the first of the two tunes provided, 683 ["O for a closer *waltz* with God"?], or contrast the tune at 552 with the text, "Fight the good fight.") Great strength derives from a traditional association of a strong tune with an appropriate text. Many of our hymns, such as "A mighty fortress" and "O come all ye faithful," fall into this category. "O God, our help in ages past" and "Jesus Christ is risen today" are other examples.

Often a judicious selection of stanzas serves the liturgy of the day much better than the use of the whole text. At times when all stanzas are sung the reason for its choice on a particular occasion is obscured. At times, for example, stanza 3 would make a much better climax for the hymn "O sacred head, sore wounded" (168, 169) than stanza 5. On most occasions either stanza 3 or stanza 4 (depending on the lections for the day) of "For all the saints, who from their labors rest" (287) would make a better climax than stanza 8. It is especially true that a selection of stanzas is often best as a Sequence because a lengthy hymn at this point, rather than highlighting the Readings, interrupts the movement of the Liturgy of the Word. An unduly long hymn at this point separates the first two Readings and the Psalm from the Gospel and sermon. For example the text of the hymn "Alleluia! sing to Jesus!" (460, 461) contains a great many biblical allusions. Although all five eight-line stanzas are too much for use as a Sequence, on Ascension Day stanzas 1 and 2 might be used, or when the New Testament Lesson is from the Epistle to the Hebrews stanzas 1 and 4 would make a good choice. However when omitting stanzas, careful consideration must be given to the integrity and completeness of the new entity being created.

The Use of the Metrical Index

Clergy and church musicians should learn to use the metrical index in 1982 Acc. Ed. Vol. 2, pp. 1039–1044. Thoughtful use of this index makes possible the use of many texts which might otherwise be unusable because they appear with a tune unknown to the congregation (In the Accompaniment Volume alternative tunes are suggested for a number of hymns.)

In the metrical index the hymns are categorized according to the number of syllables in each line. The most common metrical patterns are:

66. 86   (called Short Metre and abbreviated s.m.)
86. 86   (called Common Metre and abbreviated c.m.)
88. 88   (called Long Metre and abbreviated l.m.)
77. 77
76. 76. d.   (The "D" in this and other patterns means "doubled"; it indicates that the same metrical pattern is repeated a second time.)

In theory a text in any metrical pattern could be sung to any tune of that pattern. In practice the poetic accents of some texts make them unusable with certain tunes of the same metre. For example, though the text "Come, risen Lord, and deign to be our guest" (THE HYMNAL 1982, 305, 306) and the tune *O quanta qualia* (348, 623) are both 10 10. 10 10, they will not work together. The text is iambic and the tune dactylic.

In making substitutions one must be careful to choose tunes in keeping with the texts. Though *Bangor* and *Land of Rest* are both 86. 86 or Common Metre, *Land of Rest* would hardly be suitable for "Alone thou goest forth, O Lord" or *Bangor* for "I come with joy to meet my Lord." Though *Adon Olam* and *Woodworth* are both 88. 88 or Long Metre, *Adon Olam* would hardly do for "Just as I am, without one plea," or *Woodworth* for "Sing now with joy unto the Lord." Also, the use of tunes with strong seasonal associations should generally be avoided at other times of the year.

The Metrical Index of THE HYMNAL 1982 is reproduced in Appendix II (below) with the first lines of the texts printed out for easier recognition.

For several reasons, the choice of hymns is one of the most important aspects in planning any service. Hymns are a primary element in the participation of the people and help to gather the individuals into a corporate body. Well chosen hymns provide appropriate accompaniments or responses of the people to the various elements of the rites. And often one of the hymns stays in a person's mind, forming the "take home package," and providing material for meditation and remembrance in the following days. The choice of hymns, as much as any other element, sets the tone or mood of the season. For example, there should be a radical contrast between the hymns used in Lent and those used in the Easter Season, between those used in Advent and those used at Christmas. The placement of a hymn must receive careful consideration. Not only must the text be appropriate; the tune must also be suitable. A tune good for an opening hymn, for example, would often be too big and imposing for use as a Sequence for it would tend to separate the prior Readings from the Gospel and sermon. It might also be too imposing for use at the offering for there it would overpower the Sanctus of the Eucharistic Prayer. Careful choice of hymns can contribute significantly to the solemnity, beauty, joy, and enthusiasm which the worship of God deserves.

Psalms and Canticles

Prose psalms and/or canticles are used in most of the rites of THE BOOK OF COMMON PRAYER. A Gradual is appointed for use in the Liturgy of the Word at the Eucharist and at other rites (marriage, burial, ordination, celebration of a new ministry, consecration of a church). The Gloria in excelsis or some other appropriate canticle may be used in the entrance rite of the Eucharist except in Advent or Lent. On certain occasions a canticle may take the place of the Gradual Psalm, and at times a canticle is appropriate at the entrance of the ministers, between the Epistle and Gospel, at the Offertory or during the Communion of the People. The use of psalms and of canticles is required in the Daily Offices. It is generally appropriate to sing them.

Both plainchant (plainsong) and Anglican chant settings are provided in THE HYMNAL 1982 for all the canticles of THE BOOK OF COMMON PRAYER. For some canticles other settings are provided as well. Plainchant settings of the psalms appointed in the Eucharistic lectionary, for the various Pastoral Offices and Episcopal Services, and for Lesser Feasts and Fasts are provided in the six volumes of the publication GRADUAL PSALMS, ALLELUIA VERSES AND TRACTS (CHURCH HYMNAL SERIES VI). Two other Church Hymnal publications, THE ANGLICAN CHANT PSALTER, edited by Alec Wyton, and THE PLAINSONG PSALTER, edited by James Litton, also provide settings for all of the Psalms. Acc. Ed. Vol. 1, S 446 prints all of the Plainsong Psalm Tones with the various endings. See Acc. Ed. Vol. 1, pp. 12–17, for instructions on singing chant, and Side A of the first cassette in the series WHEN IN OUR MUSIC GOD IS GLORIFIED (Church Hymnal Corporation) for an instructional session.

Good chanting is essentially good reading on a musical tone. The rhythms and accents are essentially those of good reading. The time value of the notes is simply that of the syllables to which they are sung in Anglican chant, and for the most part, in plainchant as well. The recitation may consist of a single unaccented syllable, in which case it would be passed over lightly, or it may consist of a dozen or more syllables, in which case it would be prolonged to allow for the unhurried singing of every syllable with natural stresses.

Plainchant

A plainchant psalm tone consists of five parts:

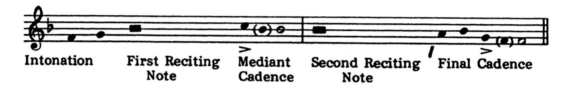

Intonation   First Reciting   Mediant   Second Reciting   Final Cadence
               Note   Cadence   Note

The intonation is sung to the first syllables of the first verse of any psalm or canticle. In responsorial psalms it is sung at the beginning of each verse which follows a refrain. In the Gospel canticles (*Benedictus Dominus Deus, Magnificat,* and *Nunc dimittis*) and sometimes in other canticles it is sung at the beginning of each verse.

All syllables in the first half of the verse not sung to the intonation or to the mediant cadence are sung to the first reciting note. (In rare instances the reciting note is omitted.)

The mediant cadence contains one or two accented notes to which are sung the final accented syllables of the first half of the verse. Other notes in the mediant cadence are sung to unaccented syllables or omitted. If the final syllable is accented, any note or notes which follow the final accented note of the music are omitted.

In the second half of the verse the second reciting note and the final cadence are used in the same manner in which the first reciting note and mediant cadence are used in the first half.

Give thanks to the Lord, for h̃e is good,* for his mercy en-/dures for év-er.

Whenever possible, plainsong should be unaccompanied. Simple accompaniments are provided in THE HYMNAL 1982; these illustrate principles of plainsong accompaniment. Four-part harmony should be avoided as much as possible. The accompaniment should be light and flexible so that it will not hinder the supple movement of the voices. Repeated notes should normally be sustained, and 16′ tone should be used sparingly, if at all. In many instances, the intonation is a sufficient introduction, but if the tune is not well known, the whole melody should be played as an introduction. If unaccompanied, the cantor should sing the first half of the first verse and the group should then join in for the remaining portion of the verse; if accompanied, however, the whole group, accompanied, should sing the whole of the first verse after an instrumental introduction consisting of the intonation or the whole verse.

Anglican Chant

Anglican chant developed from plainchant. It is an art form of great beauty when sung in four-part harmony by carefully rehearsed choirs. Many congregations sing Anglican chant with affection and enthusiasm.

An Anglican chant consists of two phrases, one of four notes in duration, followed by one of six notes. A double, triple, or quadruple chant consists of a doubling, tripling, or quadrupling of this basic pattern. Because of the fixed design of Anglican chant, a text must be pointed so that certain accented syllables will be sung to particular notes — the second and fourth notes of each section and the sixth note of the final section. The first note of each section, the reciting note, may be associated with only a single unaccented syllable (it may, in fact, on occasion be omitted) or it may be associated with a dozen or more syllables. The musical notation defines the pitch but not the duration of any note.

THE HYMNAL 1982 uses several marks to indicate the pointing. The short bar lines before accented syllables are equivalent to the bar lines in the music. Two dots over a syllable indicate that one syllable is extended over two notes. A staple over two (or sometimes three) syllables indicates that these are sung to the same note. A dash prior to a short bar line indicates that the reciting note is to be skipped.

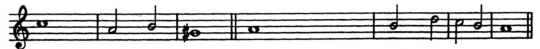

The sea is ׀ his, for he ׀ made it,* and his hands have ׀ molded the ׀ dry ׀ land.

The accompaniment should be light and flexible, and "imperceptibly ahead of the singing."* The singers must not have to pull the accompanist along. The pedals should be used sparingly, if at all.

Other Forms of Chant

Plainsong and Anglican chant form the basic musical heritage for the singing of psalms and canticles. But even as they represent the culmination of a long development, newer forms are beginning to evolve in our day. Joseph Gelineau's settings represent an imaginative, musical and singable approach, as do the settings by Peter R. Hallock in THE IONIAN PSALTER (Ionian Arts, Inc., P. O. Box 259, Mercer Island WA 98040) and those of Betty Pulkingham in CELEBRATE THE CHURCH YEAR WITH PSALMS & CANTICLES (Celebration, P. O. Box 309, Aliquippa PA 15001). THE HYMNAL 1982 also contains contemporary settings of Invitatories and Canticles by a variety of composers: Ronald Arnatt, Richard Felciano, Calvin Hampton, William Mathias, Norman Mealy, Gerald R. Near, Betty Pulkingham, John Rutter, McNeil Robinson, and Jack Noble White.

In addition THE HYMNAL 1982 includes recently devised "Simplified Anglican Chants" (S 408–S 415) which ennable a group with minimal explanation or practice to sing any Psalm or Canticle from an unpointed text.

---

*Carl Halter, THE PRACTICE OF SACRED MUSIC, St. Louis: Concordia, 1955, p. 28.

The important thing to remember is that the singing of psalms and canticles is by no means restricted to the traditional form. Congregations may want to explore new forms, keeping in mind appropriateness in the selection and excellence in preparation.

Music for the Eucharist

The Eucharistic rite involves music in several different ways: the Glory be to God / Glory to God (*Gloria in excelsis*), or other song of praise of the entrance rite; the Lord, have mercy upon us / Lord have mercy (*Kyrie*); the Kyrie eleison; the Holy God (*Trisagion*); the Creed; the Holy, holy, holy / Holy, holy, holy Lord (*Sanctus*) and Blessed is he (*Benedictus qui venit*); the Memorial Acclamation; the Great Amen; the Lord's Prayer; and the Fraction Anthem. Certain parts may be sung by the celebrant or assisting ministers. (See HEAE.) The settings for these songs should be such that priest and people are in dialogue and that the congregation can sing them well, preferably without being bookbound.

Although composers have often provided "masses" or "services" with music for each of the common texts, it is perfectly permissible to combine elements from several different composers or services within the same rite. In fact, the "masses" or "services" provided by individual composers date from a time when the choices were much more limited, when there was a so-called "ordinary" of the Mass with certain fixed elements. Sticking with the music of a "mass" or "service" or with the music of one composer can preclude the use of some texts which would be better choices for use with the particular lections or for the day or occasion. For example, any of a number of Fraction Anthems would be a better choice for use during the Easter Season than the O Lamb of God (*Agnus Dei*) even though the Holy, holy, holy (*Sanctus*) of Merbecke or of Willan was being used; and the Christ our Passover (*Pascha nostrum*), the We Praise Thee / You are God (*Te Deum laudamus*), or The Song to the Lamb (*Dignus es*) would be a better choice for the Song of Praise than the Glory be to God (*Gloria in excelsis*).

The Holy, holy, holy / Holy, holy, holy Lord (*Sanctus*) and Blessed is he (*Benedictus qui venit*) should be varied, at least seasonally. Most congregations should probably aim at learning at least three settings (for each rite if both Rite I and Rite II are used) — a more somber setting for use in Advent and Lent, a more festive one for Christmas through the First Sunday after the Epiphany (and the Last Sunday after the Epiphany) and for Easter through the Day of Pentecost, and another setting for more general use. Although in some congregations the use of additional settings might be desirable, there should not be so much variation that the congregation cannot participate with confidence.

Anthems

Judicious choice of anthems within the capability of the choir can contribute to the worship of the congregation in several ways. The use of new hymns as anthems is one of the most effective ways of teaching new hymns to the congregation. Anthems enhance a rite with music beyond the ability of the congregation and expose them to a great variety of music from the Church's heritage. They also allow the choir opportunity to make a special offering. Anthem preparation interests and challenges a choir and maintains the morale of a group of dedicated, able musicians. Close attention to textual meaning and its musical interpretation can provide a significant theological learning experience for them.

In THE BOOK OF COMMON PRAYER the word "anthem" refers to music sung by a choir or cantor rather than by the congregation. In the Roman rite anthems came into use about the fifth century in conjunction with the three processions — the entrance of the clergy, the Offertory procession, and the procession of the people to the Communion stations. The use of music by the choir (or a cantor) rather than music with congregational participation (except possibly through the singing of a responsorial verse) left the people free to listen, watch, and participate in the action.

In THE BOOK OF COMMON PRAYER an anthem is listed among the options for use at each of these three processions. Anthems are specified in the rubrics rather than hymns or psalms after the silence following the Breaking of the Bread (and the Pouring of the Wine) in the Eucharistic rites and at the lighting of the candles in An Order of Worship for Evening. At these times the congregation should not be bookbound but free to observe the liturgical actions. In addition, an anthem is also an option at the place of the Gradual and of the Sequence. On occasion an anthem setting of the Psalm of the Day would be appropriate for the Gradual, and at times a brief anthem providing a response to the Epistle or an introduction to the Gospel would be appropriate in place of a Sequence or an Alleluia Verse.

On occasion, if the congregation has participated in an entrance hymn, it is acceptable to use an anthem setting of the Gloria in excelsis or of another canticle in the entrance rite of the Eucharistic rite. Anthem settings of canticles may sometimes be appropriate in the Daily Offices. The rubric after the fixed Collects of the Daily Offices allows for an anthem. This is the point at which, in classical Anglicanism, anthems have traditionally been sung.

In addition to their use in regular services, anthems are suggested in some of the Proper Liturgies for Special Days: at the beginning of the Liturgy of the Palms on Palm Sunday and after the thanksgiving over the palms (pp. 270–271; THE HYMNAL 1982, 153); during the washing of feet on Maundy Thursday (pp. 274–275; THE HYMNAL 1982, S 344–S 347); and during the devotions before the cross on Good Friday (pp. 281–282; THE HYMNAL 1982, S 349–S 351). Among the Pastoral Offices, in addition to the anthems which may be sung for the Eucharist, an anthem is suggested at a marriage after the Declaration of Consent (p. 425) and at the wedding party's departure from the church (p. 432). At a burial an anthem is suggested at the beginning of the rite (pp. 469 and 491–492); at the Commendation (pp. 482–483 and 499); at the bearing of the body from the church (pp. 483–484 and 500); and at the committal (pp. 484–485 and 501). (See THE HYMNAL 1982, S 375–S 389.)

Evaluating Anthems for Use in Liturgical Services

Anthems should be suited to their use. The text of an anthem should relate to the particular service being celebrated. The tune should be in keeping with the mood of the service. The range, the balance of parts, and the degree of difficulty should be within the musical command of the choir. An anthem should be consonant with its position in the rite; it should enhance the flow of the service. Care should be exercised lest the anthem assume the climactic position rightly belonging to the Eucharistic Prayer.

A list of collections of suitable anthems appears in Chapter I (p. 27).

Hymns as Choir Anthems

Hymns used as choir anthems can heighten appreciation of a familiar text and/or tune and provide one of the most effective ways of teaching new hymns. Interest increases when some stanzas are sung in unison, others in harmony; some sung as solos or separately by men, women, or children; some accompanied, others a capella. Descants or fauxbourdons or varied organ accompaniments also may be used. THE HYMNAL 1982 itself is a rich resource for such variations (See Appendix I [below]; for additional resources, see above, pp. 24, 25, and 31). The publications listed below contain suitable brief preludes or introductions.

THE CONCORDIA HYMN PRELUDE SERIES (Concordia)

HYMN PRELUDES AND FREE ACCOMPANIMENTS (Augsburg)

THE PARISH ORGANIST (Concordia)

HYMN INTRODUCTIONS by Jan Bender (Concordia)

Interludes may be used between stanzas. Sometimes the last verse may be printed in the service leaflet and the congregation asked to join in. Also, when used in this manner a judicious selection of stanzas is ofter more desirable than singing the entire hymn.

Instrumental Voluntaries

This is the first edition of THE BOOK OF COMMON PRAYER which explicitly recognizes the contribution of instrumental music. Instrumental voluntaries are an effective means of teaching new music, of heightening an appreciation of familiar texts and tunes, of setting the stage for the rite, of providing opportunity for a special offering by the instrumentalists, and of exposing the congregation to a tremendous repertoire of worthy music.

Instrumental music based on hymns used in the service or on hymns or chorales thematically related to the service is normally most appropriate. The music should contribute to the rite; it should not merely entertain the congregation or exhibit the virtuosity of the instrumentalist or serve to cover worse noises.

The prelude sets the stage for the service, preparing the people to enter into the mood of the rite. It may often help the people to participate in some of the music of the rite by exposing them to it beforehand. (Note that on certain occasions a musical prelude is forbidden or undesirable [see THE BOOK OF COMMON PRAYER, pp. 142, 264, 276, 283, and 285].) The postlude sends the people on their way with a dominant theme of the service still in their minds.

In addition to the prelude and postlude, there are other opportunities for instrumental music in the rites. A rubric on page 14 states, "On occasion, and as appropriate, instrumental music may be substituted for a hymn or anthem." Instrumental music is often appropriate at the Offertory as a prelude to the Eucharistic Prayer and at the Communion of the People. On occasion it may be used appropriately as a response to a Lesson. Often it is an effective accompaniment to the entrance or exit of the ministers. Sometimes a brief selection fits in place of the Sequence or Alleluia Verse (compare p. 572) or in place of a Fraction Anthem. Instrumental music may accompany outdoor processions as is specifically suggested at the consecration of a church (p. 567).

Evaluating Instrumental Voluntaries

An instrumental voluntary makes a statement just as much as an anthem or a hymn and should be as carefully evaluated for its contribution to the particular service. It should be in keeping with the mood of the season and the rite. It should be suitable for the instrument(s) used and within the capability of the instrumentalist(s).

AN ORGANIST'S GUIDE TO RESOURCES FOR *The Hymnal 1982*, Volumes 1 and 2, compiled by Dennis Schmidt (HYMNAL STUDIES SEVEN) provides an extensive bibliography of organ music and gives references for preludes on more than two-thirds of the tunes in THE HYMNAL 1982.

Basic Collections of Organ Music _____

Listed below are several of the most useful general collections of organ music:

80 CHORALE PRELUDES. (ed. Hermann Keller) German Masters of the 17th and 18th centuries, Peters.

SEASONAL CHORALE PRELUDES. Books I and II, OUP.

THE CHURCH ORGANIST'S GOLDEN TREASURY: AN ANTHOLOGY OF CHORAL PRELUDES. (ed. Carl F. Pfatteicher and Archibald T. Davison), 3 volumes, Oliver Ditson Company.

THE PARISH ORGANIST. 12 Volumes, Concordia.

THE CONCORDIA HYMN PRELUDE SERIES. 42 Volumes, Concordia.

THE ORGANIST'S COMPANION. (ed. Wayne Leupold) a bi-monthly journal of easy organ music, mostly manuals alone, McAfee Music.

Collections of works of individual composers of particular use include the following:

J.S. Bach. ORGELBÜCHLEIN.

Johannes Brahms. ELEVEN CHORALE PRELUDES, MERCURY MUSIC (Theodore Presser).

Dietrich Buxtehude. CHORALE PRELUDES, Peters.

Johann Pachelbel. CHORALE PRELUDES, Kalmus.
PARTITAS, Kalmus.
FUGUES ON THE MAGNIFICAT, Novello.

Flor Peeters. CHORALE PRELUDES, Peters. (Various collections).

Max Reger. 30 SHORT CHORALE PRELUDES, Peters.

Samuel Scheidt. DAS GÖRLITZER TABULATURBUCH, Peters.

Georg P. Telemann. 12 EASY CHORALE PRELUDES, Kalmus.

Ralph Vaughan Williams. THREE PRELUDES FOUNDED ON WELSH HYMN TUNES, Stainer & Bell.

Louis Vierne. 24 PIECES IN FREE STYLE, Durand.

Helmut Walcha. CHORALVORSPIELE (3 Volumes), Peters.

Healey Willan. FIVE PRELUDES ON PLAINCHANT MELODIES, Oxford.
SIX CHORALE PRELUDES (2 sets), Concordia.
TEN CHORALE PRELUDES (3 sets), Peters.
36 SHORT PRELUDES AND POSTLUDES ON WELL-KNOWN HYMN TUNES, Peters.

Alec Wyton. A LITTLE CHRISTIAN YEAR, Carl Fischer.
PRELUDES FOR CHRISTIAN PRAISE, Sacred Music Press.
PRELUDES ON CONTEMPORARY HYMNS, Augsburg.

Various liturgical versets from suites and masses by French composers of the 17th and 18th centuries, especially works by Couperin, Du Mage, Clerambault, and Guilain are especially usable as organ voluntaries.

Part Three:

*Educating and
Inspiring the Congregation*

Music in Christian Education

Christian education implies that learning is going on for the entire congregation in various ways and through various structures. It is a very complex operation and varies from church to church. Imaginative opportunities must be created to talk about, present, practice, experience and participate in liturgy and its music.

An excellent resource for use with small children in introducing them to canticles and service music and more than one hundred hymns is the children's hymnal WE SING OF GOD, by Nancy and Robert Roth (Church Hymnal Corporation, 1989). Its Teacher's Guide contains valuable material on the whole process of teaching children, along with simplified accompaniments and suggestions for presentation of materials in the hymnal.

These opportunities would help children to learn hymns and service music. Adults should have seminars on liturgy and its meaning. There should also be open rehearsals for congregations at various times — before service, during the service, at a separate time. Choirs can give demonstrations as a means of showing and teaching the congregation. A hymn sing with some old favorites along with new hymns is another possibility. On occasion a hymn sing designed as a homily might be appropriate. Classes in church school can learn hymns for the current Church season. These hymns must be those for the liturgy, not the "easy" hymns which underestimate children's ability to appreciate, learn and use the best in church music. (See Acc. Ed. Vol. 1, pp. 682–683, for the Index of Hymns for use with Children and the helpful notes which precede it.)

Congregations can no longer rely on a limited number of hymns for full participation in the service. They must develop a greater musical knowledge to facilitate participation in new hymns and service music.

Teaching New Hymns and Service Music

The learning and singing of new hymns is important to the spiritual development of individuals and of congregations. An increased repertoire opens additional possibilities for relating hymnody to the lectionary. Hymn singing then becomes an integral part of the liturgy. (See TEACHING MUSIC IN SMALL CHURCHES by Marilyn J. Keiser [HYMNAL STUDIES THREE].)

Often new, strong tunes bring out the hidden worth of familiar texts. For example, compare the seriousness and intensity of the tune at 684 with the lack of such of the tune at 683 in THE HYMNAL 1982 for the text "O for a closer walk with God." In a similar vein compare the tunes at 553 and 552 for the text "Fight the good fight with all thy might," or the tunes at 200 and 199 for "Come, ye faithful, raise the strain."

One need not fear introducing new hymns because experience indicates that many congregations can maintain a repertoire of two to three hundred hymn tunes. If the repertoire is stretched too far beyond this, many tunes are not used with enough frequency for the congregation to feel at ease with them. If judicious use is made of the metrical index (see above, pp. 42–43), this number of tunes makes available an overwhelming majority of the texts of the THE HYMNAL 1982.

New hymns should be carefully chosen for their usefulness. When it is desirable to replace a familiar tune with a superior new tune, we recommend the following procedure: for example, if the congregation is familiar with the tune *Beatitudo* (683) for the text "O for a closer walk with God" and one wishes to switch to the unfamiliar tune *Caithness* (684), it might be wise to omit the use of this text for a period of time. During that time the tune *Caithness* might be taught and used with the text "Christ, when for us you were baptized" (121) or "O God, to those who here profess" (352). After this tune has been well learned, the text "O for a closer walk with God" may then be sung to it.

In introducing a new hymn, the choir should sing the melody in unison, or for the sake of absolute clarity in certain hymns, it may be desirable to have the hymn melody sung by a soloist or a cantor. The organist might play only the melody in a play-through of a new hymn. A piano might be preferable to an organ for strong, rhythmic leadership in teaching new hymns.

Much can be gained by introducing new hymns and service music in some way before expecting congregational involvement. Some churches use a "Hymn of the Month" plan in which the choir or cantor first perform it. Relevant remarks about its history and use are presented on one Sunday, in the service sheet or verbally. The hymn is then used as a congregational hymn on the remaining Sundays of the month. However, great attention should be given to its liturgical suitability for succeeding Sundays.

Some congregations have had success with a regular monthly hymn and service practice. Others have an open choir practice once a month. Church suppers, the church school, and other informal settings provide an excellent opportunity for teaching new hymns. The more relaxed atmosphere of the parish house is often more conducive to effective teaching.

Sometimes a brief pre-service warmup is desirable. This should be exceedingly well planned to make the most economical use of time. It should probably not be aimed at producing a polished performance but only at enabling the congregation to sing with some confidence one or two of the items. If lengthier pre-service practices are desired, they should probably be announced in advance and so scheduled that the service itself can begin at the usual time.

To promote interest in new hymns, notes about hymns and stories about the circumstances of their being written can be printed in the bulletin or used in sermons. The forthcoming HYMNAL 1982 COMPANION will give pertinent information for each text and tune. A COMMENTARY ON NEW HYMNS by Raymond F. Glover (HYMNAL STUDIES SIX) provides information on both text and music for seventy-seven of the hymns new to THE Hymnal 1982. Permission for the reprinting of the essays in this book is granted by the publisher. Also, since over half of both the texts and tunes in this hymnal were retained from THE HYMNAL 1940, THE HYMNAL 1940 COMPANION is still a good source of information.

People should be encouraged to possess their own copies of THE HYMNAL 1982 and THE HYMNAL 1982 COMPANION. Hymns are very useful for private and family devotions. Next to the Bible and THE BOOK OF COMMON PRAYER, THE HYMNAL 1982 is the greatest source of devotional material readily available to most people. Furthermore, people whose devotional life has been nurtured on the hymnal are more receptive to learning new hymns.

A dynamic, positive, and enthusiastic attitude from the clergy, choir, and organist can make all the difference in the acceptance of new music. A choir concerned with its educational function should not be too proud to make use of hymns in place of anthems when appropriate. Interest and variation are achieved by the use of different groupings, variation between unison singing and full harmony, and the use of canonic treatments, descants, fauxbourdons, and varied harmonizations and accompaniments. THE HYMNAL 1982 itself is a rich resource for descants, fauxbourdons, and varied harmonizations and accompaniments and canonic treatments. See Appendix I (below). (See above, pp. 24, 25 and 31, for suggested supplementary sources for descants and varied accompaniments.)

Unfamiliar hymns or service music scheduled for congregational use should be used by the organist as preludes, as postludes, and as offertory or communion voluntaries. Variations can be achieved on some of the repetitions by highlighting the melody on a solo stop and by the use of varied harmonizations. (See above, pp. 31). Suitable and useful preludes are available on more than two-thirds of the tunes in THE HYMNAL 1982 (See HYMNAL STUDIES SEVEN, Volumes 1 and 2). Using new tunes in these ways lessens the congregation's uneasiness about singing them, for the frequent hearing of a new tune lends some feeling of familiarity.

Unless the text is appropriate only for an opening or closing hymn, it is best to use a new hymn within the service. If an unfamiliar hymn used at the beginning of a service does not elicit good congregational participation, a negative reaction, difficult or impossible to counteract, may ensue. If the final hymn is unfamiliar, no matter how many familiar tunes appeared within the service, the clergy are often met at the door with, "Why do we never sing anything familiar?"

Teaching a Different Pointing for Canticles

Several steps are advisable in teaching new pointing for canticles. If there is a choir, it should be thoroughly at home with the new pointing before exposing the congregation to it. An effective approach to teaching the choir is to have them read the words of the canticle together, verse by verse, repeating until it conveys meaning, with proper stress on the words. They should then monotone the words, in the same rhythm with the same stresses. They should then sing the canticle, maintaining this same care for the text. In many situations it would be wise for the choir to sing the canticle as an anthem, possibly two or three times, before asking the congregation to participate. For the sake of absolute clarity, it would be better for a cantor rather than the choir to model the new pointing for the congregation. Then the congregation should be alerted to the difference in pointing, followed by the same procedures used with the choir — first reading, then monotoning, last of all singing the canticle.

In teaching a new canticle, it is generally best not to use a new tune with a new text or pointing, but rather to use a tune familiar to the congregation. However, when teaching a new pointing for a familiar text, a tune associated with the old pointing should not be used. If possible use some other familiar tune.

Use of Service Leaflets

Service leaflets are a basic and essential educational tool. They help the people to find their way in the service and indicate the shape of the rite. Sometimes they may specify the theme of the service. Leaflets may either provide texts and tunes needed by the congregation or indicate clearly the books within which these texts and tunes are to be found. They should usually provide translations for any texts sung in foreign languages. To facilitate participation by visitors and newcomers, brief responses, normally said or sung from memory, should be printed in the bulletin.

Information in the leaflet should assist the people in moving with ease through the service. Unfortunately, service leaflets sometimes provide more detail than the congregation needs, thus becoming more confusing than helpful. Congregations do not need to follow the whole text of a rite. Brief responses and refrains are often more effectively dealt with by reproduction in the service leaflet instead of a page reference. The refrains from GRADUAL PSALMS, ALLELUIA VERSES AND TRACTS and any items from MUSIC FOR MINISTERS AND CONGREGATION may be reproduced in the service leaflet without infringement of copyright. An increasing number of commercial publishers are giving permission to reproduce in a service leaflet the refrains or melody lines of hymns, psalms, canticles and service music. One should be sure to ascertain this freedom by checking the copyright permission statement in the source publication.

Reproduced below is a service leaflet prepared for a congregation still in the process of learning several of the regular responses from THE HYMNAL 1982. Music is reproduced in this service leaflet from MMC and GPAVT.

Second Sunday of Easter _____

Organ: Prelude on *Gelobt sei Gott* Alec Wyton
Hymn 205, "Good Christians all, rejoice and sing!" *Gelobt sei Gott*

Al - le - lu - ia. Christ is ris - en.

The Lord is ris'n in - deed. Al - le - lu - ia.

Song of Praise: S 50, "Christ our Passover" (BCP, p. 83)

Celebrant The Lord be with you.
People And also with you.
Celebrant Let us pray.

The Collect of the Day

The Word of God _____

First Reading: *Acts 3:12a, 13–15, 17–26*

After the reading

Reader The Word of the Lord.
People Thanks be to God.

Silence
Gradual: *Psalm 111* (BCP, p. 754)

REFRAIN

Hal-le-lu-jah, hal-le - lu - jah, hal-le - lu-jah!

Second Reading: *1 John 5:1–6*

After the reading

Reader The Word of the Lord.
People Thanks be to God.

Silence
Alleluia Verse: *John 20:29*

REFRAIN

Al-le-lu - ia, al - le - lu - ia, al - le - lu-ia.

Deacon The Holy Gospel of our Lord Jesus Christ according to John.
People Glory to you, Lord Christ.

The Holy Gospel: *John 20:19–31*

Deacon The Gospel of the Lord.
People Praise to you, Lord Christ.

The Sermon
The Nicene Creed (BCP, p. 358)
The Prayers of the People: Form V (BCP, p. 389)

Responses:

Lord, have mer - cy.

To you, O Lord our God.

The Peace

Celebrant The peace of the Lord be always with you.
People And also with you.
Greet one another in the name of the Lord.

The Holy Communion _____

Hymn 206, "O sons and daughters, let us sing" *O filii et filiae*
Eucharistic Prayer D (BCP, p. 372)

The Holy Eucharist II
Lift up your hearts *Sursum corda*

Celebrant *People*

The Lord be with you. And al - so with you.

Celebrant *People*

Lift up your hearts. We lift them to the Lord.

Celebrant

Let us give thanks to the Lord our God.

People

It is right to give him thanks and praise.

Sanctus: S 128   William Mathias

Memorial Acclamation: S 141   McNeil Robinson II

The Great Amen: S 147   McNeil Robinson II

The Lord's Prayer: S 148   Ambrosian

The Breaking of the Bread

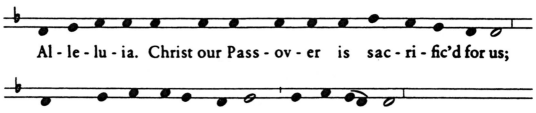

Al - le - lu - ia. Christ our Pass - ov - er is sac - ri - fic'd for us;

There - fore let us keep the feast. Al - le - lu - ia.

The Communion _____

Anthem: "This joyful Eastertide" (for text, see 192) Dutch carol
Hymn 242, "How oft, O Lord, thy face hath shone" *Jacob*

The Postcommunion Prayer (BCP, p. 365) _____

Hymn 209, "We walk by faith, and not by sight" *St. Botolph*
The Dismissal:

Let us go forth in the name of Christ, al · le · lu · ia,

al · le - lu · ia.

Thanks be to God, al · le · lu · ia,   al · le - lu · ia.

Organ: *"O sons and daughters, let us sing"* Jean Francois Dandrieu

Part Four:

*Planning Music for the
Rites of the
Book of Common Prayer and the
Book of Occasional Services*

Principles for Choosing Hymns, Service Music, Anthems, and Instrumental Voluntaries

The music used in the services of the Church should be selected according to definite principles. To fall back on the constant use of the "old," "familiar," and "well-liked" hymns, service music, anthems, and instrumental voluntaries is hardly a worthy principle. Hopefully, in the end, the new music, with frequent repetition, will become the people's own, but they cannot be expected to like every musical work on first hearing. It is important to maintain in services a balance between familiar music and that in the process of being learned.

Hymns

The hymns for a service should be chosen according to one of four principles:

(1) The Thematic or Liturgical Principle   The choice of hymn is based on the relationship of its text to the lections, theme of the day, and the particular place it will occupy in the rite. (See the Liturgical and Subject Index, Acc. Ed. Vol. 1, pp. 684–702, or the much fuller and more detailed A LITURGICAL INDEX TO THE HYMNAL 1982 by Marion J. Hatchett [HYMNAL STUDIES FIVE] and the Index of Scriptural References, Acc. Ed. Vol. 1, pp. 703–711, or A SCRIPTURAL INDEX TO THE HYMNAL 1982 by Marion J. Hatchett [HYMNAL STUDIES EIGHT], which gives the first lines of the hymns and indicates where the Scriptural texts appear in the lectionaries.)

(2) The Seasonal Principle   At points in the rite for which there is no peculiarly appropriate hymn, it is suitable to use a seasonal hymn.

(3) The Teaching Principle   Hymns which the congregation is currently learning should be used frequently at services whenever the text is suitable.

(4) The "Use in Course" Principle   Much of the lectionary is based on the use of psalms and lessons "in course" (that is, read sequentially). This is an assurance that fitting passages will not be overlooked in a given period of time. When hymns cannot be chosen according to the above principles, the gaps within a service should be filled according to the "use in course" principle. A definite record should be kept of the use of each hymn at the principal services.

Service Music

Analogous principles apply to the choice of service music. Each congregation should know more than one setting for each of the songs of the people. This makes possible some contrast between ordinary Sundays and the preparatory seasons of Advent and Lent, on the one hand, or the festal seasons of Christmas-Epiphany and Easter-Pentecost on the other. Settings currently being taught should be used almost exclusively for a period of time. This will quickly bring a sense of ease on the part of the congregation. A word of caution: in the emphasis on learning the new, do not neglect the use of the familiar for such an extended period of time that the people lose confidence in singing it.

Anthems

Ideally the anthem should enhance the proclamation of the lections for the day or occasion or provide a meditation on them or appropriate response to them. The text of an anthem should be suited to the action it accompanies (Entrance, Offertory, or Communion). When peculiarly apt texts are not available, an anthem generally suited to the season is acceptable. When choosing music for the choir, hymns and service music projected for later congregational use should be high on the list of priorities. Finally, good anthems should not fall into disuse but should be used according to a "use in course" scheme. A definite record should be kept of the use of each anthem at a principal service.

Instrumental Voluntaries

Much the same principles as those for anthems apply to the choice of instrumental voluntaries. Those with word associations for the people, thus helping to set the stage for the particular lections, or encouraging reflection on them, should have high priority. The voluntary should be used frequently to familiarize the people with new hymns or service music. At other times, it is fitting to employ music with no particular word associations but with content which helps to set the stage for a particular service or expresses an appropriate musical response to the rite.

Planning Music for the Daily Office

Two strands of tradition lie behind the Daily Office of THE BOOK OF COMMON PRAYER: the weekday forms of the Liturgy of the Word, centered in the reading and exposition of the Scriptures, and the periods of private prayer which later within monasticism developed into corporate Offices which sanctify with prayer the principal divisions of the day. Because of the nature of the Daily Office, permission to precede or follow an Office with a hymn has been withdrawn. A hymn seems inappropriate before the Opening Preces of Morning Prayer. Note that Morning or Evening Prayer may be used as the Liturgy of the Word at the Eucharist in conformity with directions on pages 142 and 322, or 354.

Daily Morning Prayer

Pre-Service Music Congregational participation can be greatly enhanced if the time immediately before the Office is devoted to familiarizing the people with the music. The music of the Office itself may be used or preludes based on it. (See HYMNAL STUDIES SEVEN Volumes 1 and 2.) In addition to music used for teaching purposes, other instrumental music is often excellent at this point.

Opening Sentences If used, the opening sentence(s) may be monotoned.

Opening Preces For the music of the Opening Preces, see THE HYMNAL 1982 S 1 (Rite I) and S 33 (Rite II).

Invitatory Psalm See THE HYMNAL 1982 S 2–S 7 and S 11–S 15 for settings of the Venite and Jubilate for Rite I and S 34–S 45 and S 295 for settings for Rite II. Antiphons are provided for every day of the year for use with the Invitatory Psalm (S 289–S 291 for Rite I, S 293–S 295 for Rite II). Traditionally this Psalm is sung responsorially. The cantor or choir begins by singing the Antiphon, then repeated by the people. The choir or cantor then sings the verses with the congregation singing the Antiphon after each division of the Venite or each verse of the Jubilate. When Anglican pointing is used for the Antiphon, however, it is sung only before and after the Invitatory Psalm. The Antiphon's purpose is to highlight the emphasis of the day or season. On occasion, the congregation may sing the Invitatory Psalm, with or without the Antiphon. A metrical version of the Invitatory Psalm may also be used. (See THE HYMNAL 1982 399 for a metrical version of Venite and 377, 378 and 391 for metrical versions of Jubilate.)

377, 378   All people that on earth do dwell
391   Before the Lord's eternal throne
399   To God with gladness sing

Psalm 95 is used in its entirety on Ash Wednesday, Holy Saturday, and all Fridays during Lent. (See BCP, pp. 950–957.) It may be used at other times. For settings of this psalm see THE HYMNAL 1982 S 8–S 10 (Rite I), with its antiphon at S 291 and S 292, and S 34 and S 36–S 40 (Rite II).

Christ our Passover (*Pascha nostrum*) is sung in Easter Week in place of the Invitatory Psalm and may be used until the Day of Pentecost. For settings see THE HYMNAL 1982 S 16–S 20 (Rite I) and S 46–S 50 (Rite II). The Easter Antiphon is not used with Christ our Passover (*Pascha nostrum*), for it has its own antiphon, "Alleluia."

Variable Psalm(s)   The variable psalms may be sung in unison, antiphonally, or responsorially. The antiphonal method is traditional; because of the length of selections for the Daily Office, this method seems best in most situations. Plainchant and Anglican chant are the usual setting of the psalms in the Daily Office. Plainchant is generally easier and more effective. Anglican chant is a desirable alternative with a group which sings together daily and can do parts with ease. Settings are provided for the whole Psalter in both of the Church Hymnal publications, THE PLAINSONG PSALTER and THE ANGLICAN CHANT PSALTER. THE PLAINSONG PSALTER provides antiphons for use before and after each Psalm (after Glory to the Father [*Gloria Patri*] if that is said at the end of the Psalm). The Psalms may also be sung to "Simplified Anglican Chant" (S 408–S 415).

Glory to the Father (*Gloria Patri*) is to be used after the last psalm and may be used after each psalm or after each section of Psalm 119. Even if the psalm is antiphonal, the Glory to the Father (*Gloria Patri*) is sung by all. If the psalm is said, so is the Gloria Patri.

Old Testament Lesson   If the Old Testament Lesson is sung, the announcement and conclusion should also be sung. See HEAE or MMC for instructions on the singing of lessons.

Silence   A period of silence may follow the reading.

Canticle   After an Old Testament Lesson, a pre-incarnational canticle (1, 2, 4, or 8–14, 16) is appropriate. (See THE HYMNAL 1982 S 177–S 184, S 190–S 195, S 208–S 241, S 248–S 252, S 394, S 400–S 402 and S 404 for plainchant, Anglican chant, and "through composed" settings.) The Canticle of Moses (8) is particularly appropriate in the Easter Season, and a Song of Penitence (14) during Lent or on penitential occasions. A table suggests canticles appropriate to each of the days of the week (BCP, pp. 144–145). Glory to the Father (*Gloria Patri*) is not required but may be used after Canticles 4, 8, 9, 10, 11, or 16. (It is probably best to omit Glory to the Father (*Gloria Patri*) if using a canticle setting with a translation different from that of THE BOOK OF COMMON PRAYER; it is also less confusing to omit it when an antiphon is sung.) Canticle texts printed in Rite One may be used in Rite Two, and vice versa. Other previously authorized translations may be used if the music requires it as well as metrical versions of the canticles. THE HYMNAL 1982 contains metrical versions of several of these canticles (See: Volume 1, Service Music, pp. 680–681): 1 and 12 A Song of Creation (*Benedicite, omnia opera Domini*, 428; 4 and 16 The Song of Zechariah (*Benedictus Dominus Deus*), 444; 9 The First Song of Isaiah (*Ecce, Deus*), 678, 679; 11 The Third Song of Isaiah (*Surge, illuminare*), 543.

428	O all ye works of God, now come
444	Blessed be the God of Israel
678, 679	Surely it is God who saves me
543	O Zion, tune thy voice

"In special circumstances, in place of a Canticle, a hymn may be sung" (BCP, p. 142). Services with a congregation unable to sing canticles or made up largely of children may use a hymn in place of the canticle. This could also apply to certain festal days.

New Testament Lesson If the New Testament Lesson is sung, the announcement and conclusion should also be sung. See HEAE or MMC for instructions on singing the lessons.

Silence A period of silence may be kept after the reading.

Sermon If two Lessons are used, the sermon will follow at this point. (See BCP, pp. 113, 142.)

Canticle After a lesson from the New Testament, a post-incarnational canticle (3, 5–7, or 15, 17–21) is appropriate. (See THE HYMNAL 1982 S 185–S 189, S 196–S 207, S 242–S 247, S 253–S 288, S 393, S 395–S 399, S 403, and S 405–S 407 for plainchant, Anglican chant, and "through composed" settings.) A table suggests canticles appropriate to each of the days of the week (BCP, pp. 144–145). It is traditional to omit either Glory be to God / Glory to God (*Gloria in excelsis*) or We Praise Thee / You are God (*Te Deum laudamus*) on ordinary days of Advent or Lent. Glory to the Father (*Gloria Patri*) is not required but may be used after canticles 3, 5, 15, 17, 19. (It is probably best to omit Glory to the Father (*Gloria Patri*) if using a canticle setting with a translation different from that of THE BOOK OF COMMON PRAYER; it is also less confusing to omit it when an antiphon is sung.) Texts appearing in Rite Two may be used in Rite One, and vice versa. Other previously authorized translations may be used if the music requires it. Metrical versions of the canticles may be used. THE HYMNAL 1982 contains metrical versions of these canticles (See: Volume 1, Service Music, pp. 680–681): 3 and 15 The Song of Mary (*Magnificat*), 437, 438; 5 and 17 The Song of Simeon (*Nunc dimittis*), 499; 6 and 20 Glory to God (*Gloria in excelsis*), 421; 7 and 21 We Praise Thee / You are God (*Te Deum laudamus*), 364 and 366; 18 A Song to the Lamb (*Dignus es*), 374 and 417, 418; 19 The Song of the Redeemed (*Magna et mirabilia*), 532, 533.

437, 438	Tell out, my soul, the greatness of the Lord!
499	Lord God, you now have set your servant free
421	All glory be to God on high
364	O God, we praise thee, and confess
366	Holy God, we praise thy Name
374	Come, let us join our cheerful songs
417, 418	This is the feast of victory for our God
532, 533	How wondrous and great thy works, God of praise!

In special circumstances a hymn may be used in place of a canticle. (See above under *Canticle.*)

Gospel If all three Lessons are used, the Gospel comes after the canticle following the

New Testament reading. If it is sung, the announcement and conclusion should also be sung. See HEAE or MMC for the singing of lessons.

There is no permission to sing a hymn between the Lesson and the sermon. Nothing should intervene between the people's response to the lection and the initial sentence of the sermon. If fewer than three Lessons are used, the sermon will follow the last Lesson and precede a canticle. (See BCP, pp. 113, 142.)

Apostles' Creed   If this is monotoned, it is not good form for an organist to accompany it. Music may intrude as well as enhance. This is an occasion on which it intrudes.

Suffrages   See THE HYMNAL 1982 S 21–S 23 (Rite I) or S 51–S 53 (Rite II). The responses should not be accompanied after the congregation has learned them. The second set of suffrages has been associated traditionally with the We Praise Thee / You are God (*Te Deum laudamus*) and the Glory be to God / Glory to God (*Gloria in excelsis*).

Collects   One or more Collects and a Prayer for mission are required except in special circumstances. See THE HYMNAL 1982 S 447–S 448 or HEAE or MMC for tones for the Collects.

Hymn or Anthem   Much of the English cathedral anthem repertoire was composed for use at this point in the Daily Office. This is also a good time for an Office hymn or one related to the lections of the day, a seasonal hymn or a general hymn of praise.

The Hymnal 1982   contains several hymns traditionally associated with the ancient morning Offices which contributed to Morning Prayer:

> 1, 2   Father, we praise thee, now the night is over
> (Matins)
> 5   O splendor of God's glory bright (Lauds)
> 3, 4   Now that the daylight fills the sky (Prime)

In addition a number of seasonal office hymns are included in the book. Hymns 6–11 are also peculiarly appropriate for morning use.

A Liturgical Index to The Hymnal 1982   by Marion J. Hatchett (HYMNAL STUDIES FIVE) lists hymns for use at Morning Prayer, related to the lections, for every day of the two-year lectionary cycle. An offering may be quietly received and placed upon the altar during the course of the hymn or anthem. Processions of a triumphal nature and presentation sentences are inappropriate in the Daily Office.

Intercessions and Thanksgivings   Prayers following the Collect structure may be sung to a collect tone. Other prayers may be monotoned.

Concluding Versicle and Response   For music see THE HYMNAL 1982 S 24–S 25 or S 54–S 55.

The Grace   This sentence of scripture may be monotoned.

Postlude   The postlude reflects or sums up the rite. This might be the occasion to use a voluntary based on that text which best sums up the rite or one introducing an unfamiliar tune. See HYMNAL STUDIES SEVEN, Volumes 1 and 2.

An Order of Service for Noonday

For the musical setting see THE HYMNAL 1982 S 296–S 304 or the separate booklet, MUSICAL SETTINGS FOR NOONDAY AND COMPLINE.

Prelude   See Morning Prayer (above).

Opening Preces   For the music for the Opening Preces see THE HYMNAL 1982 S 296.

Hymn   Though the rite is designated "An Order of Service for Noonday" it includes alternative texts appropriate for each of the traditional "Little Offices" — Terce, Sext, and Nones, and THE HYMNAL 1982 provides texts, traditional and contemporary, appropriate for each of these hours.

12, 13	The golden sun lights up the sky (Terce)
19, 20	Now Holy Spirit, ever One (Terce)
16, 17	Now let us sing our praise to God (Sext)
18	As now the sun shines down at noon (Sext)
21, 22	O God of truth, O Lord of might (Sext)
14, 15	O God, creation's secret force (Nones)
23	The fleeting day is nearly gone (Nones)

Psalm(s)   For music see S 297–S 300. The Psalm(s) may be sung as at Morning Prayer, although unison singing may be desirable because of the shorter selections. Everyone sings Glory to the Father (*Gloria Patri*) at the end of the Psalms. If the Psalm is said, Glory to the Father (*Gloria Patri*) must be said. These Psalms or other appropriate Psalms may be sung to the settings of THE PLAINSONG PSALTER or THE ANGLICAN CHANT PSALTER or to Simplified Anglican Chant (S 408–S 415). (The first Psalm is particularly appropriate for Terce, the second for Sext, and the third for Nones.)

Scripture   See THE HYMNAL 1982 S 301–S 303, or the Lesson may be monotoned and the response sung. (The first Lesson is particularly appropriate for Terce, the second for Sext, and the third for Nones.)

Prayers   See S 304. For the Collect, see S 448. (The first Collect is particularly appropriate for Terce, the second and third for Sext, and the fourth for Nones.) The Collect may be monotoned.

Dismissal   For the music see S 304.

Postlude   See Morning Prayer (above).

An Order of Worship for the Evening

This Order may be used as a complete rite; as an introduction to Evening Prayer, the Holy Eucharist, or some other rite; or as the prelude to an evening meal or other activity.

"A musical prelude or processional is not appropriate" (BCP, p. 142).

Opening Acclamation   For the music see THE HYMNAL 1982 S 56–S 57 (S 78–S 83 in Lent and Easter Season), HEAE or MMC.

Short Lesson of Scripture   It is appropriate to sing this short Lesson according to the tone provided in HYMNAL 1982 S 449 (also in HEAE and MMC) or to monotone it.

Prayer for Light   See THE HYMNAL 1982 S 447–S 448, HEAE or MMC for collect tones.

Anthem, Psalm, or Silence   For traditional anthems at the Candle Lighting, see THE HYMNAL 1982 S 305–S 320. A cantor or choir might sing one of the traditional evening psalms (8, 23, 36, 84, 93, 113, 114, 117, 121, 134, 139, 141, 143) (For music, see THE PLAINSONG PSALTER, THE ANGLICAN CHANT PSALTER, or Simplified Anglican Chant [S 408–S 415].) It is not appropriate to have a congregational hymn or psalm at this point for the attention of the people should be on the lighting of the candles rather than on a book or service sheets.

O Gracious Light (Phos hilaron)   For settings of this canticle see THE HYMNAL 1982
S 27 and S 59–S 61. For metrical settings see:

25, 26	O gracious Light, Lord Jesus Christ
36	O gladsome light, O grace
37	O brightness of the immortal Father's face

The tune at 26 for the first of these texts has particular associations with the season of
Advent. In the various seasons other hymns which stress the imagery of light would be
appropriate substitutions for the Phos hilaron.

Advent 60	Creator of the stars of night
Christmas 85, 86	O Savior of our fallen race
Epiphany 125, 126	The people who in darkness walked
Lent 144	Lord Jesus, Sun of righteousness
Ascension 217, 218	A hymn of glory let us sing
Trinity Sunday 29, 30	O Trinity of blessèd light

On occasion other evening hymns which make use of the imagery of light might be
substituted.

27, 28	O blest Creator, source of light
31, 32	Most Holy God, the Lord of heaven
33, 34, 35	Christ, mighty Savior, Light of all creation
38, 39	Jesus, Redeemer of the world
40, 41	O Christ, you are both light and day

The service may continue with Evening Prayer (beginning with the Psalms), with the
Holy Eucharist (beginning with the Salutation and Collect of the Day), or with some
other Office or devotion. If a meal or some other activity is to follow, the service may
conclude with the Lord's Prayer and a Grace or Blessing or it may continue with the
elements outlined on page 113 of THE BOOK OF COMMON PRAYER.

Psalm(s)   These may be sung as at Morning Prayer (above).

Silence   A period of silence may follow the Psalm(s).

Collect   A Collect related to the Psalm(s) may be used. It is hoped that use of traditional
psalter Collects will be revived. A full series of Psalter Collects may be found in the
Canadian BOOK OF ALTERNATIVE SERVICES (Toronto: Anglican Book Center) and
another in LUTHERAN BOOK OF WORSHIP: MINISTERS DESK EDITION (Minneapolis:
Augsburg). For collect tones see THE HYMNAL 1982 S 447–S 448, HEAE, or MMC.

Lesson   The reading, with its announcement and conclusion, may be sung. (See HEAE
or MMC for lesson tones.) A sermon, a reading, or silence may follow the Lesson.

Canticle or Hymn of Praise   The Song of Mary (*Magnificat*), a canticle including the
theme of light (for example, The Third Song of Isaiah [*Surge, illuminare*], The Song of
Zechariah [*Benedictus Dominus Deus*], or The Song of Simeon [*Nunc dimittis*]), a hymn
based on the theme of light, or a general hymn of praise may be used.

Prayers   A litany or other devotions may be sung or said.

Lord's Prayer   Even if other prayers have been said, the Lord's Prayer may be sung.
It may be monotoned as in conjunction with suffrages at Morning or Evening Prayer,
or a setting such as those in THE HYMNAL 1982 S 119 (traditional) or S 148–S 150
(contemporary) may be used.

Concluding Collect   See S 447–S 448, HEAE, or MMC for collect tones.

Blessing and Dismissal See HEAE or MMC for tones for both blessings and dismissals, or THE HYMNAL 1982 S 65–S 66 for dismissals. "Alleluia, alleluia" is added to the Dismissal and response during the Easter Season.

Postlude See Morning Prayer (above).

Daily Evening Prayer

The structure of the rite and the ceremonial action are basically the same as those for Morning Prayer (above). For music for Opening Preces see S 26 (Rite I) or S 58 (Rite II).

An Invitatory Psalm is not required as at Morning Prayer, but may be used. The optional O Gracious Light *(Phos hilaron)* is printed in the rite, with permission to make use of a metrical version or some other suitable hymn. (See An Order of Worship for the Evening [above] for references to settings of Phos hilaron and suitable hymns.)

Normally only one Lesson would be used; the Gospel in Year One and the Epistle in Year Two. Any of the canticles printed in Morning Prayer may be used at Evening Prayer. See the table of Suggested Canticles at Evening Prayer (BCP, p. 145) for canticles appropriate to the days of the week.

For music for the Suffrages and Dismissal, see THE Hymnal 1982 S 28–S 32 (Rite I) or S 62–S 66 (Rite II).

An Order for Compline

For the musical setting see THE HYMNAL 1982 S 321–S 337 or the separate booklet, MUSICAL SETTINGS FOR NOONDAY AND COMPLINE.

Prelude See Morning Prayer (above).

Preces See THE HYMNAL 1982 S 321 for music.

Psalm(s) See S 322–S 326. The Psalm(s) may be sung as at Morning Prayer. Because the selections are shorter, unison singing may be desirable. All sing Glory to the Father *(Gloria Patri)* at the end of the Psalms. If the Psalm is said, so is the Glory to the Father *(Gloria Patri)*.

Scripture See S 327–S 330. The Lesson may be monotoned, and the response sung.

Hymn An evening hymn is suitable here. Sometimes it is permissible to substitute a seasonal hymn.

Suffrages and Lord's Prayer See S 331–S 335.

Collects For collect tone see S 448, HEAE, or MMC.

Antiphon, Alleluias, and The Song of Simeon (Nunc dimittis) See S 336. For other settings of the The Song of Simeon *(Nunc dimittis)* see S 196–S 200 and S 395 (traditional) or S 253–S 260 and S 405 (contemporary).

Concluding Versicle and Response and Benedicamus and Blessing For music see S 337.

Postlude If used at the end of Compline, it should be quiet and restrained.

Planning Music for the Great Litany

The Great Litany may be sung or read by the officiant, kneeling or standing in some prominent place so as to be both seen and heard.

The Great Litany may be used as an entrance rite for the Holy Eucharist. This is a dramatic way of marking the First Sunday of Advent, the First Sunday in Lent, and/or the Rogation Days.

In some architectural situations, it is possible and sometimes desirable to sing the Litany in procession either within or outside the church building. The ministers and choir or the whole congregation may participate in the procession. Where appropriate, the invocations might be sung before the altar. The procession might circle the church, then return to the altar or the chancel steps for the Lord's Prayer and the concluding collect.

For music for the Great Litany see S 67 (the entire text of the Great Litany is printed at S 67 in the Accompaniment Volume).

Two settings of the Supplication are provided at S 338–S 339.

Planning Music for the Church Year

Advent Season _____

The emphasis for the First Sunday of Advent is eschatological; for the next two Sundays the emphasis shifts to John the Baptist, and for the Last Sunday to the Annunciation. For suggestions for appropriate hymns for the different Sundays, see the Liturgical and Subject Index, Acc. Ed. Vol. 1, pp. 684–685, or for a fuller and more detailed listing for each of the three years of the Eucharistic Lectionary cycle, see HYMNAL STUDIES FIVE: A LITURGICAL INDEX TO THE HYMNAL 1982 (New York: Church Hymnal Corporation) (hereafter this volume will be referred to simply as HYMNAL STUDIES FIVE).

Advent might be set apart from the Sundays after Pentecost preceding it and from the festal Christmas Season following it by beginning the Eucharistic rite with the Great Litany, possibly in procession, or with the Penitential Order.

THE BOOK OF OCCASIONAL SERVICES provides an order for an Advent Festival of Lessons and Music. See below, pp. 98–99.

Christmas Season _____

THE HYMNAL 1982 contains a large section of hymns specific to Christmas Day or to the Christmas Season (77–115). In addition a number of hymns printed in other sections of The Hymnal are appropriate. See Acc. Ed. Vol. 1, pp. 685–686, and HYMNAL STUDIES FIVE, pp. 177–181.

THE BOOK OF OCCASIONAL SERVICES provides a vigil for use prior to the first Eucharist of Christmas, a station at a Christmas creche, and a Christmas Festival of Lessons and Music (See below).

At some point within the Christmas Season, either on New Year's Eve, or on a Sunday after Christmas, it is appropriate to mark the New Year. This may be the Service for New Year's Eve (BOS) (See below), or, on the other hand, a simple inclusion of appropriate petitions and hymns within the rites of the First or Second Sunday after

Christmas or the Feast of the Holy Name. Suitable hymns are provided in THE HYMNAL 1982 at 250–251, and others are listed in Acc. Ed. Vol. 1, p. 685.

January 1 is the Feast of the Holy Name. This day takes precedence over the Sunday. THE HYMNAL 1982 provides two texts specifically for this day (248, 249 and 252). Other suitable hymns are listed in Acc. Ed. Vol. 1, p. 690, and in HYMNAL STUDIES FIVE, pp. 179–180.

When there is a Second Sunday after Christmas, one of three Gospels may be read: the flight into Egypt and return to Nazareth; the visit to the temple at the age of twelve; or the visit of the magi. If the emphasis is on the Holy Family and family life, related Christmas hymns or hymns with family themes may be used. Recommendations for use with each of these Gospels may be found in Acc. Ed. Vol. 1, pp. 685–686, and in HYMNAL STUDIES FIVE, pp. 180–181.

Epiphany Season

On the feast of the Epiphany the Gospel is the story of the visit of the magi. Suitable hymns are listed in Acc. Ed. Vol. 1, p. 686, and in HYMNAL STUDIES FIVE, p. 181.

For the First Sunday after the Epiphany, the Baptism of our Lord, THE BOOK OF OCCASIONAL SERVICES provides a vigil for use in connection with baptism and the Eucharist. (See below.) For hymns suitable for the Sunday, see Acc. Ed. Vol. 1, p. 686, and HYMNAL STUDIES FIVE, pp. 181–182. The First Sunday after the Epiphany is one of the five baptismal days of the Church Year.

For special texts and ceremonies for use in connection with the Presentation of Our Lord Jesus Christ in the Temple, "Candlemas," another feast taking precedence over the Sunday, see BOS. For the musical settings see THE HYMNAL 1982 S 340–S 343 (See below.) THE HYMNAL 1982 provides two hymns proper to the day (257 and 259). Other suitable hymns are listed in Acc. Ed. Vol. 1, pp. 690–691, and HYMNAL STUDIES FIVE, pp. 263–264.

On the Last Sunday after the Epiphany the Gospel is the story of the Transfiguration. As the climax of the Christmas-Epiphany Season and the last Sunday before Lent, this day should receive special attention. THE HYMNAL 1982 contains several texts devoted to the Transfiguration (129, 130; 133, 134; and 136, 137). Hymn 135 encapsulates the major emphases of the season, ending with a newly written last stanza devoted to the Transfiguration. The text at 122 and 123, which bids good-by to the use of Alleluia for the season of Lent, might suitably be used as the final hymn. Other hymns are also suggested in Acc. Ed. Vol. 1, p. 686, and HYMNAL STUDIES FIVE, pp. 185, 218, and 242 (Years A, B, and C).

Lenten Season

See the PROPER LITURGIES FOR SPECIAL DAYS (below) for Ash Wednesday, Palm Sunday, Maundy Thursday, Good Friday, and Holy Saturday.

Lent might be set apart from the surrounding festal seasons by beginning the Eucharistic rite with the Great Litany, possibly in procession, or with the Penitential Order.

THE BOOK OF OCCASIONAL SERVICES provides special material for Lenten services relating to the adult catechumenate. It also contains an allocution and directions for the reservation of the Sacrament and the stripping of the altar at the Maundy Thursday liturgy, and two special rites for Lent, the Way of the Cross for Fridays other than Good Friday, and Tenebrae for Wednesday in Holy Week. (See below.) LESSER FEASTS AND FASTS provides propers for a daily Eucharist in Lent.

For hymns appropriate to the season (in addition to those in the Lent and Holy Week sections [140–173]) see Acc. Ed. Vol. 1, pp. 686–687, and HYMNAL STUDIES FIVE, pp. 185–191, 218–221, and 242–244 (Years A, B, and C).

For the Great Vigil of Easter see the PROPER LITURGIES FOR SPECIAL DAYS (below).

The Easter season is again, as in the early Church, a season fifty days in length; the Paschal celebration should be sustained throughout this time. THE HYMNAL 1982 contains a large section of hymns devoted to Easter (174–213). In addition, a number of hymns in other sections of the book are suitable. See Acc. Ed. Vol. 1, pp. 687–689, and HYMNAL STUDIES FIVE, pp. 191–199, 221–223, and 244–247 (Years A, B, and C).

The ancient Tonus Peregrinus has been associated traditionally with the Jewish Passover and the Christian Easter Season. This tone is provided in THE HYMNAL 1982 for the Opening Acclamation (S 79), the Pascha nostrum (S 50), the Fraction Anthem (S 151), and the Dismissal (S 176). Both THE PLAINSONG PSALTER and THE ANGLICAN CHANT PSALTER set the Gradual Psalm of the Easter Vigil (Psalm 114) to this tone. THE PLAINSONG PSALTER also sets Psalm 105, Part II, Psalm 115, and Psalm 136 to this tone. Furthermore, several of the canticles are set to this tone (A Song of Creation [*Benedicite, omnia opera Domini*], S 177 and S 228; The Song of Mary [*Magnificat*], S 242; The Song of Zechariah [*Benedictus Dominus Deus*], S 190; The Song of Moses (*Cantemus Domino*], S 208). The use of these settings for these psalms and canticles would be particularly appropriate during the Easter Season.

Propers are provided in the Prayer Book for a daily Eucharist the first week of Easter and in LESSER FEASTS AND FASTS for the remainder of the Season.

The traditional time for the celebration of the Rogation Days is the Monday, Tuesday, and Wednesday after the Sixth Sunday of Easter. See BOS for the Rogation procession. (See below.) These days might be marked by the use of the Great Litany, possibly in procession. (See above, pp. 71.) Suitable hymns are suggested in Acc. Ed. Vol. 1, p. 694, and in HYMNAL STUDIES FIVE, p. 286.

THE HYMNAL 1982 includes several hymns specifically for Ascension Day (214–222). Other suitable hymns are recommended in Acc. Ed. Vol. 1, pp. 688–689, and in HYMNAL STUDIES FIVE, p. 198.

For the vigil of Pentecost see PROPER LITURGIES FOR SPECIAL DAYS (below).

Pentecost ranks next after Easter Day as a primary feast day of the Church Year. Many hymns dealing with the Holy Spirit are not suitable for use on the Day of Pentecost because they either do not celebrate the event of the outpouring of the Holy Spirit or they lack a festive character.

THE HYMNAL 1982 contains two translations of the traditional Sequence for Pentecost:

226, 227 Come, thou Holy Spirit bright
    228 Holy Spirit, font of light

It also contains other hymns proper to the day:

223, 224 Hail this joyful day's return
    225 Hail thee, festival day!
    229 Spirit of mercy, truth, and love
    230 A mighty sound from heaven

Other suitable hymns are listed in Acc. Ed. Vol. 1, p. 689, and in HYMNAL STUDIES FIVE, pp. 199–200. Pentecost is one of the five baptismal days or occasions of the Church Year. Particularly appropriate baptismal hymns for this occasion are:

    297 Descend, O Spirit, purging flame
    299 Spirit of God, unleashed on earth
    513 Like the murmur of the dove's song

Particularly appropriate hymns for use immediately after the baptisms would include:

294 Baptized in water, sealed by the Spirit

295 Sing praise to our creator

296 We know that Christ is raised and dies no more

The Season after Pentecost

The First Sunday after Pentecost is Trinity Sunday. Particularly appropriate are the hymns in the section headed "The Holy Trinity" (362–371). Other related hymns are listed in Acc. Ed. Vol. 1, p. 689, and in HYMNAL STUDIES FIVE, pp. 200–201, 223–224, and 247–248 (Years A, B, and C).

The major feast within this Season is All Saints. This day, or the Sunday after All Saints' Day, is one of the five baptismal days of the Church year. A baptismal vigil is provided in the BOS; also included here is a quite different type of service for All Hallows' Eve. (See below.) Hymns particularly appropriate for All Saints are listed in Acc. Ed. Vol. 1, p. 692, and in HYMNAL STUDIES FIVE, pp. 273–274.

The final Sundays of the Season after Pentecost have an eschatological emphasis. Suitable hymns are listed in Acc. Ed. Vol. 1, p. 689, and in HYMNAL STUDIES FIVE, pp. 212, 235–236, and 259 (Years A, B, and C).

On the Last Sunday after Pentecost the emphasis is on the kingship of Christ. Suitable hymns are listed in Acc. Ed. Vol. 1, pp. 689–690, and in HYMNAL STUDIES FIVE, pp. 213, 236–237, and 260 (Years A, B, and C).

Proper Liturgies for Special Days

For music see Supplement to HEAE (PROPER LITURGIES FOR SPECIAL DAYS).

Ash Wednesday

(Supplement to HEAE, pp. 240–245)

On Ash Wednesday there should be no music before the service, and the entrance of the ministers should be in silence. The rite begins with the Salutation (*Celebrant:* The Lord be with you. *People:* And also with you.) and the Collect of the Day. A full series of Readings is provided: Old Testament Lesson, Gradual, Epistle, and Gospel. A Tract (see GPAVT) or a Sequence is appropriate between the Epistle and the Gospel. There is a sermon, but the Nicene Creed is omitted. An exhortation and a period of silence follow the sermon.

Prayer (BCP, p. 265). See THE HYMNAL 1982 S 447–S 448, HEAE, or MMC for collect tones.

Psalm 51 The choir or congregation may sing this in unison, antiphonally, or responsorially. See THE PLAINSONG PSALTER or THE ANGLICAN CHANT PSALTER for musical settings (Note that only verses 1–18 are to be used). If desired, a verse from the Psalm or other verse of Scripture may be used as an Antiphon. It would be fitting for the singing of the Psalm to begin during the imposition of ashes if a large number are receiving the imposition.

Litany of Penitence If singing the Litany is desired, the tones used for the Great Litany can be adapted for the Suffrages and Responses.

See HYMNAL STUDIES FIVE, pp. 185–186, for hymn recommendations.

Palm Sunday

(Supplement to HEAE, pp. 246–257; MMC, pp. 28–31.) THE HYMNAL 1982 153)

Pre-Service Music   A bell or other musical instrument might call the people to silence for the opening anthem. Brass, strings, or other portable musical instruments, later used to accompany the procession, might perform a brief, informal prelude.

Anthem   The text in THE BOOK OF COMMON PRAYER or some other suitable anthem may be sung by the choir. In some situations this anthem might be sung as a simple versicle and response between priest, deacon, or cantor and choir or congregation (See THE HYMNAL 1982 153).

Collect and Reading   See THE Hymnal 1982 S 447–S 448, HEAE, or MMC for collect tones, and HEAE or MMC for Lesson tones.

Blessing of the Palms   Even if the Collect and Reading are said, the form of the blessing of the palms may be sung. (See HEAE.)

Anthem   The choir may sing this or some other fitting text. Sometimes this anthem could be sung as a simple versicle and response between a priest or a deacon or a cantor and the choir or the congregation (See THE HYMNAL 1982 153).

Procession   Hymns with easily memorized refrains (such as "All glory, laud, and honor," THE HYMNAL 1982 154 or 155) and responsorial psalmody (Ps. 118, vv. 19–29, HYMNAL 1982 157, or MMC) are best for the procession.

The cantor sings the refrain of either hymn or Psalm; the congregation then repeats it after the cantor and after each verse or group of verses sung by cantor or choir. This avoids the awkwardness for the people of singing from a printed sheet as they process. Portable musical instruments help to give support and keep the group together.

Station   The procession may halt at some landmark on the grounds or at the church entrance for the station Collect, sung to a common collect tone.

Since congregational singing often deteriorates while people climb steps or go through entrances, it is usually wise to end the singing at the door with the station Collect. Then the people enter the church during an instrumental voluntary or choir anthem. "Ride on, ride on in majesty" (THE HYMNAL 1982, 156) is particularly suited here as it points from the entry into Jerusalem to the impending crucifixion, the theme of the lections of the Liturgy of the Word.

The Ministry of the Word begins with the Salutation and Collect. Provisions are made for a full series of readings: Old Testament Lesson, Gradual, Epistle, and Gospel. A Tract or Sequence is appropriate between the Epistle and Gospel. Appropriate hymns include:

> 156   Ride on! ride on in majesty!
> 164   Alone thou goest forth, O Lord
> 458   My song is love unknown

Passion Gospel   Laypersons may read or chant the Passion Gospel. For traditional music for singing it, see THE PASSIONS, published by Music for Liturgy, 175 West 72nd St., New York, NY 10023 (RSV) and CHANTS OF THE PASSION ACCORDING TO MATTHEW, MARK, LUKE AND JOHN arranged for singing by Jan Kern (GIA Publications, 7404 South Mason, Bedford Park, IL 60638) (New American Bible).

After the reading of the Gospel and for the remainder of the service, all hymns, anthems, and instrumental music should be devoted to the crucifixion. For example, it is highly inappropriate after the Gospel to use a text such as "All glory, laud, and honor" or instrumental music with Palm Sunday entry associations. Useful hymns include:

158	Ah, holy Jesus, how hast thou offended
161	The flaming banners of our King
162	The royal banners forward go
168, 169	O sacred head, sore wounded
170	To mock your reign, O dearest Lord
313	Let thy Blood in mercy poured
337	And now, O Father, mindful of the love (sts. 1–2)
474	When I survey the wondrous cross

See Acc. Ed. Vol. 1, p. 687, and HYMNAL STUDIES FIVE, pp. 188–189.

The Nicene Creed and the Confession of Sin seem redundant and should probably be omitted after use of the Liturgy of the Palms.

Maundy Thursday

The two primary emphases of the Maundy Thursday rite are the institution of the Eucharist and the "maundy," the washing of feet with its attendant command to love one another. Particularly fitting are hymns referring to the institution of the Eucharist:

315	Thou, who at thy first Eucharist didst pray
320	Zion, praise thy Savior, singing
322	When Jesus died to save us
329, 331	Now, my tongue, the mystery telling (sts. 1–4)

The liturgy begins in the usual manner. Even though it is Lent, it has been traditional in some areas to sing the Glory be to God / Glory to God (*Gloria in excelsis*) or some other song of praise in the entrance rite, possibly with the ringing of bells; then organ, bells, and other musical instruments are silent until the Eucharist of the Easter Vigil. Often this is not practical. Also, many people feel strongly that use of the Lord, have mercy upon us / Lord, have mercy (*Kyrie*), Kyrie eleison, or Holy God (*Trisagion*) instead of a song of praise is more in keeping with the Maundy Thursday rite.

Washing of Feet During the washing of feet, following the sermon, the choir or cantor may sing the anthems provided in THE BOOK OF COMMON PRAYER or some other suitable ones. (See THE HYMNAL 1982 S 344–S 347 for musical settings of the anthems.) The congregation should not sing a hymn or psalm at this point for their total attention should be directed to the washing of feet. However, a cantor or choir might sing a hymn with a congregational refrain.

576, 577	God is love, and where true love is *(Ubi caritas)*
602	Jesu, Jesu, fill us with your love
606	Where true charity and love dwell *(Ubi caritas)*

After the washing of the feet, the service continues with the Prayers of the People. Normally associated with the offertory is the ancient text *Ubi caritas,* for which THE HYMNAL 1982 provides three translations.

576, 577	God is love, and where true love is
581	Where charity and love prevail
606	Where true charity and love dwell

The service proceeds in the usual manner through the postcommunion prayer. Then (a hymn and) a Dismissal may follow, or the congregation may remain for the removal of the Sacrament to the place of repose and/or the stripping of the altar. The hymn "Now, my tongue, the mystery telling" (329, 330, 331) is normally associated with the removal of the Sacrament to the place of repose.

Stripping of the Altar If the stripping of the altar is a public ceremony, it follows the postcommunion prayer (and hymn). It may occur in silence, or Psalm 22 (said or sung by a solo voice) could accompany it. Verse 17b and c of that Psalm, "They divide my garments among them; they cast lots for my clothing," is an appropriate antiphon. After this, the congregation may leave or remain for a vigil. An instrumental postlude would not be appropriate. See BOS for additional provisions for Maundy Thursday.

See Acc. Ed. Vol. 1, p. 687, and HYMNAL STUDIES FIVE, p. 190, for additional hymn suggestions for the Maundy Thursday rite.

Good Friday

(Supplement to HEAE, pp. 258–276; MMC, p. 31)

On Good Friday there should be no music before the service; the entrance of the ministers should be silent and should be followed by an appreciable period of silent prayer. The liturgy begins with an optional special Opening Acclamation (for music see S 348) followed immediately by the Collect of the Day. A full series of readings is provided: Old Testament Lesson, Gradual, Epistle, and Gospel. A Tract or Sequence between the Epistle and Gospel is appropriate.

Passion Gospel For traditional music for this, see above (Palm Sunday Passion Gospel).

Hymn On Good Friday a hymn may follow the sermon.

Solemn Collects For traditional music, see HEAE, pages 264–270.

Anthems and/or hymns Anthems (three are provided and others may also be used) may be read or sung after the bringing in of a wooden cross. Music for these anthems is found in THE HYMNAL 1982 S 349–S 351. "Sing, my tongue, the glorious battle" (165, 166, or S 352) or some other suitable hymn extolling the glory of the cross is then sung.

After the anthems and the hymn have been sung before the cross, it is probably best not to use any more music in the service. The ministers and people depart in silence. In some situations, however, appropriate hymns, psalms or anthems during the ministration of Communion might be effective.

For appropriate hymns for the Good Friday rite, see Acc. Ed. Vol. 1, p. 687, and HYMNAL STUDIES FIVE, pp. 190–191.

Holy Saturday

On Holy Saturday there should be no music before the service; the entrance of the clergy should be silent. The rite begins with the Collect of the Day. A full series of readings is given: Old Testament Lesson, Gradual, Epistle, and Gospel. A Tract or a Sequence is fitting between the Epistle and Gospel. Hymns 173, "O sorrow deep!," 172, "Were you there when they crucified my Lord?," or 458, "My song is love unknown," would be a suitable Sequence.

Anthem The anthem "In the midst of life" (BCP, pp. 484 or 492) may be sung by priest, deacon, cantor, or choir. For musical settings, see THE HYMNAL 1982 S 379 and S 382. The setting at S 382 is well suited for choir or congregation singing the refrain, the cantor singing the verses.

Lord's Prayer and Grace The Lord's Prayer may be monotoned, or sung to one of the musical settings in THE HYMNAL 1982 S 119 (traditional) or S 148–S 150 (contemporary). The Grace (BCP, pp. 59 or 102) may be monotoned.

The Great Vigil of Easter

(Supplement to HEAE, pp. 278–320; MMC, p. 32; THE HYMNAL 1982 S 68–S 70)

Lighting of the Paschal Candle The opening address may be monotoned, and the Collect may be sung to a common collect tone. (See THE HYMNAL 1982 S 447–S 448, HEAE, or MMC.)

Acclamation The Acclamation (S 68) is sung or said three times. It is sung at a higher pitch each time. For additional information see HEAE.

Exsultet Even if little else is sung, this should be. If a deacon is not available, a priest or the best cantor available should sing it. (See HEAE.)

The Liturgy of the Word The address of the celebrant may be monotoned, the Lessons and Collects sung to common tones. Great restraint must be exercised in the use of psalms, canticles, and hymns other than those listed as responses to the Lessons. This is not an Easter festival carol service, but rather a vigil of readings set off by silences and responses in the words of Scripture and by solemn prayers. It is probably best for the congregation to sit during the Psalms. Responsorial singing is recommended. (See GPAVT for responsorial settings of the recommended psalms and canticles.) If accompaniment is necessary, recorders, harpsichord, or other quiet instruments are preferred, thus reserving the organ, bells, brass and other loud instruments for the initial song of praise at the Eucharist.

Holy Baptism A suitable psalm, such as Psalm 42, or a hymn may accompany the procession to the font. Singing the Prayers for the Candidates, the Thanksgiving over the Water and the Consecration of the Chrism and singing or monotoning other prayers or forms is appropriate. (See HEAE or MMC.) Psalm 23 or some other psalm or hymn may be sung at the time of a procession to the front of the church after the Baptism. In the rite of Confirmation, Reception, or Reaffirmation, one may sing the prayers.

Renewal of Baptismal Vows It is appropriate to sing the concluding prayer.

At the Eucharist Bells and/or an instrumental fanfare are suitable at the lighting of the altar and chancel candles. The acclamation of the celebrant and the response of the people may be repeated several times. If sung, each repetition might be at a higher pitch.
   The ancient Tonus Peregrinus has been associated traditionally with the Jewish Passover and the Christian Easter. This tone is provided in THE HYMNAL 1982 for the Opening Acclamation (S 79), the Christ our Passover (*Pascha nostrum*) (S 50), the Fraction Anthem (S 151), and the Dismissal (S 176). Both THE PLAINSONG PSALTER and THE ANGLICAN CHANT PSALTER set Psalm 114 to this tone as well. Furthermore, several of the canticles are set to this tone (A Song of Creation [*Benedicite, omnia opera Domini*], S 177 and S 228; The Song of Mary [*Magnificat*], S 242; The Song of Zechariah [*Benedictus Dominus Deus*], S 190; The Song of Moses [*Cantemus Domino*], S 208), and the use of these settings for these canticles would be particularly appropriate during the Easter Season.

Canticle After the restrained psalmody of the vigil, the canticle setting should be popular, festive, and congregational. If the congregation can join heartily in a setting of Christ our Passover (*Pascha nostrum*) (S 16–S 20 [traditional] or S 46–S 50 [contemporary]) or We Praise Thee / You are God (*Te Deum laudamus*) (S 205–S 207) [traditional] or S 282–S 288 and S 407 [contemporary]) because of the references in the texts to the resurrection, one of these would be more appropriate to the occasion than Glory be to God / Glory to God (*Gloria in excelsis*). The organ, silent until this point in the rite, might have brass, percussion and/or bell accompaniment.

Ministry of the Word The Epistle and Gospel may be sung, separated by the sung Great Alleluia (S 70) and Psalm 114 (See THE PLAINSONG PSALTER and THE ANGLICAN CHANT PSALTER for settings of this psalm to the Tonus Peregrinus) or some other suitable psalm or hymn. Hymn 83, "Christians, to the Paschal victim," is a traditional Easter Sequence. Hymn 184, "Christ the Lord is risen again!," may be sung in alternation between two groups. (See note at 184 in Acc. Ed. Vol. 2.) The Nicene Creed is omitted. The sermon is followed by (the Baptism or Renewal of Baptismal Vows and) the Prayers of the People and the Peace.

The hymns, psalms, or anthems at the Offertory, during the Communion, and before and/or after the postcommunion prayer should stress the passover event. The following hymns are suggested:

174	At the Lamb's high feast we sing
187	Through the Red Sea brought at last
199, 200	Come, ye faithful, raise the strain
202	The Lamb's high banquet called to share
210	The day of resurrection!

See Acc. Ed. Vol. 1, pp. 687–688, and HYMNAL STUDIES FIVE, p. 191, for additional suggestions.

Note that "Alleluia, alleluia" may be added at the end of the Dismissal and of its response from the Easter Vigil through the Day of Pentecost. For music see THE HYMNAL 1982 S 175–S 176, HEAE, or MMC.

The Vigil of Pentecost

The Service of Light The Vigil of Pentecost (BCP, p. 175 or 227) begins with An Order of Worship for the Evening (See above, pp. 68–70). If the Vigil is kept on Saturday evening, the first of the prayers on page 110, BCP, is especially fitting. See S 315 for a traditional lucernaria text for Pentecost. Another canticle or hymn may replace O Gracious Light (*Phos hilaron*).

The Ministry of the Word The Ministry of the Word begins with the Salutation and Collect of the Day, which may be sung to a common collect tone. At least three Lessons precede the Gospel. Any hymn substituted for a psalm or canticle prior to the Alleluia or Sequence should invoke the Holy Spirit. For translations of Veni Creator Spiritus see:

500	Creator Spirit, by whose aid
501, 502	O Holy Spirit, by whose breath
503, 504	Come, Holy Ghost, our souls inspire

For translations of Veni Sancte Spiritus, the traditional Sequence for Pentecost, see:

226, 227	Come, thou Holy Spirit bright
228	Holy Spirit, font of light

Holy Baptism The procession to the font may be accompanied by the singing of an appropriate psalm, such as Psalm 42, or a baptismal hymn invoking the Holy Spirit:

297	Descend, O Spirit, purging flame
299	Spirit of God, unleashed on earth
513	Like the murmur of the dove's song

It is appropriate to sing the Prayers for the Candidates, the Thanksgiving over Water, and the Consecration of the Chrism, and to sing or monotone other prayers or forms as well (See THE HYMNAL 1982 S 75 or MMC and HEAE). Psalm 23, some other related psalm, or a hymn celebrating the outpouring of the Holy Spirit in Baptism may be sung at the procession to the front of the church following the Baptism, such as:

294	Baptized in water, sealed by the Spirit
295	Sing praise to our Creator
296	We know that Christ is raised and dies no more

If the rite of Confirmation, Reception, or Reaffirmation is administered, it is suitable to sing the prayers of that rite.

Renewal of Baptismal Vows   The concluding prayer may be sung. The Prayers of the People and the Peace follow the Renewal or Baptism.

At the Holy Communion   The hymns, psalms, and anthems at the Offertory, during the Communion, and before and/or after the postcommunion prayer should be festive. Suggested hymns are:

223, 224	Hail this joyful day's return
225	Hail thee, festival day!
229	Spirit of mercy, truth, and love
230	A mighty sound from heaven
506, 507	Praise the Spirit in creation
514	To thee, O Comforter divine
531	O Spirit of the living God

Note that "Alleluia, alleluia" may be added at the end of the Dismissal and its response (See S 175–S 176).

Planning Music for Holy Baptism

The Prayer Book provides a special entrance rite for Holy Baptism. Sentences of Scripture sung or said responsively take the place of the Lord, have mercy upon us / Lord, have mercy (*Kyrie*), *Kyrie* eleison, Holy God (*Trisagion*), or song of praise. For music, see THE HYMNAL 1982 S 71–S 74, HEAE, or MMC. Though the rubrics allow the insertion of a song of praise after these special versicles and responses (BCP, p. 312), to make such an insertion would very much clutter what is a very direct and admirable entrance rite and take attention away from its baptismal emphasis. At the Great Vigil of Easter or the Vigil of Pentecost, this entrance rite is not used. These primary baptismal times have their own special entrance rites with a service of light and a special Ministry of the Word. See BOS for baptismal vigils for the First Sunday after Epiphany and All Saints, and for a "Vigil on the Eve of Baptism."

Procession to the Font   This may precede or follow the presentation and examination of candidates and the baptismal covenant. Psalm 42, some other suitable psalm, or Canticle 9, or a baptismal hymn may be sung during the procession. (See THE PLAIN-SONG PSALTER or THE ANGLICAN CHANT PSALTER for Psalm 42, or Hymn 658 for a metrical version of it; see S 213–S 216 or S 400–S 401 for Canticle 9, or 678, 679 for a metrical version of it.) The following are suitable hymns for use at the procession to the font:

297   Descend, O Spirit, purging flame
298   All who believe and are baptized
299   Spirit of God, unleashed on earth
370   I bind unto myself today
547   Awake, O sleeper, rise from death
686   Come, thou fount of every blessing
697   My God, accept my heart this day

Prayers for the Candidates   Music for these prayers is in HEAE or MMC, and the people's response is printed in THE HYMNAL 1982 at S 75. The procession may move to the font during the singing of these prayers. The celebrant's concluding prayer may be sung to a common collect tone.

Thanksgiving over the Water and Consecration of the Chrism   For the music, see HEAE. The people's responses are printed in THE HYMNAL 1982 at S 75. It is appropriate to sing other prayers to a common collect tone and also to monotone other forms.

Procession to the Altar   Psalm 23, some other suitable psalm, or a hymn may be sung. (See THE PLAINSONG PSALTER or THE ANGLICAN CHANT PSALTER for Psalm 23, or see Hymn 645, 646; 663; or 664 for a metrical version of it.) Suitable hymns include the following:

176, 177   Over the chaos of the empty waters
213   Come away to the skies
294   Baptized in water, sealed by the Spirit
295   Sing praise to our Creator
296   We know that Christ is raised and dies no more
432   O praise ye the Lord! Praise him in the height
473   Lift high the cross

Confirmation, Reception, or Reaffirmation   If this rite is administered, the prayers may be sung.

Peace   For music, see THE HYMNAL 1982 S 110–S 111, HEAE, or MMC.

After the Peace, the Eucharistic rite continues with the Prayers of the People or the Offertory.

For additional recommendations, see HYMNAL STUDIES FIVE, pp. 175–176.

Planning Music for The Holy Eucharist

Quite early in Church history a classic shape evolved for the Eucharistic rite. The Liturgy of the Word consisted of: 1. Old Testament Lesson(s), 2. Psalmody, 3. New Testament Lesson(s), 4. A reading from the Gospels, 5. Homily, 6. Prayers of the People, and 7. The Peace. A four-action shape developed for the Liturgy of the Table: 1. The preparation of the Table, 2. The Great Thanksgiving, 3. The Breaking of the Bread, and 4. The giving of the Bread and Wine. Over the years these basic structures were somewhat obscured, and certain elements were lost. The current BOOK OF COMMON PRAYER restores the basic components of both the Liturgy of the Word and the Liturgy of the Table. These elements should stand out. Other items in the liturgy should function as preparation and reinforcement for the basic elements.

The Entrance Rite

The real beginning of the liturgy is the first Lesson. That which precedes this reading is often called "the entrance rite." It serves to call the congregation together and set the stage for the readings and all that follows. In planning, it is best to begin with the Ministry of the Word and move on to the Holy Communion. After these are worked out, plan an entrance rite which best prepares the people. This rite must not be so lengthy or so emotionally demanding that it exhausts the people; rather it should call them together and prepare them for hearing the proclamation of the Word.

Certain days or occasions have their own entrance rites. For other occasions there are often five available options; an entrance song may precede the first three.

Prelude Congregational participation can be enhanced if the time immediately before the entrance song is used to familiarize them with new music in the rite. The music itself or preludes based on it will serve this purpose. See HYMNAL STUDIES SEVEN, Volumes 1 and 2.

Occasionally it is advisable to have a congregational hymn and service music practice just before the prelude. In addition to music for teaching, musical offerings by instrumentalists, choir, or vocalists are also appropriate.

Entrance Song A hymn, psalm, or anthem may be used at the entrance of the ministers. The choir should be in place prior to this song, or at least well into the nave when the singing begins. Although a psalm or anthem may be used sometimes, this song should be ideally a familiar hymn of praise related to the theme of the Lessons for the day. When this is impossible, a seasonal hymn is suitable; if not a seasonal hymn, then a general hymn of praise.

> *Option I:* The normal use from Christmas Day through the Feast of the Epiphany, on Sundays from Easter Day through the Day of Pentecost, on all the days of Easter Week, and on Ascension Day; and permitted at other times except in Advent and Lent (BCP, p. 406).

Opening Acclamation Music is given in THE HYMNAL 1982 (S 76–S 79), HEAE and MMC.

Collect for Purity This collect, required in Rite One but optional in Rite Two, may be sung in the same manner as the Collect of the Day. That would not be appropriate with a sung Opening Acclamation Lord, have mercy upon us / Lord, have mercy (*Kyrie*), Kyrie eleison, or Holy God (*Trisagion*), or song of praise. In Rite Two, the Collect for Purity is not required and should generally be omitted for it interrupts the movement from the entrance song and Opening Acclamation to the song of praise.

Lord, have mercy upon us / Lord, have mercy (Kyrie), Kyrie eleison, or Trisagion.
In Rite One, one or another of these may be used even on those occasions calling for a song of praise, though it should be omitted for it adds an incongruent note to an already cluttered entrance rite.

Song of Praise Glory be to God / Glory to God (*Gloria in excelsis*) is an excellent choice for Christmastide. The other Daily Office canticles are desirable alternatives for other seasons. We Praise Thee / You are God (*Te Deum laudamus*) is appropriate for the Easter Season, saints' days, and Trinity Sunday; Christ our Passover (*Pascha nostrum*) or The Song to the Lamb (*Dignus es*) for the Easter Season; The Song of Zechariah (*Benedictus Dominus Deus*) or The Third Song of Isaiah (*Surge, illuminare*) or The Song of the Redeemed (*Magna et mirabilia*) for Epiphany; The Song of Mary (*Magnificat*) for

Marian feasts, *et al.* This Song of Praise should be chosen with the lections for the day in mind. See THE HYMNAL 1982 S 355 for "A Canticle Use Chart."

Option II: The normal option for Advent and Lent, permissible at other times.

Opening Acclamation Music is provided in THE HYMNAL 1982 (S 76–S 83), HEAE, and MMC.

Collect for Purity This collect, required in Rite One but optional in Rite Two, may be sung in the same manner as the Collect of the Day. It would not be inappropriate if the Opening Acclamation and the Lord, have mercy upon us / Lord, have mercy (*Kyrie*), Kyrie eleison, or Holy God (*Trisagion*) are sung.

Lord, have mercy upon us / Lord, have mercy (Kyrie), Kyrie eleison, or Holy God (Trisagion). The Kyrie in either English or Greek may be be sung or said in a three-fold, six-fold, or nine-fold form. Holy God (*Trisagion*) may be be sung or said antiphonally and/or three times in accordance with Eastern custom. For music see THE HYMNAL 1982 S 84–S 102.

Option III: The use of A Penitential Order (Rite One, pp. 319–321; Rite Two, pp. 351–353), appropriate in Lent and on certain other occasions.

Opening Acclamation Music for it appears in THE HYMNAL 1982 (S 76–S 83), HEAE, and MMC.

Lord, have mercy upon us / Lord, have mercy (Kyrie), Kyrie eleison, Holy God (Trisagion), Glory be to God / Glory to God (Gloria in excelsis) or other song of praise. See Option I or Option II (above).

Option IV: The use of the Great Litany (BCP, pp. 148–153), appropriate in Lent and on certain other occasions. When used as an entrance rite, it is concluded with the Lord, have mercy upon us or Kyrie eleison on page 153. For music see THE HYMNAL 1982 S 67. (The complete text is printed at S 67 in the Accompaniment Edition.) For the concluding Lord, have mercy upon us or Kyrie eleison the music printed at S 67 may be used or S 84–S 93.

Option V: The use of An Order of Worship for the Evening (BCP, pp. 108–112). The Order of Worship for the Evening, ending with O Gracious Light (*Phos hilaron*), may be used in place of all that precedes the Salutation and Collect of the Day. (See above, pp. 68–70.)

The Ministry of the Word

Salutation and Collect Two tones for the Collect are provided in THE HYMNAL 1982 (S 447–S 448), HEAE, and MMC.

First Reading If the Lesson is sung, the announcement and conclusion should also be sung. See HEAE or MMC for the tone.

Silence A period of silence may be observed after the reading.

Gradual Whereas other psalms are accompaniments to actions, this psalm has a unique rationale and integrity. Sometimes the early Church Fathers spoke of it as the Lesson from the Psalms. Traditionally this Psalm is sung by a cantor from the pulpit (or lectern). The congregation remains seated while the psalm is sung responsorially, with the cantor singing the verses and the congregation repeating the refrain after each verse or group of verses. (This presupposes a teaching session prior to the first time that it is used in a congregation.) It is not traditional to use Glory to the Father (*Gloria Patri*) after the Gradual. For music, see GPAVT. Alternative plainsong settings for cantor with newly composed congregational refrains (with accompaniments) are available in THE PSALM-NARY: GRADUAL PSALMS FOR CANTOR AND CONGREGATION by James E. Barrett (The Hymnary Press, P. O. Box 5782, Missoula MT 59806).

Though the Gradual Psalm should normally be sung by a cantor from the pulpit (the name *Gradual* supposedly comes from the fact that this was sung from the *gradus* or step of the pulpit), it may be desirable to make occasional use of a plainsong or Anglican chant setting (See THE PLAINSONG PSALTER or THE ANGLICAN CHANT PSALTER); Simplified Anglican Chant (S 408–S 415); a metrical version (See Acc. Ed. Vol. 1, p. 679, for a list of "Metrical Psalms and Hymns based on Psalms"); a setting from THE IONIAN PSALTER (See above, page 45), or a restrained anthem setting.

Second Reading If this is sung, the announcement and conclusion are also sung. See HEAE or MMC for the tone.

Silence A period of silence may be kept after the reading.

Alleluia or Tract An acclamation consisting of alleluias with a verse of Scripture has traditionally in the West accompanied the procession to the pulpit for the reading of the Gospel. A psalm, without Gloria Patri, known as the Tract, has been a traditional substitute for the Alleluia and Verse during Lent. See GPAVT for settings of Alleluias and Tracts.

Sequence A hymn may replace the Alleluia or Tract at this point. It should sum up, highlight or respond to the Epistle or anticipate the Gospel. Both an Alleluia and a Sequence may be used on occasion.

Gospel See HEAE or MMC for the tone. The Gloria tibi and Laus tibi should not be sung unless the announcement and the conclusion are sung.

There is no longer permission to sing a hymn or any other text (or to make any announcement or say any prayer, for that matter) between the people's Praise be to thee, O Christ / Praise to you, Lord Christ and the sermon; nothing should intervene between the people's response to the Gospel and the initial sentence of the sermon. Particularly reprehensible (in addition to being unrubrical) is the practice sometimes seen of postponing concluding stanzas of the Sequence and singing them after the Gospel. This destroys the integrity of the text as well as interrupting the flow of the liturgy. Also, there is no longer blanket permission to follow the sermon with a hymn. It is fitting to have there a period of silence or to lead directly into the Creed or the Prayers of the People.

Creed The Creed is required only on Sundays and on other major feasts. On the great baptismal days (Easter, Pentecost, All Saints' Day or the Sunday after All Saints' Day, and The Baptism of our Lord) when there are no baptismal candidates, the Renewal of Baptismal Vows (BCP, pp. 292–294) may take the place of the Nicene Creed. If the congregation knows a setting of the Creed, it is suitable to sing it. (See THE HYMNAL 1982 S 103–S 105 and S 361 for settings.) It is not good form for the organist to play during the congregation's monotoning of the Creed.

Prayers of the People See THE HYMNAL 1982 S 106–S 109 and S 362–S 363 for musical settings for the six forms of the Prayers of the People. See HEAE or MMC for additional settings of Form I and Form V.

Concluding Collect The concluding Collect may be sung to the tone of the Collect of the Day, even though the petitions have been said, or vice versa.

Peace See THE HYMNAL 1982 S 110–S 111 or HEAE or MMC. The organist should allow adequate time for the exchange of the Peace but avoid an undue lag.

The Holy Communion

Offertory Sentence It is often more effective for the organist simply to begin a hymn, anthem, or organ voluntary than for the priest to say or sing a sentence of Scripture to initiate the Offertory, especially if the people are enthusiastic in exchanging the Peace.

Hymn, psalm, or anthem Music during the preparation of the Table and the placing on it of the bread, wine, alms, and other offerings is in itself an offering. It should serve as a meditative aid to the people, preparing them for their participation in the Great Thanksgiving. The music should be restrained in length and emotional content. The historic liturgical reason for the singing of a hymn, psalm, or anthem at this point in the structure of the rite is to provide a musical accompaniment to the offering of the gifts and preparation of the table; the music is an accompaniment to the actions of the preparation of the table, not an addition to the sequence. Triumphal processions and the saying or singing of a presentation Sentence are highly inappropriate, for the Great Thanksgiving is, in itself, the verbalization of the offering and the climax toward which the Offertory moves. If the action of the Offertory is not completed by the conclusion of the hymn, anthem, or voluntary, a period of silence is in order.

The Great Thanksgiving See THE HYMNAL 1982 for music for the Lift up your hearts (Sursum corda), S 112 (Rite I) and S 120 (Rite II). Music for the Lift up your hearts (Sursum corda), the Prefaces, and the conclusions of the Eucharistic Prayers is provided in HEAE. The older tradition of singing the entire Eucharistic Prayer, now being restored, is commendable. Two musical settings, one traditional and one contemporary, for Prayer C are provided in THE HYMNAL 1982 (S 369 and S 370). Musical settings for the entire text of the other Eucharistic Prayers is available from Mason Martens, 175 West 72nd Street, New York, NY 10023.

Even if the celebrant sings no portion of the Eucharistic Prayer, the people should sing the Holy, holy, holy / Holy, holy, holy Lord (*Sanctus*) and may sing the Memorial Acclamation. See THE HYMNAL 1982 for settings of the Holy, holy, holy / Holy, holy, holy Lord (*Sanctus*) (S 113–S 119 [Rite I] and S 121–S 131 and S 364–S 365 [Rite II]), and of the Memorial Acclamations (S 132–S 135 and S 366 [Prayer A], S 136–S 138 and S 367–S 368 [Prayer B], and S 139–S 141 [Prayer D]).

If the entire prayer, or its conclusion, has been sung the Great Amen would also be sung (See THE HYMNAL 1982 S 118 or S 142–S 147).

Lord's Prayer Congregational singing of the Lord's Prayer is appropriate, at least occasionally, especially if the Eucharistic Prayer has been sung. For settings, see S 119 (traditional) or S 148–S 150 (contemporary).

Fraction Anthem After the Bread has been broken (and after the Wine has been poured into any additional chalices needed for the distribution), a silence is kept. A Fraction Anthem *may* follow the silence as an introduction to "The Gifts of God for the People of God." Two texts are provided in THE BOOK OF COMMON PRAYER (p. 337 and pp. 364 and 407), though both should not be used together. Musical settings for additional Fraction Anthems printed in BOS are provided in THE HYMNAL 1982. See S 151–S 172 and S 373–S 374. The anthem should be varied, being chosen on the basis of the lessons for the day and/or the season of the Church Year. The omission of a Fraction Anthem is often highly effective, as is, on occasion, the substitution of an instrumental fanfare.

Invitation   See HEAE for the proper music.

Hymn, Psalm, or Anthem during Communion   This is a fitting time for a choir anthem. Responsorial psalmody is traditional here. It works well because it enables the people to continue singing as they move to and from the Communion station. Certain hymns with refrains can also be used. Canticles particularly appropriate to the season may also be used (see THE HYMNAL 1982 S 355, "A Canticle Use Chart").

Music of great length or dramatic quality which is inappropriate at the offering, where music should lead up to the climactic prayer of the rite, is often well suited to the Communion procession. Joyous music is especially good. Historically, great psalms of praise, especially Psalms 145, 148, and 150, have been associated with this point in the rite.

Hymn   A hymn is often needed prior to the postcommunion prayer to get the congregation back on their feet and to cover the ablutions or removal of the elements. A hymn associated with this moment in historic liturgies is appropriate.

312   Strengthen for service, Lord
326   From glory to glory advancing, we praise thee, O
       Lord
346   Completed, Lord, the Holy Mysteries

A hymn proper to the season or related to the day's lections or a general hymn of praise may also be used.

Postcommunion Prayer   If desired, this prayer may be monotoned.

Hymn   This is the last point within the rite for a hymn. The choir should remain in place throughout the hymn to provide congregational support. Ideally, this hymn should be a very familiar hymn based on the propers of the day which sends the people out to love and serve the Lord.

Blessing and/or Dismissal   A blessing is required in Rite One and a dismissal in Rite Two. "Alleluia, Alleluia" may be added at the end of the dismissal and of its response throughout the Great Fifty Days. See HEAE or MMC for tones for both blessings and dismissals, or THE HYMNAL 1982 S 173–S 176 for responses to the Episcopal Blessing and for Dismissals. See BOS for seasonal blessings and Lenten prayers over the people.

Postlude   The music at the exit of the clergy and people should ideally derive from that hymn or text which best sums up the service. The time might be used to familiarize the people with a tune intended for future use. See HYMNAL STUDIES SEVEN, Volumes 1 and 2. The choir, like the congregation, should leave informally.

An Order for Celebrating the Holy Eucharist ("Rite III") _____

This order, which lists the elements considered essential for a eucharistic celebration, follows the traditional form which has been adopted in Rite I and Rite II, but provides for experimentation or adaptation to particular circumstances. The initial rubrics emphasize that this order does not provide license for a casually improvised service, but demands more careful attention and preparation than Rite I or Rite II in which the choices are more limited and the structure largely detailed, and that it is not intended for use as the principal service on the Lord's Day.

From the standpoint of the choice of music it is important to note that the more inclusive word "song" is used, in contrast to "hymn, psalm, or anthem" of the rubrics of Rite I and Rite II.

Planning Music for the Pastoral Offices

Confirmation, Reception, or Reaffirmation of Baptismal Vows ___

Material from the baptismal rite is repeated under this heading to make the service easier to follow at times when there is no one to be baptized at the bishop's parochial visit but there are persons who wish to make public affirmation or reaffirmation, or to be received from other communions.

THE BOOK OF COMMON PRAYER provides a special entrance rite: Sentences of Scripture for use at Confirmation, Reception, or Reaffirmation of Baptismal Vows. Sentences of Scripture are sung or said responsively in place of the Kyrie, Trisagion, or song of praise. For music, see S 71–S 74, HEAE, or MMC. At the Great Vigil of Easter or the Vigil of Pentecost this entrance rite is not used, for those primary times of Baptism and Renewal of Baptismal Vows have their own special entrance rites with a service of light and a special Ministry of the Word.

The prayers of the rite may be sung. For the music of the (optional) petitions see HEAE or MMC. The people's responses are printed in THE HYMNAL 1982 at S 75. The other prayers may be sung to a common collect tone (THE HYMNAL 1982 S 447–S 448, HEAE, or MMC). For the music of the Peace, see THE HYMNAL 1982 S 110–S 111, HEAE, or MMC.

After the Peace, the Eucharistic rite continues with the Prayers of the People or the Offertory.

Chrism for use at subsequent baptisms may be consecrated after the postcommunion prayer (See BOS, pp. 224–225). For music, see HEAE.

A Form of Commitment to Christian Service ___

This rite must be tailored to each individual situation. Occasionally it may be appropriate to include a hymn or psalm as a portion of the statement of intention and/or to monotone or sing the prayers to a common collect tone.

Celebration and Blessing of a Marriage ___

The celebration and blessing of a marriage is a sacramental rite of the Church; the music should reflect this. As at other rites of the Church, the canon and rubrics govern the choices.

Prelude Preludes based on hymns or service music to be used within the rite are especially appropriate. Since congregations at weddings often include a large number of people unfamiliar with some of the hymns and service music, participation is greatly enhanced by the organist's playing the hymns and service music or preludes based on them. (See HYMNAL STUDIES SEVEN, Volumes 1 and 2.) Since many weddings are, in fact, ecumenical occasions, it might be wise to refer to the Index of Hymns on the Consultation on Ecumenical Hymnody List (Acc. Ed. Vol. 1, pages 712–713). Instrumentalists, a choir, or soloists may also make musical offerings at this time.

Entrance Hymn, Psalm, Anthem, or Instrumental Music A strong general hymn of praise is probably better at the entrance than any of the hymns in the marriage section of THE HYMNAL 1982. Some suitable hymns are:

364   O God, we praise thee, and confess
366   Holy God, we praise thy Name

373	Praise the Lord! ye heavens adore him
375	Give praise and glory unto God
376	Joyful, joyful, we adore thee
377, 378	All people that on earth do dwell
390	Praise to the Lord, the Almighty
396, 397	Now thank we all our God
398	I sing the almighty power of God
399	To God with gladness sing
400	All creatures of our God and King
401	The God of Abraham praise
408	Sing praise to God who reigns above
409	The spacious firmament on high
410	Praise, my soul, the King of heaven
413	New songs of celebration render
414	God, my King, thy might confessing
416	For the beauty of the earth
421	All glory be to God on high
423	Immortal, invisible, God only wise
428	O all ye works of God, now come
430	Come, O come, our voices raise
431	The stars declare his glory
432	O praise ye the Lord! Praise him in the height
492	Sing, ye faithful, sing with gladness
518	Christ is made the sure foundation

Appropriate psalms for the entrance include the Invitatory Psalms 95 and 100 (See THE HYMNAL 1982 S 2–S 15 and S 34–S 45) and the psalms appointed for use at a wedding — 67, 127, and 128 (See GPAVT, THE PLAINSONG PSALTER and THE ANGLICAN CHANT PSALTER). Other useful Psalms are 148 and 150. Several collections of organ music contain music suited for use at the entrance:

PARISH ORGANIST — WEDDING MUSIC VOLUME IX. Concordia.

WEDDING MUSIC, I AND II. Concordia.

WEDDING MUSIC, I AND II. (Ed. David Johnson) Augsburg.

A BOOK OF WEDDING PIECES. OUP.

A SECOND BOOK OF WEDDING PIECES. (Ed. C.H. Trevor & Christopher Morris) OUP.

CEREMONIAL MUSIC — PURCELL. (Ed. E. Power Biggs) Mercury (Presser).

CEREMONIAL MUSIC I AND II. OUP.

Various trumpet voluntaries by English composers (Boyce, Stanley, et al.) are especially useful.

Hymn, Psalm, or Anthem A hymn, psalm, or anthem may follow the Declaration of Consent (and Giving in Marriage). A hymn from the wedding section of THE HYMNAL 1982 would be appropriate:

350	O God of love, to thee we bow
351	May the grace of Christ our Savior
352	O God, to those who here profess
353	Your love, O God, has called us here

Other suitable hymns are:

138   All praise to you, O Lord

612   Gracious Spirit, Holy ghost

709   O God of Bethel, by whose hand

The Ministry of the Word   See THE HYMNAL 1982 S 447–S 448, HEAE or MMC for tones for the Salutation and Collect. There is provision for a full series of lections: Old Testament Lesson, Gradual, Epistle, and Gospel. An Alleluia, Tract, or Sequence is appropriate between the Epistle and Gospel. (See GPAVT.)

Any of the seven hymns listed immediately above would make a suitable Sequence.

Prayers and Blessing   The prayers and blessing could be monotoned or sung to a common collect tone.

Peace   For the music for the Peace, see THE HYMNAL 1982 S 110–S 111, HEAE, or MMC.

At the Eucharist   The Offertory would be an appropriate time for a meditative hymn, anthem, or solo if desired. Suitable hymns include:

138   All praise to you, O Lord

351   May the grace of Christ our Savior

581   Where charity and love prevail

593   Lord, make us servants of your peace

612   Gracious Spirit, Holy Ghost

709   O God of Bethel, by whose hand

Several collections contain suitable vocal music:

WEDDING BLESSINGS. Concordia.

SACRED SONGS. Bach, Concordia.

WEDDING SONGS. F. Peeters, Peters.

WEDDING SONGS. Jan Bender, Concordia.

THREE WEDDING SONGS. Robert Powell, Concordia.

THREE WEDDING SOLOS. G. Winston Cassler, Augsburg.

BELOVED LET US LOVE. R. Proulx, Augsburg.

The time of the Communion would be an appropriate time for an anthem or solo, or for one of the hymns listed above, or for Psalm 23 (See THE PLAINSONG PSALTER or THE ANGLICAN CHANT PSALTER) or a metrical version of it.

645, 646   The King of love my shepherd is *(but omit stanzas 3 and 4)*

663   The Lord my God my shepherd is

664   My Shepherd will supply my need

Appropriate hymns for use after the Communion of the people (before or after the postcommunion prayer) include:

312   Strengthen for service, Lord

351   May the grace of Christ our Savior

635   If thou but trust in God to guide thee

Hymn, Psalm, Anthem, or Instrumental Music   A hymn, psalm, or anthem may be sung or instrumental music played as the wedding party leaves the church. Appropriate hymns are:

373	Praise the Lord! ye heavens adore him
375	Give praise and glory unto God
376	Joyful, joyful, we adore thee
390	Praise to the Lord, the Almighty
396, 397	Now thank we all our God
408	Sing praise to God who reigns above
410	Praise, my soul, the King of heaven
414	God, my King, thy might confessing
416	For the beauty of the earth
421	All glory be to God on high
432	O praise ye the Lord! Praise him in the height
635	If thou but trust in God to guide thee

Suitable instrumental music is in the collections listed above and in J.S. Bach, ORGELBÜCHLEIN (various editions) ("In thee is gladness," "If thou but suffer God to guide thee").

Blessing of a Civil Marriage

Music appropriate for use at the Celebration and Blessing of a Marriage is also suited to the blessing of a civil marriage.

An Order for Marriage

Music appropriate for the Celebration and Blessing of a Marriage should constitute the norm for music used in this order.

Thanksgiving for the Birth or Adoption of a Child

On occasion it may be appropriate to sing the Magnificat or Psalm, to monotone or sing the prayers to a common collect tone, and to sing the blessing. The music for the Aaronic blessing in HEAE and MMC can be adapted for this blessing.

Ministration to the sick

When used as a public service, the Ministry of the Word and the Holy Communion may include music suitable for a regular Eucharistic rite. Hymns stressing the healing power of God are fitting. See Acc. Ed. Vol. 1, pp. 694–695, and HYMNAL STUDIES FIVE, p. 287, for recommendations.

The prayers of the Laying on of Hands and Anointing (Part II) may be monotoned or sung to a common collect tone. Singing the blessing of oil for the Anointing of the Sick (to a collect tone, a blessing tone or a preface tone) gives it a desired emphasis, whether it is used within this rite or, as is more desirable, at a principal Sunday Eucharist.

Ministration at the Time of Death

Litany at the Time of Death   Within a monastic or collegiate community, it may be appropriate to sing the Litany at the Time of Death (adapting the music of the Great Litany, S 67). This Litany may also be used within the Vigil (see below).

Prayers for a Vigil   In some circumstances it may be possible to use music at the Vigil, singing the Litany at the Time of Death (see above) or prayers from the Burial of the

Dead (see below). Psalms appointed for use in the burial rite might also be sung (See GPAVT, THE PLAINSONG PSALTER, or THE ANGLICAN CHANT PSALTER). Responsorial singing of the psalms would probably be most practicable since it eliminates the need for books or sheets of music.

Burial of the Dead _____

The same principles as those for any other regular or proper liturgies apply to the choice of music for a burial.

Prelude Preludes based on hymns or service music to appear within the rite are particularly appropriate. Since a congregation gathered for a burial includes a number of persons unfamiliar with some hymns and service music, participation will improve greatly if the organist familiarizes them with the music by using it or preludes based on it. (See HYMNAL STUDIES SEVEN, Volumes 1 and 2.) Since burials often draw people from different traditions it might be wise in making choices to refer to the Index of Hymns on the Consultation on Ecumenical Hymnody List (Acc. Ed. Vol. 1, pages 712–713). Instrumentalists, a choir, or soloists may also make a musical offering.

Entrance Anthems The Entrance Anthems may be sung by the minister, or by a cantor or choir, or by minister and people. For music, see Acc. Ed. Vol. 1, S 375–S 378 (Rite I) or S 380–S 382 (Rite II). In Rite Two a hymn, psalm, or other suitable anthem may be sung in place of anthems in BCP. Suitable hymns include:

388	O worship the King, all glorious above!
429	I'll praise my Maker while I've breath
526	Let saints on earth in concert sing
636, 637	How firm a foundation, ye saints of the Lord
680	O God, our help in ages past
687, 688	A mighty fortress is our God

Salutation and Collect. For the common collect tones, see THE HYMNAL 1982 S 447–S 448, HEAE, or MMC.

Liturgy of the Word A full series of readings is provided: Old Testament Lesson, Gradual (or hymn or canticle), New Testament Lesson, Tract (or Sequence or canticle) and Gospel. (See GPAVT, "Burial of the Dead" and "For the Departed.") Suitable hymns include:

14, 15	O God, creation's secret force
188, 189	Love's redeeming work is done
191	Alleluia, alleluia! Hearts and voices heavenward raise
194, 195	Jesus lives! thy terrors now
447	The Christ who died but rose again
635	If thou but trust in God to guide thee
668	I to the hills will lift mine eyes

Prayers The prayers of Rite One or the concluding collect of Rite Two may be monotoned or sung to a common collect tone (THE HYMNAL 1982 S 447–S 448, HEAE, or MMC).

At the Eucharist The Eucharist commences with the Peace and continues as usual (with the Preface for the Commemoration of the Dead if a Eucharistic Prayer allowing a Proper Preface is used) until the special postcommunion prayer. Suitable hymns at the Offertory include:

<table>
<tr><td>208</td><td>Alleluia, alleluia, alleluia! The strife is o'er</td></tr>
<tr><td>379</td><td>God is Love, let heaven adore him</td></tr>
<tr><td>455, 456</td><td>O love of God, how strong and true</td></tr>
<tr><td>457</td><td>Thou art the Way, to thee alone</td></tr>
<tr><td>690</td><td>Guide me, O thou great Jehovah</td></tr>
</table>

Suitable hymns at the time of Communion include:

<table>
<tr><td>338</td><td>Wherefore, O Father, we thy humble servants</td></tr>
<tr><td>357</td><td>Jesus, Son of Mary</td></tr>
<tr><td>526</td><td>Let saints on earth in concert sing</td></tr>
<tr><td>645, 646</td><td>The King of love my shepherd is</td></tr>
<tr><td>663</td><td>The Lord my God my shepherd is</td></tr>
<tr><td>664</td><td>My Shepherd will supply my need</td></tr>
</table>

Commendation   See THE HYMNAL 1982 355 and S 383 for musical settings of the prose text of the anthem, and S 358 for a metrical version. The commendation, "Into your hands . . . ," may be monotoned or sung to a blessing tone (HEAE or MMC).

Dismissal   For music, see THE HYMNAL 1982 S 174.

Hymn, Anthem, or Canticle   For musical settings of the anthems, see THE HYMNAL 1982 S 384–S 388. For an expanded text of the last of these anthems, see THE HYMNAL 1982 354, or for a metrical version, see 356. Suitable hymns include:

<table>
<tr><td>373</td><td>Praise the Lord! ye heavens adore him</td></tr>
<tr><td>492</td><td>Sing, ye faithful, sing with gladness</td></tr>
<tr><td>618</td><td>Ye watchers and ye holy ones</td></tr>
<tr><td>620</td><td>Jerusalem, my happy home</td></tr>
<tr><td>621, 622</td><td>Light's abode, celestial Salem</td></tr>
<tr><td>623</td><td>O what their joy and their glory must be</td></tr>
<tr><td>624</td><td>Jerusalem the golden</td></tr>
<tr><td>625</td><td>Ye holy angels bright</td></tr>
</table>

For settings of the recommended canticles, see THE HYMNAL 1982 S 190–S 195, S 248–S 252, S 394, and S 404 (The Song of Zechariah [*Benedictus*]) S 196–S 200, S 253–S 260, S 395, and S 405 (The Song of Simeon [*Nunc dimittis*]), and S 16–S 20 and S 46–S 50 (Christ our Passover [*Pascha nostrum*]).

The Committal

Anthem   The minister, cantor, or choir may sing or say the anthem. For music see THE HYMNAL 1982 S 379 and S 389.

The Committal   The Committal may be monotoned or sung to a collect tone or a blessing tone (See HEAE or MMC).

Prayers   The Lord's Prayer may be monotoned or sung to one of the settings in THE HYMNAL 1982 S 119 (traditional) or S 148–S 150 (contemporary). Other prayers may be monotoned or sung to a collect tone.

Dismissal   For musical settings of the texts of the Rite II dismissal, see THE HYMNAL 1982 S 78–S 79 and S 174.

Blessing   See HEAE or MMC for the tone for blessings.

An Order for Burial

For suggestions for appropriate music, see the Burial of the Dead (above).

Planning Music for Episcopal Services

An Ordination (Bishop, Priest, or Deacon)

Prelude   People at an ordination rite normally come from differing parishes and traditions. The participation is likely to be enhanced if the musicians familiarize the congregation with the music by using it as a prelude or by using preludes based on it. (See HYMNAL STUDIES SEVEN, Volumes 1 and 2.) Instrumentalists or choristers may make other musical offerings.

Entrance Hymn, Psalm, or Anthem   Suitable hymns for the entrance are:

> 359   God of the prophets, bless the prophets' heirs (Of a
>   Priest)
> 370   I bind unto myself today
> 511   Holy Spirit, ever living
> 518   Christ is made the sure foundation
> 524   I love thy kingdom, Lord
> 525   The Church's one foundation
> 528   Lord, you give the great commission

Opening Acclamation and Collect for Purity   For the music for the Opening Acclamation, see THE HYMNAL 1982 S 76–S 83, HEAE, or MMC. For the Collect for Purity a common collect tone may be used (THE HYMNAL 1982 S 447–S 448, HEAE, or MMC).

Litany   For music, see S 390. A common collect tone may be used for the concluding Collect.

Ministry of the Word   Three lessons are required. A Gradual is provided after the Old Testament Lesson, and an Alleluia, Tract, or Sequence may be used after the New Testament Lesson (See GPAVT). Suitable hymns for use as a Sequence include:

> 359   God of the prophets, bless the prophets' heirs (Of a
>   Priest)
> 511   Holy Spirit, ever living
> 513   Like the murmur of the dove's song
> 521   Put forth, O God, thy Spirit's might

The Nicene Creed may be sung. See S 104–S 105 and S 361 for musical settings.

Hymn, Veni Creator Spiritus, or Veni Sancte Spiritus   For translations of Veni Creator Spiritus, see:

> 500   Creator Spirit, by whose aid
> 501, 502   O Holy Spirit, by whose breath
> 503, 504   Come, Holy Ghost, our souls inspire

For translations of Veni Sancte Spiritus, see:

226, 227 Come, thou Holy Spirit bright
228 Holy Spirit, font of light

A period of silent prayer follows the hymn.

Prayer of Consecration This prayer may be sung. In the Roman rite it is sung to the Preface tone.

At the Vesting of a New Bishop At the Ordination of a Bishop, the Additional Directions (BCP, p. 553) allow for instrumental music.
Peace. For music, see THE HYMNAL 1982 S 110–S 111, HEAE, or MMC.

At the Holy Communion The liturgy continues with the Offertory. Suitable hymns for the Offertory or at the Communion or before or after the postcommunion prayer include:

321 My God, thy table now is spread
505 O Spirit of Life, O Spirit of God
530 Spread, O spread, thou mighty word
531 O Spirit of the living God
535 Ye servants of God, your Master proclaim
539 O Zion, haste, thy mission high fulfilling
540 Awake, thou Spirit of the watchmen
541 Come, labor on
556, 557 Rejoice, ye pure in heart!
593 Lord, make us servants of your peace
610 Lord, whose love through humble service

Blessing For tones for blessings, see HEAE or MMC. For the people's responses to the Episcopal Blessing, see THE HYMNAL 1982 S 173.

Dismissal For music, see THE HYMNAL 1982 S 174–S 176, HEAE, or MMC.

At the Ordination of a Bishop At the Ordination of a Bishop, the Additional Directions (BCP, p. 553) allow for a hymn of praise after the blessing and dismissal. Suitable hymns include We Praise Thee / You are God (*Te Deum laudamus*) and general metrical hymns of praise.

Postlude Ideally, the music at the exit of the clergy and people should be based on that hymn or text which best sums up the service. (See HYMNAL STUDIES SEVEN, Volumes 1 and 2.)

Celebration of a New Ministry

Prelude People usually come from differing parishes and traditions for a Celebration of a New Ministry. The participation is likely to be enhanced if the musicians will familiarize the congregation with the music by using it as a prelude or by using preludes based on it. (See HYMNAL STUDIES SEVEN, Volumes 1 and 2.) Other musical offerings may be made by instrumentalists or choristers.

Entrance Hymn, Psalm, or Anthem Suitable hymns for use at the entrance include:

359 God of the prophets, bless the prophets' heirs
370 I bind unto myself today
511 Holy Spirit, ever living

517 How lovely is thy dwelling-place
518 Christ is made the sure foundation
524 I love thy kingdom, Lord
525 The Church's one foundation

Litany   For music, see S 390. The concluding collect may be sung to a common collect tone (THE HYMNAL 1982 S 447–S 448, HEAE, or MMC).

Liturgy of the Word   There is provision for a full series of readings: Old Testament Lesson, Gradual, Epistle and Gospel. It is appropriate to sing an Alleluia, Tract, or Sequence between the Epistle and the Gospel. (See GPAVT.) Suitable hymns for use as a Sequence include:

359 God of the prophets, bless the prophets' heirs
511 Holy Spirit, ever living
521 Put forth, O God, thy Spirit's might

Hymn   The sermon (and any response to it) is followed by a hymn during which representatives of the congregation and clergy process or move forward with the symbols of office to be presented. Appropriate hymns include:

359 God of the prophets, bless the prophets' heirs
511 Holy Spirit, ever living
528 Lord, you give the great commission
531 O Spirit of the living God
535 Ye servants of God, your Master proclaim

Peace   For music, see THE HYMNAL 1982 S 110–S 111, HEAE, or MMC.

At the Eucharist   The liturgy continues with the Offertory. Suitable hymns for use at the Offertory or at the Communion or before or after the postcommunion prayer include hymns listed above and also the following:

321 My God, thy table now is spread
530 Spread, O spread, thou mighty word
540 Awake, thou Spirit of the watchmen
541 Come, labor on
593 Lord, make us servants of your peace
610 Lord, whose love through humble service

Blessing and Dismissal   For tones for the blessing, see HEAE or MMC. For the dismissal, see THE HYMNAL 1982 S 174–S 176, HEAE, or MMC.

Postlude   Ideally, the music at the exit of the clergy and people should be based on that hymn or text which best sums up the service. (See HYMNAL STUDIES SEVEN, Volumes 1 and 2.)

Dedication and Consecration of a Church

Pre-service Music   A bell or other musical instrument might call the people to silence for the bishop's opening words. Brass, strings, or other portable musical instruments which could later accompany the procession might perform a brief, informal prelude to the rite.

Prayer   A common collect tone may be used for the initial prayer (THE HYMNAL 1982 S 447–S 448, HEAE, or MMC.

Procession   Especially appropriate are hymns with an easily memorized congregational refrain, or responsorial psalms. Fitting psalms include 48, 84, 95, 100, and 118. See THE HYMNAL 1982 S 2–S 10 and S 34–S 40 for settings of Psalm 95 or S 11–S 15, S 41–S 45, and S 295 for settings of Psalm 100. See GPAVT, THE PLAINSONG PSALTER, and THE ANGLICAN CHANT PSALTER for settings of these and of the other recommended psalms.

Opening of the Doors and Marking of the Threshold   These forms may be monotoned.

Entrance Psalm   Psalm 122 and/or one of the psalms listed above may be sung responsorially as the procession comes into the church. (See GPAVT, THE PLAINSONG PSALTER, and THE ANGLICAN CHANT PSALTER for settings of Psalm 122.) Hymns and anthems may also be sung. Appropriate hymns include:

360, 361	Only-begotten, Word of God eternal
509	Spirit divine, attend our prayers
517	How lovely is thy dwelling-place
518	Christ is made the sure foundation
519, 520	Blessed city, heavenly Salem
522, 523	Glorious things of thee are spoken
524	I love thy kingdom, Lord

Prayer for the Consecration of the Church   This may be sung.

Processional Psalm, Hymn, or Instrumental Music   As the procession moves to the font, selected verses of Psalm 42, or Canticle 9, or a hymn may be sung. See GPAVT, THE PLAINSONG PSALTER, and THE ANGLICAN CHANT PSALTER for settings of Psalm 42, or THE HYMNAL 1982 658 for a metrical version. See THE HYMNAL 1982 S 213–S 216 and S 400–S 401 for settings of Canticle 9 or 678, 679 for a metrical version. Appropriate hymns include:

176, 177	Over the chaos of the empty waters
213	Come away to the skies
294	Baptized in water, sealed by the Spirit
295	Sing praise to our Creator
296	We know that Christ is raised and dies no more
298	All who believe and are baptized
299	Spirit of God, unleashed on earth

Dedication of the Font   The dedication form may be sung. For the music for the Thanksgiving over the Water, see HEAE; for the people's responses, see THE HYMNAL 1982 S 75.

Processional Psalm, Hymn, or Instrumental Music   As the procession moves to the lectern-pulpit, selected verses of a psalm or hymn, or instrumental music, may be used, but not the organ or other instrument to be dedicated. Appropriate psalms include 25, 111, 119:1–16, and 119:89–112. (For musical settings, see THE PLAINSONG PSALTER or THE ANGLICAN CHANT PSALTER.) Appropriate hymns include:

627	Lamp of our feet, whereby we trace
630	Thanks to God, whose Word was spoken
631	Book of books, our people's strength

Dedication of the Lectern and/or Pulpit   This form may be sung.

Liturgy of the Word   Provision is made for an Old Testament Lesson, a Gradual, and an Epistle to be said or sung (see GPAVT).

Processional Psalm, Hymn, or Instrumental Music   As the procession moves to an appropriate place, selected verses of a psalm or hymn, or instrumental music, may be used. Suitable psalms are 92, 98, and 150. (For musical settings, see THE PLAINSONG PSALTER or THE ANGLICAN CHANT PSALTER.) Fitting hymns include:

390	Praise to the Lord, the Almighty
402, 403	Let all the world in every corner sing
413	New songs of celebration render
420	When in our music God is glorified
426	Songs of praise the angels sang
432	O praise ye the Lord! Praise him in the height

Dedication of an Instrument of Music   This form may be sung. "Instrumental music may now be played, or a hymn or anthem sung." Now for the first time in the service the newly dedicated instrument is sounded. A brief fanfare would be in order, or a strong hymn of praise such as one of those listed immediately above.

Nicene Creed   The Nicene Creed may be sung or said if the Apostles' Creed has not already been said (that is, at a Baptism or Confirmation within the rite). (For musical settings of the Nicene Creed, see THE HYMNAL 1982 S 104–S 105 and S 361.)

Prayers of the People   Music is provided in THE HYMNAL 1982 for all six Forms (S 106–S 109 and S 362–S 363). Additional tones are provided for Forms I and V in HEAE and MMC. A common collect tone may be used for the concluding collect (See THE HYMNAL 1982 S 447–S 448, HEAE, or MMC).

Dedication of the Altar   This form may be sung. The dialogue could be sung to a Suffrage tone (S 52) and the concluding paragraph to a blessing tone or preface tone (See HEAE or MMC).
Bells or instrumental music. Joyous music is suitable at the vesting of the altar.
Peace. For music, see THE HYMNAL 1982 S 110–S 111, HEAE, or MMC.

At the Eucharist   The liturgy continues with the Offertory. Suitable hymns for use at the Offertory or at the Communion or before or after the postcommunion prayer include those suggested above for use at the entrance into the church, and also: 51 We the Lord's people, heart and voice uniting (except on Sunday omit stanza 3).

Blessing and Dismissal   For tones for blessings, see HEAE or MMC. For the people's responses to the Episcopal Blessing, see THE HYMNAL 1982 S 173. For music for dismissals, see THE HYMNAL 1982 S 174–S 176, HEAE, or MMC.

Postlude   Ideally, the music at the exit of the clergy and people should be based on that hymn or text which best sums up the service. (See HYMNAL STUDIES SEVEN, Volumes 1 and 2.)

Planning Music For Occasional Services

THE BOOK OF OCCASIONAL SERVICES provides supplementary texts for use in rites of THE BOOK OF COMMON PRAYER (Anthems at the Candle Lighting, Anthems at the Breaking of Bread, Seasonal Blessings, Station at a Christmas Creche, Candlemas Procession, et al.). It also provides supplementary rites for a number of occasions in the Church Year, and additional Pastoral Services and Episcopal Services. THE HYMNAL 1982 provides music for many of these texts.

Anthems at the Candle Lighting

For musical settings for these anthems see S 305–S 320.

Anthems at the Breaking of Bread

For musical settings see S 151–S 172 and S 373–S 374. For settings of the Psalm Verses see THE PLAINSONG PSALTER or THE ANGLICAN CHANT PSALTER. Simplified Anglican Chants (S 408–S 415) could be used for these verses.

Seasonal Blessings

For tones for blessings see MMC or HEAE. The Lenten Prayers over the People may be monotoned or sung to a common collect tone or to a blessing tone.

Advent Festival of Lessons and Music

The Advent Festival of Lessons and Music (BOS, pages 23–32) differs from the Christmas Festival of Lessons and Music (BOS, pages 36–39) in several important particulars. Aside from different Short Lesson, Prayer for Light, Anthem or Psalm at the Candle Lighting, and hymn in place of Phos hilaron in the Service of Light, the readings in the Advent service lead up to a Gospel announcing the forthcoming birth of John the Baptist (appropriate when the service is held within the second or third weeks of Advent) or a Gospel announcing the forthcoming birth of the Messiah (appropriate when the service is held within the fourth week of Advent). The rubrics of the service for Advent also suggest that a period of silence might follow each lesson. In the service for Advent the lessons are to be interspersed with "appropriate Advent hymns, canticles, and anthems," whereas in the service for Christmas they are to be interspersed with "appropriate carols, hymns, canticles, and anthems." The services end with blessings proper to the different seasons. The service for Advent has more of the nature of a vigil, whereas that for Christmas is a festal celebration.

If the service begins with An Order of Worship for the Evening, "A musical prelude or processional is not appropriate" (BCP, p. 142).

Opening Acclamation   For music, see THE HYMNAL 1982 S 56–S 57.

Short Lesson of Scripture   One of the Short Lessons for Advent (See BCP, p. 108) may be monotoned or sung to the tone provided in THE HYMNAL 1982 S 449, HEAE, or MMC.

Prayer for Light   This collect may be sung to one of the usual collect tones (THE HYMNAL 1982 S 447–S 448, HEAE, or MMC).

Anthem, Psalm, or Silence   The Anthem at the Candle Lighting for Advent (S 309) or Psalm 85:7–13 (For music, see THE PLAINSONG PSALTER, or THE ANGLICAN CHANT PSALTER, or Simplified Anglican Chant [S 408–S 415]) may be sung or silence may be kept during the lighting of the candles.

O Gracious Light (Phos hilaron) or Hymn   For music for the Phos hilaron, see THE HYMNAL 1982 S 27 and S 59–S 61. For metrical versions, see:

     25, 26   O gracious Light, Lord Jesus Christ
         36   O gladsome Light, O grace
         37   O brightness of the immortal Father's face

Appropriate hymns would include:

       60   Creator of the stars of night
496, 497   How bright appears the Morning Star
    6, 7   Christ, whose glory fills the skies
      56   O come, O come, Emmanuel

Bidding Prayer　The Bidding Prayer may be monotoned, and the Lord's Prayer monotoned or sung to one of the settings in THE HYMNAL 1982 S 119 (traditional) or S 148–S 150 (contemporary).

The Lessons　The Lessons and the concluding Gospel may be sung to the usual tones (See HEAE or MMC).

Advent Hymns, Canticles, and Anthems　See HYMNAL STUDIES FIVE, pp. 297–299, for recommendations of hymns to follow each of the suggested lessons. Luke 1:5–25 might appropriately be followed by The Song of Zechariah (*Benedictus Dominus Deus*) (See THE HYMNAL 1982 S 190–S 195, S 248–S 252, S 394, and S 404), or Luke 1:26–38 *or* 1:26–56 by The Song of Mary (*Magnificat*) (S 185–S 189, S 242–S 247, S 393, and S 403).

Collect　The collect may be sung to one of the usual collect tones (THE HYMNAL 1982 S 447–S 448, HEAE, or MMC).

Seasonal Blessing for Advent (BOS, p. 20)　For the tone for blessings, see HEAE or MMC.

Vigil for Christmas Eve

The service begins with An Order of Worship for the Evening (BCP, p. 109). "A musical prelude or processional is not appropriate" (BCP, p. 142).

Short Lesson of Scripture　If used, the Short Lesson for Christmas (BCP, p. 108) may be monotoned or sung to the tone provided in THE HYMNAL 1982 S 449, HEAE, or MMC.

Prayer for Light　This collect may be sung to one of the usual collect tones (THE HYMNAL 1982 S 447–S 448, HEAE, or MMC).

Anthem, Psalm, or Silence　The Anthem at the Candle Lighting for Christmas (S 310) or Psalm 113 (For music see THE PLAINSONG PSALTER, or THE ANGLICAN CHANT PSALTER, or Simplified Anglican Chant [S 408–S 415]) may be sung or silence may be kept during the lighting of the candles.

O Gracious Light (Phos hilaron), The Song of Mary (Magnificat), or Hymn　For music for the Phos hilaron, see THE HYMNAL 1982 S 27 and S 59–S 61. For metrical versions, see:

    25, 26   O gracious Light, Lord Jesus Christ
      36   O gladsome Light, O grace
      37   O brightness of the immortal Father's face

For settings of the Song of Mary (*Magnificat*), see THE HYMNAL 1982 S 185–S 189, S 242–S 247, S 393, and S 403. Suitable hymns would include:

      82   Of the Father's love begotten
    85, 86   O Savior of our fallen race

91   Break forth, O beauteous heavenly light

103   A child is born in Bethlehem, Alleluia!

The Lessons   The Lessons may be sung to the usual tones (See HEAE or MMC).

Anthems, Canticles, Hymns, Carols, or Instrumental Music   See HYMNAL STUDIES FIVE, pp. 299–302, for recommendations of hymns or carols to follow each of the suggested lessons. After the last reading, there may be a procession to the creche (see below), after which the procession continues to the chancel, and the Eucharist begins in the usual way.

Station at a Christmas Creche

The station at a Christmas Creche could precede the Entrance Hymn for a Christmas Eucharist. It might be preceded by a hymn sung in procession to the creche or by the Vigil for Christmas Eve (above). The Versicle and Response and the Collect may be monotoned or the Versicle and Response sung to the setting for the Suffrages (S 52) and the Collect to Tone II (S 448).

Christmas Festival of Lessons and Music

If the service begins with An Order of Worship for the Evening (BCP, p. 109) "A musical prelude or processional is not appropriate" (BCP, p. 142).

Opening Acclamation   For music, see THE HYMNAL 1982 S 56–S 57.

Short Lesson of Scripture   If used, the Short Lesson for Christmas (BCP, p. 108) may be monotoned or sung to the tone provided in THE HYMNAL 1982 S 449, HEAE, or MMC.

Prayer for Light   This collect may be sung to one of the usual collect tones (THE HYMNAL 1982 S 447–S 448, HEAE, or MMC).

Anthem, Psalm, or Silence   The Anthem at the Candle Lighting for Christmas (S 310) may be sung, or Psalm 113 (For music see THE PLAINSONG PSALTER, or THE ANGLICAN CHANT PSALTER, or Simplified Anglican Chant [S 408–S 415]), or silence may be kept, during the lighting of the candles.

Phos Hilaron or Hymn   For music for the Phos hilaron, see THE HYMNAL 1982 S 27 and S 59–S 61. For metrical versions, see:

25, 26   O gracious Light, Lord Jesus Christ

36   O gladsome Light, O grace

37   O brightness of the immortal Father's face

Appropriate hymns would include:

82   Of the Father's love begotten

85, 86   O Savior of our fallen race

91   Break forth, O beauteous heavenly light

103   A child is born in Bethlehem, Alleluia!

Bidding Prayer   The Bidding Prayer may be monotoned, and the Lord's Prayer monotoned or sung to one of the settings in THE HYMNAL 1982 S 119 (traditional) or S 148–S 150 (contemporary).

The Lessons   The Lessons and the concluding Gospel may be sung to the usual tones (See HEAE or MMC).

Carols, Hymns, Canticles, and Anthems See HYMNAL STUDIES FIVE, pp. 299–302, for recommendations of hymns or carols to follow each of the suggested lessons. Luke 1:39–46 *or* 1:39–56 might appropriately be followed by The Song of Mary (*Magnificat*) [See THE HYMNAL 1982 S 185–S 189, S 242–S 247, S 393, and S 403] or Luke 1:57–80 by The Song of Zechariah (*Benedictus Dominus Deus*) [S 190–S 195, S 248–S 252, S 394, and S 404].

Collect The collect may be sung to one of the usual collect tones (THE HYMNAL 1982 S 447–S 448, HEAE, or MMC).

Seasonal Blessing for Christmas (BOS, p. 21) For the tone for blessings, see HEAE or MMC.

Service for New Year's Eve

The service begins with An Order of Worship for the Evening (BCP, p. 109). "A musical prelude or processional is not appropriate" (BCP, p. 142).

Opening Acclamation For music, see THE HYMNAL 1982 S 56–S 57.

Short Lesson of Scripture If a Short Lesson is used, it may be monotoned or sung to the tone provided in THE HYMNAL 1982 S 449, HEAE, or MMC.

Prayer for Light This collect may be sung to one of the usual collect tones (THE HYMNAL 1982 S 447–S 448, HEAE, or MMC).

Anthem, Psalm, or Silence The Anthem at the Candle Lighting for Christmas (S 310) may be sung, or a psalm (See THE PLAINSONG PSALTER, or THE ANGLICAN CHANT PSALTER, or Simplified Anglican Chant [S 408–S 415] for music), or silence may be kept during the lighting of the candles.

O Gracious Light (Phos Hilaron) or Hymn For music for the Phos hilaron, see THE HYMNAL 1982 S 27 and S 59–S 61. For metrical versions, see:

25, 26	O gracious Light, Lord Jesus Christ
36	O gladsome Light, O grace
37	O brightness of the immortal Father's face

Appropriate hymns would include:

82	Of the Father's love begotten
85, 86	O Savior of our fallen race
91	Break forth, O beauteous heavenly light
103	A child is born in Bethlehem, Alleluia!

The Lessons The Lessons may be sung to the usual tones (See HEAE or MMC).

The Psalms or Hymns For music for the psalms, see THE PLAINSONG PSALTER, or THE ANGLICAN CHANT PSALTER, or Simplified Anglican Chant (S 408–S 415). HYMANL STUDIES FIVE, pp. 302–303, recommends suitable hymns related to each of the lessons that might be used in place of recommended psalms.

The Collects The collects may be sung to one of the usual collect tones (THE HYMNAL 1982 S 447–S 448, HEAE, or MMC).

The service may end with the Great Litany (See S 67) or some other form of intercession (See S 106–S 109 and S 362–S 363 for musical settings for all six forms of the Prayers of the People).

Another way to end the service is to sing the We Praise Thee / You are God (*Te*

Deum laudamus) or some other hymn of praise, followed by the Lord's Prayer, the Collect for Holy Name, and a blessing or dismissal, or both. For music for the Te Deum, see S 205–S 207, S 282–S 288, and S 407. The Lord's Prayer may be monotoned, and the collect sung to one of the usual tones (See S 447–S 448, HEAE, or MMC). For tones for blessings, see HEAE or MMC; for dismissals, see S 174.

This service may also be used as an introduction to the Eucharist for the Feast of the Holy Name, which would begin with the Gloria in excelsis or some other song of praise. For hymn suggestions, see HYMNAL STUDIES FIVE, pp. 179–180.

Blessing in Homes at Epiphany

The Greeting The greeting may be sung to the tone of the Opening Acclamation (S 76).

The Antiphons The antiphons may be sung to a Plainsong Psalm Tone (See S 446) that is congruent with the setting of the Magnificat.

The Song of Mary (Magnificat) For musical settings, see THE HYMNAL 1982 S 185–S 189, S 242–S 247, S 393, and S 403.

Salutation and Prayer(s) These may be sung to one of the usual collect tones (See THE HYMNAL 1982 S 447–S 448, HEAE, or MMC).

The Blessing For tones for the blessing, see HEAE or MMC.

The Peace For music for the peace, see S 110–S 111.

Vigil for the Eve of the Baptism of Our Lord

The service begins with An Order of Worship for the Evening (BCP, p. 109). "A musical prelude or processional is not appropriate" (BCP, p. 142).

Opening Acclamation For music, see THE HYMNAL 1982 S 56–S 57.

Short Lesson of Scripture If the Short Lesson (See BCP, p. 108) is used, it may be monotoned or sung to the tone provided in THE HYMNAL 1982 S 449, HEAE, or MMC.

Prayer for Light This collect may be sung to one of the usual collect tones (THE HYMNAL 1982 S 447–S 448, HEAE, or MMC).

Anthem, Psalm, or Silence The Anthem at the Candle Lighting for Epiphany (S 311) may be sung, or a psalm (See THE PLAINSONG PSALTER, or THE ANGLICAN CHANT PSALTER, or Simplified Anglican Chant [S 408–S 415] for music), or silence may be kept during the lighting of the candles.

O Gracious Light (Phos Hilaron), Glory be to God / Glory to God (Gloria in Excelsis), or Hymn For music for the Phos hilaron, see THE HYMNAL 1982 S 27 and S 59–S 61. For metrical versions, see:

> 25, 26 O gracious Light, Lord Jesus Christ
> 36 O gladsome Light, O grace
> 37 O brightness of the immortal Father's face

For settings of the Gloria in excelsis, see THE HYMNAL 1982 S 201–S 204, S 272–S 281, and S 396–S 399. An appropriate hymn to use as an alternative to the Phos hilaron would be Hymn 125, 126, "The people who in darkness walked."

Salutation and Collect This collect may be sung to one of the usual collect tones (THE HYMNAL 1982 S 447–S 448, HEAE, or MMC).

The Lessons The Lessons may be sung to the usual tones (See HEAE or MMC).

The Psalms, Canticles, or Hymns For music for the psalms, see THE PLAINSONG PSALTER, or THE ANGLICAN CHANT PSALTER, or Simplified Anglican Chant (S 408–S 415). HYMNAL STUDIES FIVE, pp. 303–304, recommends suitable hymns related to each of the lessons that might be used in place of recommended psalms.

The Gospel The Gospel may be sung to the usual tones (See HEAE or MMC).

The service continues, following the sermon, with Baptism or Confirmation (beginning with the Presentation of the Candidates), or with Renewal of Baptismal Vows (BCP, p. 292). (See above.)

Candlemas Procession

Opening Acclamation For music, see THE HYMNAL 1982 S 340.

The Song of Simeon (Nunc Dimittis) with Antiphon For music, see THE HYMNAL 1982 S 341.

Collect The collect may be sung to one of the usual collect tones (THE HYMNAL 1982 S 447–S 448, HEAE, or MMC).

The Procession For music for the versicle and response and the appointed psalm (the concluding psalm of the procession), see THE HYMNAL 1982 S 342 and S 343. For the stational collect either of the usual collect tones is appropriate (THE HYMNAL 1982 S 447–S 448, HEAE, or MMC). At the beginning of the procession other appropriate psalms or hymns may be used. Appropriate psalms include Psalms 27, 43, 67, 97, and 112 (See THE PLAINSONG PSALTER, or THE ANGLICAN CHANT PSALTER, or Simplified Anglican Chant [THE HYMNAL 1982 S 408–S 415]). Appropriate hymns include:

6, 7	Christ, whose glory fills the skies
257	O Zion, open wide thy gates
259	Hail to the Lord who comes
496, 497	How bright appears the Morning Star
499	Lord God, you now have set your servant free

The Eucharist begins with the Glory be to God / Glory to God (*Gloria in excelsis*) or some other Song of Praise.

The Way of the Cross

Prelude Any prelude should be quiet and meditative, normally based upon a hymn or chant that will be used in the service or another hymn associated with the passion. (See HYMNAL STUDIES SEVEN, Volumes 1 and 2.)

Entrance Hymn The entrance hymn should normally be chosen from among those in the Holy Week section of THE HYMNAL 1982 (158–172), but also see 471, "We sing the praise of him who died," and 474, "When I survey the wondrous cross."

Opening Devotions The Invocation ("In the Name of . . .") and the Versicle and Response may be sung to the tone of Suffrages A (S 52), the Lord, have mercy and the Kyrie and Lord's Prayer to the tones for the Noonday Office (S 304), and the collect to one of the usual collect tones (THE HYMNAL 1982 S 447–S 448, HEAE, of MMC).

The Stations Both the anthem and the Versicle and Response could be sung to the tone of Suffrages A (S 52), or the anthem could be sung to the tone at S 350. The lessons could be sung to the tone for Short Lessons (S 449), and the collects to one of the usual collect tones (THE HYMNAL 1982 S 447–S 448, HEAE, or MMC). For settings of the Holy God (*Trisagion*), see THE HYMNAL 1982 S 99–S 102 and S 360.

Concluding Prayers before the Altar The anthem could be sung to the tone of Suffrages A (S 52), or the setting at S 351 could be used. A collect tone (THE HYMNAL 1982 S 447–S 448, HEAE, or MMC) could be used for the prayer and a blessing tone (HEAE or MMC) for the concluding form.

Tenebrae

A complete musical setting of the office of Tenebrae of BOS, arranged from medieval sources by James M. Thompson, is available from the Music Commission of the Diocese of Chicago. Even if the traditional music cannot be used, the service is still very effective read, or using settings from THE PLAINSONG PSALTER for the psalms and from THE HYMNAL 1982 for the Benedictus, or using Simplified Anglican Chant (THE HYMNAL 1982 S 408–S 415) for psalms and Benedictus.

Blessing in Homes at Easter

The Greeting The greeting may be sung to the tone of the Opening Acclamation (S 76).

The Antiphons The antiphons may be sung to a Plainsong Psalm Tone (See S 446) that is congruent with the setting of the psalm or canticle. (For the first Antiphon, see S 294.)

Psalm 114 or an Alternative Psalm or Canticle For settings of Psalm 114, or the alternative Psalm 118, see THE PLAINSONG PSALTER or THE ANGLICAN CHANT PSALTER. For musical settings of Christ our Passover, see THE HYMNAL 1982 S 16–S 20 and S 46–S 50; for the Song of Moses, see S 208–S 212; for the Song to the Lamb, see S 261–S 266.

The Collect and Prayer These may be sung to one of the usual collect tones (See THE HYMNAL 1982 S 447–S 448, HEAE, or MMC).

The Blessing For tones for the blessing, see HEAE or MMC.

The Peace For music for the peace, see S 110–S 111.

Rogation Procession

Hymns, Psalms, Canticles, and Anthems For musical settings of Canticle 1 or 12 (A Song of Creation [*Benedicite*]), see THE HYMNAL 1982 S 177–S 179 and S 228–S 230. For settings of Psalms 103 and 104, see THE PLAINSONG PSALTER and THE ANGLICAN CHANT PSALTER or Simplified Anglican Chant (THE HYMNAL 1982 S 408–S 415). Suitable hymns include:

291 We plow the fields and scatter
292 O Jesus, crowned with all renown
388 O worship the King, all glorious above!
389 Let us, with a gladsome mind
390 Praise to the Lord, the Almighty

400 All creatures of our God and King
405 All things bright and beautiful
406, 407 Most High, omnipotent, good Lord
428 O all ye works of God, now come
709 O God of Bethel, by whose hand

The Lessons   The lessons may be sung to the usual tones (See HEAE or MMC).

The Prayers   The prayers may be sung to one of the usual collect tones (THE HYMNAL 1982 S 447–S 448, HEAE, or MMC).

The Great Litany   For music for the litany, see S 67 (the entire text is printed at S 67 in Acc. Ed. Vol. 1).

The service ends after the Great Litany with a suitable prayer and blessing (See THE HYMNAL 1982 S 447–S 448, HEAE, or MMC for collect tones, and HEAE or MMC for blessing tones), or continues, after the Lord, have mercy upon us or Kyrie eleison of the Litany, with the Eucharist for Rogation Days, beginning with the Salutation and proper Collect.

Vigil for the Eve of All Saints' Day or the Sunday After All Saints' Day

The service begins with An Order of Worship for the Evening (BCP, p. 109). "A musical prelude or processional is not appropriate" (BCP, p. 142).

Opening Acclamation   For music, see THE HYMNAL 1982 S 56–S 57.

Short Lesson of Scripture   If the Short Lesson (See BCP, p. 108) is used, it may be monotoned or sung to the tone provided in THE HYMNAL 1982 S 449, HEAE, or MMC.

Prayer for Light   This collect may be sung to one of the usual collect tones (THE HYMNAL 1982 S 447–S 448, HEAE, or MMC).

Anthem, Psalm, or Silence   The Anthem at the Candle Lighting for All Saints (S 318) may be sung, or a psalm (See THE PLAINSONG PSALTER, or THE ANGLICAN CHANT PSALTER, or Simplified Anglican Chant [S 408–S 415] for music), or silence may be kept during the lighting of the candles.

O Gracious Light (Phos hilaron), Glory be to God / Glory to God (Gloria in excelsis), or Hymn   For music for the Phos hilaron, see THE HYMNAL 1982 S 27 and S 59–S 61. For metrical versions, see:

25, 26 O gracious Light, Lord Jesus Christ
36 O gladsome Light, O grace
37 O brightness of the immortal Father's face

For settings of the Gloria in excelsis, see THE HYMNAL 1982 S 201–S 204, S 272–S 281, and S 396–S 399. An appropriate hymn to use as an alternative to the Phos hilaron would be Hymn 545, "Lo! what a cloud of witnesses."

Salutation and Collect   This collect may be sung to one of the usual collect tones (THE HYMNAL 1982 S 447–S 448, HEAE, or MMC).

The Psalms, Canticles, or Hymns   For music for the psalms, see THE PLAINSONG PSALTER, or THE ANGLICAN CHANT PSALTER, or Simplified Anglican Chant (S 408–S 415). HYMNAL STUDIES FIVE, pp. 305–306, recommends suitable hymns related to each of the lessons that might be used in place of recommended psalms.

The Gospel The Gospel may be sung to the usual tones (See HEAE or MMC).

The service continues, following the sermon, with Baptism or Confirmation (beginning with the Presentation of the Candidates), or with Renewal of Baptismal Vows (BCP, p. 292). (See above.)

Service for All Hallows' Eve

The service begins with An Order of Worship for the Evening (BCP, p. 109). "A musical prelude or processional is not appropriate" (BCP, p. 142).

Opening Acclamation For music, see THE HYMNAL 1982 S 56–S 57.

Short Lesson of Scripture If a Short Lesson is used, it may be monotoned or sung to the tone provided in THE HYMNAL 1982 S 449, HEAE, or MMC.

Prayer for Light The prayer appointed for Festivals of Saints (BCP, p. 111) may be sung to one of the usual collect tones (THE HYMNAL 1982 S 447–S 448, HEAE, or MMC).

Anthem, Psalm, or Silence The Anthem at the Candle Lighting for All Saints (S 318) or some other anthem, or a psalm (See THE PLAINSONG PSALTER, or THE ANGLICAN CHANT PSALTER, or Simplified Anglican Chant [S 408–S 415] for music), or silence may be kept during the lighting of the candles.

O Gracious Light (Phos Hilaron) or Hymn For music for the Phos hilaron, see THE HYMNAL 1982 S 27 and S 59–S 61. For metrical versions, see:

> 25, 26 O gracious Light, Lord Jesus Christ
> 36 O gladsome Light, O grace
> 37 O brightness of the immortal Father's face

Appropriate hymns to use in place of the Phos hilaron would include:

> 286 Who are these like stars appearing
> 545 Lo! what a cloud of witnesses

The Lessons The Lessons may be sung to the usual tones (See HEAE or MMC).

The Psalms, Canticles, or Hymns For music for the psalms, see THE PLAINSONG PSALTER, or THE ANGLICAN CHANT PSALTER, or Simplified Anglican Chant (S 408–S 415). HYMNAL STUDIES FIVE, pp. 306–307, recommends suitable hymns related to each of the lessons that might be used in place of recommended psalms.

The Prayers The prayers may be sung to one of the usual collect tones (THE HYMNAL 1982 S 447–S 448, HEAE, or MMC).

We Praise Thee / You are God (Te Deum Laudamus) or Other Song of Praise For settings of the Te Deum, see THE HYMNAL 1982 S 205–S 207, S 282–S 288, and S 407. Also appropriate would be the A Song of Creation (*Benedicite*), S 179 (Parts I & IV) or S 228–S 230 (Invocation, Part III, Doxology).

The Lord's Prayer The Lord's Prayer may be monotoned.

Collect of All Saints' Day This may be sung to one of the usual collect tones (THE HYMNAL 1982 S 447–S 448, HEAE, or MMC).

Blessing or Dismissal See BOS, pp. 26–27, for blessings for All Saints. For tones for blessings, see HEAE or MMC. For music for the dismissal, see THE HYMNAL 1982 S 174, HEAE, or MMC.

A Vigil on The Eve of Baptism

The service begins with An Order of Worship for the Evening (BCP, p. 109). "A musical prelude or processional is not appropriate" (BCP, p. 142).

Opening Acclamation   For music, see THE HYMNAL 1982 S 56–S 57.

Short Lesson of Scripture   If a Short Lesson is used, it may be monotoned or sung to the tone provided in THE HYMNAL 1982 S 449, HEAE, or MMC.

Prayer for Light   This collect may be sung to one of the usual collect tones (THE HYMNAL 1982 S 447–S 448, HEAE, or MMC).

Anthem, Psalm, or Silence   An anthem may be sung at the candle lighting (See THE HYMNAL 1982 S 305–S 320), or a psalm (See THE PLAINSONG PSALTER, THE ANGLICAN CHANT PSALTER, or Simplified Anglican Chant [S 408–S 415] for music), or silence may be kept.

O Gracious Light (Phos Hilaron) or Hymn   For music for the Phos hilaron, see THE HYMNAL 1982 S 27 and S 59–S 61. For metrical versions, see:

25, 26	O gracious Light, Lord Jesus Christ
36	O gladsome Light, O grace
37	O brightness of the immortal Father's face

Appropriate hymns would include:

500	Creator Spirit, by whose aid
501, 502	O Holy Spirit, by whose breath
503, 504	Come, Holy Ghost, our souls inspire
512	Come, gracious Spirit, heavenly Dove
516	Come down, O Love divine

Salutation and Collect   This collect may be sung to one of the usual collect tones (THE HYMNAL 1982 S 447–S 448, HEAE, or MMC).

The Lessons   The Lessons may be sung to the usual tones (See HEAE or MMC).

The Psalms, Canticles, or Hymns   For music for the psalms, see THE PLAINSONG PSALTER, or THE ANGLICAN CHANT PSALTER, or Simplified Anglican Chant (S 408–S 415). HYMNAL STUDIES FIVE, pp. 307–308, recommends suitable hymns related to each of the lessons that might be used in place of recommended psalms.

The Gospel   The Gospel may be sung to the usual tones (See HEAE or MMC).

The Prayers   Either form may be sung to the Suffrage tone (S 52).

Hymn   Appropriate hymns include:

297	Descend, O Spirit, purging flame
298	All who believe and are baptized
299	Spirit of God, unleashed on earth
697	My God, accept my heart this day

Blessing and/or dismissal   For tones for blessings, see HEAE or MMC. For dismissals, see THE HYMNAL 1982 S 174–S 176.

Celebration for a Home

Prelude   Since those present for this rite would often include people unfamiliar with some of the hymns or other music that might be used, participation might be greatly enhanced if the instrumentalists play music that will be used in the rite or preludes based on it. (See HYMNAL STUDIES SEVEN, Volumes 1 and 2.) A choir or soloists might also make musical offerings at this time of gathering.

Salutation and Collect   The collect might be sung to one of the usual collect tones (See THE HYMNAL 1982 S 447–S 448, HEAE, or MMC).

The Lessons   The Lessons may be sung to the usual tones (See HEAE or MMC).

Psalm or Song   A Psalm may be sung after or between readings. For Psalm 112:1–7, or other psalms, see THE PLAINSONG PSALTER, THE ANGLICAN CHANT PSALTER, or Simplified Anglican Chant (THE HYMNAL 1982 S 408–S 415). Note the use of the more inclusive word "song" rather than "hymn" in the rubric. One of the following hymns might be appropriate:

251	O God, whom neither time nor space (omit st. 2)
396, 397	Now thank we all our God
416	For the beauty of the earth
612	Gracious Spirit, Holy Ghost

Gospel   See HEAE or MMC for the tone.

Invocation   If this is used, it might be sung to one of the usual collect tones (See THE HYMNAL 1982 S 447–S 448, HEAE, or MMC).

At the Procession   The antiphons might be set to Plainsong Psalm Tones (See THE HYMNAL 1982 S 446), the versicles and responses to the Suffrage tone (See S 52), and the collects to the usual collect tones (See S 447–S 448, HEAE, or MMC). It might be appropriate for one or more of the following hymns to be sung in the course of the procession or by any remaining in the living room during the procession:

350	O God of love, to thee we bow
352	O God, to those who here profess
353	Your love, O God, has called us here
396, 397	Now thank we all our God
581	Where charity and love prevail
587	Our Father, by whose Name
612	Gracious Spirit, Holy Ghost

The Blessing of the Home   The antiphon might be set to a Plainsong Psalm Tone (See THE HYMNAL 1982 S 446), the versicle and response to the Suffrage tone (S 52), the blessing to a blessing tone (See HEAE or MMC), and the peace to the usual tone (S 110 or S 111).

For various reasons it may be desirable not to proceed to the Holy Communion, but if Communion is celebrated one of more of the following hymns might be appropriate at the offertory, during Communion, and/or before or after the postcommunion prayer:

138	All praise to you, O Lord
312	Strengthen for service, Lord
350	O God of love, to thee we bow
351	May the grace of Christ our Savior
352	O God, to those who here profess
353	Your love, O God, has called us here

581	Where charity and love prevail
587	Our Father, by whose Name
593	Lord, make us servants of your peace
635	If thou but trust in God to guide thee
645, 646	The King of love my shepherd is
663	The Lord my God my shepherd is
664	My Shepherd will supply my need
709	O God of Bethel, by whose hand

If there is not to be a Communion, the Lord's Prayer might be monotoned or sung to one of the usual settings (THE HYMNAL 1982 S 119 [traditional] or S 148–S 150 [contemporary]), and the blessing sung to one of the usual tones (See HEAE or MMC).

Blessing of a Pregnant Woman

The Prayer The prayer might be sung to one of the usual collect tones (See THE HYMNAL 1982 S 447–S 448, HEAE, or MMC).

The Blessing The blessing might be sung to one of the usual blessing tones (See HEAE or MMC).

Anniversary of a Marriage

This rite is set within the context of the Holy Eucharist. The blessing (p. 146) might be sung to one of the usual blessing tones (HEAE or MMC).

A Public Service of Healing

The Opening Acclamation could be monotoned, the Litany of Healing sung to the tone of the petitions of the Great Litany and their responses (THE HYMNAL 1982 S 67), and the prayers to one of the usual collect tones (S 447–S 448, HEAE, or MMC). The anthem, "O Savior of the world," can be sung to the setting in THE HYMNAL 1982 S 351. Both blessings ("The Almighty Lord, who is a strong tower . . ." and "May God the Father bless you . . .") can be sung to one of the usual blessing tones (See HEAE or MMC).

Burial of One Who Does Not Profess the Christian Faith

One or more of the following hymns might be appropriate:

372	Praise to the living God!
379	God is Love, let heaven adore him
423	Immortal, invisible, God only wise
635	If thou but trust in God to guide thee
645, 646	The King of love my shepherd is
663	The Lord my God my shepherd is
664	My Shepherd will supply my need
665	All my hope on God is founded
668	I to the hills will lift mine eyes
669	Commit thou all that grieves thee
680	O God, our help in ages past

For references to musical settings for other elements in the rite, see Burial of the Dead (above, pp. 91–92).

Commissioning for Lay Ministries in the Church _____

The Antiphons might be sung to a Plainsong Psalm Tone (See THE HYMNAL 1982 S 446), the versicles and responses to a Suffrage tone (See S 52), and the collects to one of the usual collect tones (See S 447–S 448, HEAE, or MMC).

Dedication of Church Furnishings and Ornaments _____

The Antiphons might be sung to a Plainsong Psalm Tone (See THE HYMNAL 1982 S 446), the versicles and responses to a Suffrage tone (See S 52), and the collects (Forms 3–22) to one of the usual collect tones (See S 447–S 448, HEAE, or MMC) or to a blessing tone (See HEAE or MMC). For music for the Thanksgiving Over the Water at the consecration of a font, see HEAE. (The people's responses are printed in THE HYMNAL 1982 S 75.) The dialogue portion of the prayer for the dedication of an altar could be sung to a Suffrage tone (See S 52) and the concluding paragraph to a blessing tone (See HEAE or MMC).

The Founding of a Church

Ground Breaking _____

Pre-Service Music A bell or other musical instrument might call the people to silence for the procession, or instruments which might later accompany the hymn and psalms might perform a brief prelude.

Litany for the Church The setting for the Litany for Ordinations (THE HYMNAL 1982 S 390) can be adapted for this litany.

Collect The collect can be sung to one of the usual collect tones (See THE HYMNAL 1982 S 447–S 448, HEAE, or MMC), and the form which follows to a blessing tone (See HEAE or MMC).

Hymn Appropriate hymns would include:

509	Spirit divine, attend our prayers
517	How lovely is thy dwelling-place
522, 523	Glorious things of thee are spoken
524	I love thy kingdom, Lord
525	The Church's one foundation

Lesson For tones for lessons, see HEAE or MMC.

Psalms and Antiphons For settings for the psalms, see THE PLAINSONG PSALTER, THE ANGLICAN CHANT PSALTER, or Simplified Anglican Chant (THE HYMNAL 1982 S 408–S 415). The antiphons might be set to Plainsong Psalm Tones (S 446).

The Ground Breaking This might be sung to a blessing tone (See HEAE or MMC).

Concluding Prayers The Lord's Prayer might be monotoned, the versicles and responses sung to a Suffrage tone (S 52), and the prayer to a collect tone (S 447–S 448, HEAE, or MMC). For music for the dismissal see S 174–S 176.

Laying of a Cornerstone

Pre-Service Music A bell or other musical instrument might call the people to silence for the opening hymn or anthem, or instruments which might later be used to accompany the hymns and acclamations might perform a brief prelude.

Hymn or Anthem Appropriate hymns would include:

509	Spirit divine, attend our prayers
517	How lovely is thy dwelling-place
518	Christ is made the sure foundation (sts. 1–2)
519, 520	Blessèd city, heavenly Salem
522, 523	Glorious things of thee are spoken
524	I love thy kingdom, Lord
525	The Church's one foundation

Lessons For lesson tones, see HEAE or MMC.

Prayer For collect tones, see THE HYMNAL 1982 S 447–S 448, HEAE, or MMC.

The Laying of the Cornerstone The prayer which follows might be sung to a blessing tone (See HEAE or MMC), the celebrant's acclamation to a Plainsong Psalm Tone (See S 446), and the people's response to one of the Alleluia tones in GPAVT or to the tone of the Great Alleluia (See THE HYMNAL 1982 S 70).

Hymn For an appropriate hymn, see list above.

Blessing and Dismissal For blessing tones, see HEAE or MMC; for dismissals, see S 174–S 176.

Consecration of Chrism Apart From Baptism

If at a visitation of the bishop there are no baptisms, the consecration of chrism for subsequent baptisms takes place immediately after the postcommunion prayer. Music for the prayer of consecration is in HEAE. (The preface might be monotoned.)

Recognition and Investiture of a Diocesan Bishop

Prelude. People gathered for such an occasion normally come from differing parishes and traditions. The participation is likely to be enhanced if the musicians familiarize the congregation with the music by using it as a prelude or by using preludes based on it. (See HYMNAL STUDIES SEVEN, Volumes 1 and 2.) Instrumentalists or choristers may make other musical offerings as well.

Procession Instrumental music would be appropriate during the procession.

Opening of the Door The bishop's words and the warden's response might be sung to a Plainsong Psalm Tone (See THE HYMNAL 1982 S 446).

Psalm or Anthem For settings of Psalm 23 or another psalm, see THE PLAINSONG PSALTER, THE ANGLICAN CHANT PSALTER, or Simplified Anglican Chant (THE HYMNAL 1982 S 408–S 415). The antiphon might be set to a Plainsong Psalm Tone (S 446).

Litany For music for the Litany for Ordinations, see THE HYMNAL 1982 S 390.

After the Litany the Eucharist proceeds in the usual manner, from the salutation and collect through the sermon (and creed). After the seating, "Bells may be rung and trumpets sounded." The Eucharist continues, beginning with the peace. For the setting for the bishop's blessing, see HEAE or MMC (the people's responses are printed in THE HYMNAL 1982 S 173).

Welcoming and Seating of a Bishop in the Cathedral _____

Prelude and Procession Instrumental music would be appropriate as a prelude and for the procession.

Greeting The greeting and the people's response may be monotoned.

Psalm or Anthem For settings of the psalms, see THE PLAINSONG PSALTER, THE ANGLICAN CHANT PSALTER, or Simplified Anglican Chant (THE HYMNAL 1982 S 408–S 415).

Instrumental music may be played as the bishop is escorted to the Cathedra, and bells may be rung and trumpets sounded after the bishop is seated.

We Praise Thee / You are God (Te Deum laudamus), Glory be to God / Glory to God (Gloria in excelsis), or Other Song of Praise For settings for the Te Deum, see THE HYMNAL 1982 S 205–S 207, S 282–S 288, and S 407; for settings for Gloria in excelsis, see S 201–S 204, S 272–S 281, and S 396–S 399.

The liturgy continues, beginning with the salutation and collect of the day. For the setting for the bishop's blessing, see HEAE or MMC (the people's responses are printed in THE HYMNAL 1982 S 173).

Appendix I:

Descants, Fauxbourdons,
Varied Harmonizations, Varied Accompaniments,
Suggested Alternative Treatments of Hymns,
and Hymns Scored for other Instruments in
THE HYMNAL 1982

Descants		Tune Name & Other Uses of Tune
59	Hark! a thrilling voice is sounding	(Merton)
72	Hark! the glad sound! the Savior comes	(Richmond, 212)
74	Blest be the King whose coming	(Valet will ich dir geben, 154)
94	While shepherds watched their flocks by night	(Winchester Old)
109	The first Nowell the angel did say	(The First Nowell)
137	O wondrous type! O vision fair	(Wareham, 20, 353)
178	Alleluia, alleluia! Give thanks to the risen Lord	(Alleluia No. 1)
181	Awake and sing the song	(St. Ethelwald, 628)
207	Jesus Christ is risen today	(Easter Hymn)
210	The day of resurrection	(Ellacombe)
241	Hearken to the anthem glorious	(Laus Deo)
268	Ye who claim the faith of Jesus	(Julion, 507)
290	Come, ye thankful people, come	(St. George's, Windsor)
305	Come, risen Lord, and deign to be our guest	(Rosedale)
335	I am the bread of life	(I Am the Bread of Life)
368	Holy Father, great Creator	(Regent Square, 93)
382	King of glory, King of peace	(General Seminary)
390	Praise to the Lord, the Almighty	(Lobe den Herren)
399	To God with gladness sing	(Camano)
405	All things bright and beautiful	(Royal Oak)
410	Praise, my soul, the King of heaven	(Lauda anima)
414	God, my King, thy might confessing	(Stuttgart, 66, 127)
450	All hail the power of Jesus' Name	(Coronation)
473	Lift high the cross	(Crucifer)
477	All praise to thee, for thou, O King divine	(Engelberg, 296, 420)
494	Crown him with many crowns	(Diademata)
518	Christ is made the sure foundation	(Westminster Abbey)
521	Put forth, O God, thy Spirit's might	(Chelsea Square)
522	Glorious things of thee are spoken	(Austria)
576	God is love, and where true love is	(Mandatum)
625	Ye holy angels bright	(Darwell's 148th)
637	How firm a foundation	(Lyons, 533)
646	The King of love my shepherd is	(Dominus regit me)

Melody in the tenor (Fauxbourdons)

118	Brightest and best of the stars of the morning	(Star in the East)
378	All people that on earth do dwell	(Old 100th, 377, 380)
439	What wondrous love is this	(Wondrous Love)
580	God, who stretched the spangled heavens	(Holy Manna, 238)
709	O God of Bethel, by whose hand	(Dundee, 126, 526)

Harmonizations for tunes printed for singing in unison

193	That Easter day with joy was bright	(Puer nobis, 124)
206	O sons and daughters, let us sing	(O filii et filiae, 203)
301	Bread of the world, in mercy broken	(Rendez à Dieu, 302)
348	Lord, we have come at your own invitation	(O quanta qualia, 623)
374	Come, let us join our cheerful songs	(Nun danket all und bringet Ehr, 509, 627)

| 413 | New songs of celebration render | (Rendez à Dieu, 302) |
| 709 | O God of Bethel, by whose hand | (Dundee, 126, 526) |

Varied harmonizations

48	O day of radiant gladness	(Es flog ein kleins Waldvögelein, 616)
66	Come, thou long-expected Jesus	(Stuttgart, 127, 414)
68	Rejoice! rejoice, believers	(Llangloffan, 607)
74	Blest be the King whose coming	(Valet will ich dir geben, 154)
127	Earth has many a noble city	(Stuttgart, 66, 414)
154	All glory, laud, and honor	(Valet will ich dir geben, 74)
321	My God, thy table now is spread	(Rockingham, 474)
343	Shepherd of souls, refresh and bless	(St. Agnes, 510)
344	Lord, dismiss us with thy blessing	(Sicilian Mariners, 708)
414	God, my King, thy might confessing	(Stuttgart, 66, 127)
474	When I survey the wondrous cross	(Rockingham, 321)
510	Come, Holy Spirit, heavenly Dove	(St. Agnes, 343)
607	O God of every nation	(Llangloffan, 68)
616	Hail to the Lord's Anointed	(Es flog ein kleins Waldvögelein, 48)
708	Savior, like a shepherd lead us	(Sicilian Mariners, 344)
716	God bless our native land	(America, 717)
717	My country, 'tis of thee	(America, 716)

Varied Accompaniments

(See listings above: Melody in the tenor (Fauxbourdons)
Harmonizations for tunes printed for singing in unison
Varied Harmonizations)

Also:

4	Now that the daylight fills the sky	(Verbum supernum prodiens, 311)
9	Not here for high and holy things	(Morning Song, 583)
10	New every morning is the love	(Kedron, 163)
15	O God, creation's secret force	(Te lucis ante terminum, 44)
18	(4 acc) As now the sun shines down at noon	(Jesu dulcis memoria, 134, 650)
38	Jesus, Redeemer of the world	(Jesu, nostra redemptio, 236 [2 acc])
41	(2 acc) O Christ, you are both light and day	(Compline)
44	To you before the close of day	(Te lucis ante terminum, 15)
56	(2 acc) O come, O come, Emmanuel	(Veni, veni, Emmanuel)
63	O heavenly Word, eternal Light	(Verbum supernum prodiens, 311)
98	(5 acc) Unto us a boy is born	(Puer nobis nascitur)

432	(2 acc) O praise ye the Lord! Praise him in the height	(Laudate Dominum)
438	(2 acc) Tell out, my soul, the greatness of the Lord	(Woodlands)
449	(2 acc) O love, how deep, how broad, how high	(Deo gracias, 218)
482	Lord of all hopefulness, Lord of all joy	(Slane, 488)
488	Be thou my vision, O Lord of my heart	(Slane, 482)
491	(2 acc) Where is this stupendous stranger	(Kit Smart)
495	Hail, thou once despisèd Jesus	(In Babilone, 215)
502	O Holy Spirit, by whose breath	(Veni Creator Spiritus, 504)
504	Come, Holy Ghost, our souls inspire	(Veni Creator Spiritus, 502)
519	(2 acc) Blessèd city, heavenly Salem	(Urbs beata Jerusalem, 122)
550	(2 acc) Jesus calls us; o'er the tumult	(Restoration)
583	O holy city, seen of John	(Morning Song, 9)
585	(2 acc) Morning glory, starlit sky	(Bingham)
636	(2 acc) How firm a Foundation, ye saints of the Lord	(Foundation)
650	O Jesus, joy of loving hearts	(Jesu dulcis memoria, 18 [4 acc], 134)
675	Take up your cross, the Savior said	(Bourbon, 147)

Verses which may be used as antiphons for the Magnificat

| 56 | O come, O come, Emmanuel | (Veni, veni, Emmanuel) |

Hymns which might be sung by alternating groups

183	Christians, to the Paschal victim	(Victimae Paschali laudes)
381	Thy strong word did cleave the darkness	(Ton-y-Botel)
400	All creatures of our God and King	(Lasst uns erfreuen)
403	Let all the world in every corner sing	(MacDougall)
406	Most High, omnipotent, good Lord	(Assisi)
407	Most High, omnipotent, good Lord	(Lukkason)
513	Like the murmur of the dove's song	(Bridegroom)
618	Ye watchers and ye holy ones (concluding Alleluias)	(Lasst uns erfreuen)
640	Watchman, tell us of the night	(Aberystwyth)

Hymns for Cantor or Choir and People

128	We three kings of Orient are	(Three Kings of Orient)
154	All glory, laud, and honor	(Valet will ich dir geben)
155	All glory, laud, and honor	(Gloria, laus, et honor)
175	Hail thee, festival day (Easter)	(Salve festa dies)
196	Look there! the Christ, our Brother, comes	(Petrus)
216	Hail thee, festival day (Ascension)	(Salve festa dies)
225	Hail thee, festival day (Pentecost)	(Salve festa dies)
402	Let all the world in every corner sing	(Augustine)
417	This is the feast of victory for our God	(Festival Canticle)
418	This is the feast of victory for our God	(Raymond)
468	It was poor little Jesus	(Poor Little Jesus)

576	God is love, and where true love is	(Mandatum)
577	God is love, and where true love is	(Ubi caritas [Murray])
606	Where true charity and love dwell	(Ubi caritas)
611	Christ the worker	(African Work Song)
676	There is a balm in Gilead	(Balm in Gilead)

Hymns That May Be Sung as Rounds or Canons

9	Not here for high and holy things	(Morning Song, 583)
25	O gracious Light, Lord Jesus Christ	(The Eighth Tune, 43)
43	All praise to thee, my God, this night	(The Eighth Tune, 25)
25C	Now greet the swiftly changing year	(Sixth Night)
254	You are the Christ, O Lord	(Wyngate Canon)
534	God is working his purpose out	(Purpose)
671	Amazing grace! how sweet the sound	(New Britain)
710	Make a joyful noise unto the Lord	(Singt dem Herren)
711	Seek ye first the kingdom of God	(Seek Ye First)
712	Dona nobis pacem	(Dona nobis pacem)
713	Christ is arisen	(Christ is arisen)
714	Shalom, my friends	(Shalom chaverim)
715	When Jesus wept	(When Jesus Wept)

Other tunes not designated as Rounds or Canons in THE HYMNAL 1982 which may be sung as such (normally at a distance of one or two measures and a space of one octave)

78	O little town of Bethlehem	(Forest Green, 398, 705)
97	Dost thou in a manger lie	(Dies est laetitiae)
98	Unto us a boy is born!	(Puer nobis nascitur)
105	God rest you merry, gentlemen	(God Rest You Merry)
119	As with gladness men of old	(Dix, 288)
124	What star is this, with beams so bright	(Puer nobis, 193)
147	Now let us all with one accord	(Bourbon, 675)
158	Ah, holy Jesus, how hast thou offended	(Herzliebster Jesu)
182	Christ is alive! Let Christians sing	(Truro, 436)
193	That Easter day with joy was bright	(Puer nobis, 124)
238	Blessèd feasts of blessèd martyrs	(Holy Manna, 580)
287	For all the saints, who from their labors rest	(Sine Nomine)
288	Praise to God, immortal praise	(Dix, 119)
304	I come with joy to meet my Lord	(Land of Rest, 620)
349	Holy Spirit, Lord of love	(Aberystwyth, 640, 699)
359	God of the prophets, bless the prophets' heirs!	(Toulon)
398	I sing the almighty power of God	(Forest Green, 78, 705)
436	Lift up your heads, ye mighty gates	(Truro, 182)
439	What wondrous love is this, O my soul	(Wondrous Love)
550	Jesus calls us; o'er the tumult	(Restoration)
571	All who love and serve your city	(Charlestown)
580	God, who stretched the spangled heavens	(Holy Manna, 238)
583	O holy city, seen of John	(Morning Song, 9)
620	Jerusalem, my happy home	(Land of Rest, 304)
636	How firm a foundation	(Foundation)
640	Watchman, tell us of the night	(Aberystwyth, 349, 699)
641	Lord Jesus, think on me	(Southwell)
645	The King of love my shepherd is	(St. Columba)
664	My Shepherd will supply my need	(Resignation)

666	Out of the depths I call	(St. Bride)
674	"Forgive our sins as we forgive"	(Detroit)
675	Take up your cross, the Savior said	(Bourbon, 147)
699	Jesus, Lover of my soul	(Aberystwyth, 349, 640)
705	As those of old their first fruits brought	(Forest Green, 78, 398)

Hymns scored for other instruments

Flute or Violin

| 469 | There's a wideness in God's mercy | (St. Helena) |

Guitar

8	Morning has broken	(Bunessan)
9	Not here for high and holy things	(Morning Song, 583)
10	New every morning is the love	(Kedron, 163)
99	Go tell it on the mountain	(Go Tell It on the Mountain)
101	Away in a manger	(Cradle Song)
105	God rest you merry, gentlemen	(God Rest You Merry)
110	The snow lay on the ground	(Venite adoremus)
111	Silent night, holy night	(Stille Nacht)
113	Oh, sleep now, holy babe	(A la ru)
115	What child is this, who, laid to rest	(Greensleeves)
118	Brightest and best of the stars of the morning	(Star in the East)
178	Alleluia, alleluia! Give thanks to the risen Lord	(Alleluia #1)
204	Now the green blade riseth	(Noël nouvelet)
206	O sons and daughters, let us sing	(O filii et filiae, 203)
213	Come away to the skies	(Middlebury)
238	Blessèd feasts of blessèd martyrs	(Holy Manna, 580)
250	Now greet the swiftly changing year	(Sixth Night)
266	Nova, nova	(Nova, nova)
276	For thy blest saints, a noble throng	(Dunlap's Creek)
292	O Jesus, crowned with all renown	(Kingsfold, 480)
293	I sing a song of the saints of God	(Grand Isle)
304	I come with joy to meet my Lord	(Land of Rest, 620)
335	I am the bread of life	(I Am the Bread of Life)
405	All things bright and beautiful	(Royal Oak)
439	What wondrous love is this	(Wondrous Love)
453	As Jacob with travel was weary one day	(Jacob's Ladder)
480	When Jesus left his Father's throne	(Kingsfold, 292)
482	Lord of all hopefulness, Lord of all joy	(Slane, 488)
488	Be thou my vision, O Lord of my heart	(Slane, 482)
490	I want to walk as a child of the light	(Houston)
529	In Christ there is no East or West	(McKee)
554	'Tis the gift to be simple	(Simple Gifts)
583	O holy city, seen of John	(Morning Song, 9)
586	Jesus, thou divine Companion	(Pleading Savior)
620	Jerusalem, my happy home	(Land of Rest, 304)
636	How firm a foundation, ye saints of the Lord	(Foundation)
638	Come, O thou Traveler unknown	(Vernon)
648	When Israel was in Egypt's land	(Go Down, Moses)

664	My Shepherd will supply my need	(Resignation)
671	Amazing grace! how sweet the sound	(New Britain)
673	The first one ever, oh, ever to know	(Ballad)
674	"Forgive our sins as we forgive"	(Detroit)
675	Take up your cross, the Savior said	(Bourbon, 147)
679	Surely it is God who saves me	(Thomas Merton)
686	Come, thou fount of every blessing	(Nettleton)
693	Just as I am, without one plea	(Woodworth)
711	Seek ye first the kingdom of God	(Seek Ye First)
714	Shalom, my friends	(Shalom chaverim)

Handbells

22	O God of truth, O Lord of might	(Rector potens, verax Deus)
27	O blest Creator, source of light	(Lucis creator optime)
103	A child is born in Bethlehem	(Puer natus in Bethlehem)
146	Now let us all with one accord	(Ex more docti mystico)
155	All glory, laud, and honor	(Gloria, laus, et honor)
213	Come away to the skies	(Middlebury)
236	King of the martyrs' noble band	(Jesu, nostra redemptio, 38, 233)

Handbells and other instruments

123	Alleluia, song of gladness	(Tibi, Christe, splendor Patris)
155	All glory, laud, and honor	(Gloria, laus, et honor)
193	That Easter day with joy was bright	(Puer nobis, 124)
303	Father, we thank thee who hast planted	(Albright)

Percussion

| 155 | All glory, laud, and honor | (Gloria, laus, et honor) |
| 385 | Many and great, O God, are thy works | (Dakota Indian Chant [Lacquiparle]) |

Solo Instrument

456	O Love of God, how strong and true	(de Tar, 659)
507	Praise the Spirit in creation	(Julion, 268)
659	O Master, let me walk with thee	(de Tar, 456)

Tambourine

| 155 | All glory, laud, and honor | (Gloria, laus, et honor) |
| 204 | Now the green blade riseth | (Noël nouvelet) |

Tambourine and Drum

| 155 | All glory, laud, and honor | (Gloria, laus, et honor) |
| 319 | You, Lord, we praise in songs of celebration | (Gott sei gelobet) |

Appendix II

Metrical Index of Tunes in
The Hymnal 1982 with the
First Lines of the Texts

METRICAL INDEX OF TUNES with the First Lines of the Texts
SM 66. 86 Short Metre

Bellwoods	600	O day of God, draw nigh
Carlisle	138	All praise to you, O Lord
	592	Teach me, my God and King
Festal Song	551	Rise up, ye saints of God
Franconia	656	Blest are the pure in heart
Nova Vita	508	Breathe on me, Breath of God
St. Bride	666	Out of the depths I call
St. Ethelwald	181	Awake and sing the song
	628	Help us, O Lord, to learn
St. George	267	Praise we the Lord this day
	279	For thy dear saints, O Lord
St. Michael	601	O day of God, draw nigh
St. Thomas (Williams)	411	O bless the Lord, my soul
	524	I love thy kingdom, Lord
Silver Street	548	Soldiers of Christ, arise
Southwell	641	Lord Jesus, think on me

SM with Refrain 66. 86 with Refrain Short Metre with Refrain

Marion	556	Rejoice, ye pure in heart
Vineyard Haven	392	Come, we that love the Lord
	557	Rejoice, ye pure in heart

SMD 66. 86. D Short Metre Double

Diademata	494	Crown him with many crowns
Mercer Street	651	This is my Father's world

CM 86. 86 Common Metre

Azmon	493	O for a thousand tongues to sing
Bangor	164	Alone thou goest forth, O Lord
	672	O very God of very God
Beatitudo	683	O for a closer walk with God
Bristol	71	Hark! the glad sound! the Savior comes
Burford	668	I to the hills will lift mine eyes
Caithness	121	Christ, when for us you were baptized
	352	O God, to those who here profess
	684	O for a closer walk with God
Call Street	588	Almighty God, your word is cast
Chelsea Square	521	Put forth, O God, thy Spirit's might
Cheshire	581	Where charity and love prevail
Cornhill	144	Lord Jesus, Sun of Righteousness
Crimond	663	The Lord my God my shepherd is
Culross	584	God, you have given us power to sound
Detroit	674	"Forgive our sins as we forgive"
Dundee	126	The people who in darkness walked
	526	Let saints on earth in concert sing
	709	O God of Bethel, by whose hand
Dunlap's Creek	276	For thy blest saints, a noble throng
Durham	415	When all thy mercies, O my God

| Windsor (rhythmic) | 642 | Jesus, the very thought of thee |
| York | 462 | The Lord will come and not be slow |

CM with Repeat   86. 86 with Repeat   Common Metre with Repeat

| Antioch | 100 | Joy to the world! the Lord is come |

CMD   86. 86. D   Common Metre Double

Carol	89	It came upon the midnight clear
Forest Green	78	O little town of Bethlehem
	398	I sing the almighty power of God
	705	As those of old their first fruits brought
Halifax	459	And have the bright immensities
	629	We limit not the truth of God
Kingsfold	292	O Jesus, crowned with all renown
	480	When Jesus left his Father's throne
Laramie	647	I know not where the road will lead
Materna	719	O beautiful for spacious skies
Noel	90	It came upon the midnight clear
	245	Praise God for John, evangelist
Resignation	664	My Shepherd will supply my need
St. Louis	79	O little town of Bethlehem
St. Matthew	567	Thine arm, O Lord, in days of old
Salvation	243	When Stephen, full of power and grace
The Church's Desolation	566	From thee all skill and science flow
The Third Tune	170	To mock your reign, O dearest Lord
	692	I heard the voice of Jesus say

LM   88. 88   Long Metre

A la venue de Noël	152	Kind Maker of the world, O hear
Ach bleib bei uns	465	Eternal light, shine in my heart
Ad cenam Agni providi	202	The Lamb's high banquet called to share
Adon Olam	425	Sing now with joy unto the Lord
Aeterne Rex altissime	136	O wondrous type! O vision fair
	220	O Lord Most High, eternal King
Bourbon	147	Now let us all with one accord
	675	Take up your cross, the Savior said
Breslau	281	He sat to watch o'er customs paid
	471	We sing the praise of him who died
Bromley	28	O blest Creator, source of light
	29	O Trinity of blessèd light
Christe, qui Lux es et dies	40	O Christ, you are both light and day
Christe, Redemptor omnium	85	O Savior of our fallen race
Compline	41	O Christ, you are both light and day
Conditor alme siderum	26	O gracious Light, Lord Jesus Christ
	60	Creator of the stars of night
Cornish	229	Spirit of mercy, truth, and love
	256	A light from heaven shone around
Danby	12	The golden sun lights up the sky
de Tar	456	O Love of God, how strong and true

568. 558

| St. Elizabeth | 383 | Fairest Lord Jesus |
| Schönster Herr Jesu | 384 | Fairest Lord Jesus |

65. 65

| Merrial | 42 | Now the day is over |
| Wem in Leidenstagen | 479 | Glory be to Jesus |

65. 65. D

| King's Weston | 435 | At the Name of Jesus |

65. 65. D with Refrain

| St. Gertrude | 562 | Onward, Christian soldiers |

65. 65. 6665

| St. Dunstan's | 564 | He who would valiant be |

664. 6664

America	716	God bless our native land
	717	My country, 'tis of thee
Moscow	365	Come, thou almighty King
	371	Thou, whose almighty word
	537	Christ for the world we sing
Olivet	691	My faith looks up to thee

665. 665. 786

| Jesu, meine Freude | 701 | Jesus, all my gladness |

66. 66

Moseley	700	O love that casts out fear
Quam dilecta	626	Lord, be thy word my rule
St. Cecilia	613	Thy kingdom come, O God

66. 66 with Refrain

Augustine	402	Let all the world in every corner sing
Gopsal	481	Rejoice, the Lord is King
MacDougall	402	Let all the world in every corner sing

66. 66. 33. 6

| Sharpthorne | 605 | What does the Lord require |

66. 66. 44. 44

Camano	399	To God with gladness sing
Croft's 136th	284	O ye immortal throng
Darwall's 148th	625	Ye holy angels bright
Love Unknown	458	My song is love unknown

O Gott, du frommer Gott	681	Our God, to whom we turn
St. Joan	542	Christ is the world's true Light
Was frag' ich nach der Welt	108	Now yield we thanks and praise

74. 74. D

General Seminary	382	King of glory, King of peace

76. 76

Ave caeli janua	273	Two stalwart trees both rooted
Christus, der is mein Leben	295	Sing praise to our Creator
	356	May choirs of angels lead you
De Eersten zijn de laatsten	274	Two stalwart trees both rooted

76. 76 with Refrain

Gloria, laus, et honor	155	All glory, laud, and honor
Go Tell It on the Mountain	99	Go tell it on the mountain
Royal Oak	405	All things bright and beautiful
Valet will ich dir geben	154	All glory, laud, and honor

76. 76. D

Ach Gott, vom Himmelreiche	235	Come sing, ye choirs exultant
Aurelia	525	The Church's one foundation
Distler	572	Weary of all trumpeting
Ellacombe	210	The day of resurrection
Es flog ein Kleins Waldvögelein	48	O day of radiant gladness
	616	Hail to the Lord's Anointed
Ewing	624	Jerusalem the golden
Gaudeamus pariter	200	Come, ye faithful, raise the strain
	237	Let us now our voices raise
Herzlich tut mich verlangen (rhythmic)	169	O sacred head, sore wounded
Herzlich tut mich verlangen [Passion Chorale] (isometric)	168	O sacred head, sore wounded
	669	Commit thou all that grieves thee
King's Lynn	231	By all your saints still striving
	591	O God of earth and altar
Lancashire	555	Lead on, O King eternal
	563	Go forward, Christian soldier
Light	667	Sometimes a light surprises
Llangloffan	68	Rejoice! rejoice, believers
	607	O God of every nation
Morning Light	561	Stand up, stand up, for Jesus
Munich	255	We sing the glorious conquest
	632	O Christ, the Word Incarnate
Nyland	232	By all your saints still striving
	655	O Jesus, I have promised
St. Kevin	199	Come, ye faithful, raise the strain
Thornbury	444	Blessed be the God of Israel
Valet will ich dir geben	74	Blest be the King whose coming
Wolvercote	289	Our Father, by whose servants

76. 76. D with Refrain

Wir pflügen	291	We plow the fields, and scatter

76. 76. 66. 76

Andújar	104	A stable lamp is lighted

76. 76. 676

Es ist ein Ros	81	Lo, how a Rose e'er blooming
Straf mich nicht	187	Through the Red Sea brought at last

76. 76. 77 with Refrain

Bereden väg för Herran	65	Prepare the way, O Zion

76. 76. 775. 775

Dies est laetitiae	97	Dost thou in a manger lie

76. 76. 86 with Refrain

God Rest You Merry	105	God rest you merry, gentlemen

76. 76. 887. 87

Song of the Holy Spirit	230	A mighty sound from heaven

76. 76. 86

Aldine	431	The stars declare his glory

76. 86. 86. 86

St. Christopher	498	Beneath the cross of Jesus

776. 778

O Welt, ich muss dich lassen	46	The duteous day now closeth

776. D

O Welt, ich muss dich lassen	309	O Food to pilgrims given
Psalm 6	308	O Food to pilgrims given

777 with Refrain

Angelus emittitur	270	Gabriel's message does away

777. 5

Troen	612	Gracious Spirit, Holy Ghost

77. 77

Aus der Tiefe rufe ich	150	Forty days and forty nights
Beata nobis gaudia	223	Hail this joyful day's return
Bingham	585	Morning glory, starlit sky

Geneva	515	Holy Ghost, dispel our sadness
Holy Manna	238	Blessèd feasts of blessèd martyrs
	580	God, who stretched the spangled heavens
Hyfrydol	460	Alleluia! sing to Jesus
	657	Love divine, all loves excelling
Hymn to Joy	376	Joyful, joyful, we adore thee
In Babilone	215	See the Conqueror mounts in triumph
	495	Hail, thou once despisèd Jesus
Lux eoi	191	Alleluia, alleluia! Hearts and voices heavenward raise
Moultrie	275	Hark! the sound of holy voices
Nettleton	686	Come, thou fount of every blessing
Pleading Savior	586	Jesus, thou divine Companion
Raquel	277	Sing of Mary, pure and lowly
Rustington	278	Sing we of the blessèd Mother
	367	Round the Lord in glory seated
St. Helena	469	There's a wideness in God's mercy
Thomas Merton	679	Surely it is God who saves me
Ton-y-Botel	381	Thy strong word did cleave the darkness
	527	Singing songs of expectation
Werde munter	336	Come with us, O blessed Jesus

87. 87. 337

Michael	665	All my hope on God is founded

87. 87. 6

Bridegroom	513	Like the murmur of the dove's song

87. 87. 66. 66. 7

Ein feste Burg (isometric)	688	A mighty fortress is our God
Ein feste Burg (rhythmic)	687	A mighty fortress is our God

87. 877

St. Andrew	549	Jesus calls us; o'er the tumult

87. 87. 77

Irby	102	Once in royal David's city
Unser Herrscher	180	He is risen, he is risen
Zeuch mich, zeuch mich	286	Who are these like stars appearing

87. 87. 77. 88

Psalm 42	67	Comfort, comfort ye my people

87. 87. 78. 74

Christ lag in Todesbanden (isometric)	186	Christ Jesus lay in death's strong bands
Christ lag in Todesbanden (rhythmic)	185	Christ Jesus lay in death's strong bands

138

87. 87. 87

Dulce carmen	559	Lead us, heavenly Father, lead us
Finnian	492	Sing, ye faithful, sing with gladness
	506	Praise the Spirit in creation
Grafton	249	To the Name of our salvation
	331	Now, my tongue, the mystery telling
Julion	268	Ye who claim the faith of Jesus
	507	Praise the Spirit in creation
Komm, o komm, du Geist des Lebens	596	Judge eternal, throned in splendor
Lauda anima	410	Praise, my soul, the King of heaven
Lowry	454	Jesus came, adored by angels
Mannheim	595	God of grace and God of glory
Oriel	248	To the Name of our salvation
	520	Blessèd city, heavenly Salem
Pange lingua (Mode 1)	165	Sing, my tongue, the glorious battle
Pange lingua (Mode 3)	166	Sing, my tongue, the glorious battle
	329	Now, my tongue, the mystery telling
Picardy	324	Let all mortal flesh keep silence
Regent Square	93	Angels, from the realms of glory
	368	Holy Father, great Creator
Rhuddlan	621	Light's abode, celestial Salem
St. Thomas	58	Lo! he comes, with clouds descending
Sicilian Mariner's	344	Lord, dismiss us with thy blessing
	708	Savior, like a shepherd lead us
Tantum ergo Sacramentum	330	Therefore we, before him bending
Tibi, Christe, splendor Patris	123	Alleluia, song of gladness
Urbs beata Jerusalem (equalist rhythm)	122	Alleluia, song of gladness
	519	Blessèd city, heavenly Salem
	622	Light's abode, celestial Salem
Urbs beata Jerusalem (syllabic rhythm)		
Westminster Abbey	518	Christ is made the sure foundation

87. 87. 87 with Refrain

Den des Vaters Sinn geboren	269	Ye who claim the faith of Jesus
Divinum mysterium	82	Of the Father's love begotten
Rowthorn	528	Lord, you give the great commission

87. 87. 877

Cwm Rhondda	594	God of grace and God of glory
	690	Guide me, O thou great Jehovah

87. 87. 87. 877

Christ unser Herr zum Jordan kam	139	When Jesus went to Jordan's stream

87. 87. 88

Mach's mit mir, Gott	198	Thou hallowed chosen morn of praise

87. 87. 887

Allein Gott in der Höh	421	All glory be to God on high
Aus tiefer Not	151	From deepest woe I cry to thee
Du Lebensbrot, Herr Jesu Christ	375	Give praise and glory unto God
Es ist das Heil	298	All who believe and are baptized
Fisk of Gloucester	190	Lift your voice rejoicing, Mary
Mit Freuden zart	408	Sing praise to God who reigns above
	598	Lord Christ, when first thou cam'st to earth

87. 87. 88. 77

Ermuntre dich	91	Break forth, O beauteous heavenly light

87. 87. 12 7

Helmsley	57	Lo! he comes with clouds descending

87. 87. 12 77

Bryn Calfaria	307	Lord, enthroned in heavenly splendor

88

Come Holy Ghost	503	Come, Holy Ghost, our souls inspire

88 with Alleluias and Refrain

Puer natus in Bethlehem	103	A child is born in Bethlehem

88 with Refrain

Alleluia No. 1	178	Alleluia, alleluia! Give thanks to the risen Lord

88. 446 with Refrain

Three Kings of Orient	128	We three kings of Orient are

88. 44. 88 with Refrain

Lasst uns erfreuen	400	All creatures of our God and King
	618	Ye watchers and ye holy ones

886. 886

Cornwall	386	We sing of God, the mighty source
	422	Not far beyond the sea, nor high
Magdalen College	387	We sing of God, the mighty source

887. D

Stabat Mater dolorosa	159	At the cross her vigil keeping

88. 77. D

Psalm 86	258	Virgin-born, we bow before thee

887. 88

| Assisi | 406 | Most High, omnipotent, good Lord |
| Lukkason | 407 | Most High, omnipotent, good Lord |

887. 887

Ach Herr, du allerhöchster Gott	219	The Lord ascendeth up on high
Alles ist an Gottes Segen	244	Come, pure hearts, in joyful measure
	334	Praise the Lord, rise up rejoicing
Lauda Sion Salvatorem	320	Zion, praise thy Savior, singing

888 with Alleluias

Gelobt sei Gott	205	Good Christians all, rejoice and sing
Hilariter	211	The whole bright world rejoices now
O filii et filiae (carol)	203	O sons and daughters, let us sing
O filii et filiae (chant)	206	O sons and daughters, let us sing
Victory	208	The strife is o'er, the battle done

888. 6

| St. Mary Magdalene | 350 | O God of love, to thee we bow |

88. 86

| St. Mark's, Berkeley | 69 | What is the crying at Jordan |
| Sixth Night | 250 | Now greet the swiftly changing year |

88. 88. 5

| Salem Harbor | 443 | From God Christ's deity came forth |

88. 88. 88

Meadville	49	Come, let us with our Lord arise
Melita	579	Almighty Father, strong to save
	608	Eternal Father, strong to save
St. Catherine	558	Faith of our fathers! living still
St. Petersburg	574	Before thy throne, O God, we kneel
Surrey	500	Creator Spirit, by whose aid
Vater unser im Himmelreich	575	Before thy throne, O God, we kneel
Vernon	638	Come, O thou Traveler unknown
Woodbury	639	Come, O thou Traveler unknown

888. 888

| Christus Rex | 614 | Christ is the King! O friends upraise |
| Old 113th | 429 | I'll praise my Maker while I've breath |

88. 10

| St. Bartholomew's | 514 | To thee, O Comforter divine |

96. 99. 96

| Dakota Indian Chant [Lacquiparle] | 385 | Many and great, O God, are thy works |

98. 96 with Refrain

Torah Song [Yisrael V'oraita]   536   Open your ears, O faithful people

98. 98

Albright   303   Father, we thank thee who hast planted
St. Clement   24   The day thou gavest, Lord, is ended

98. 98. 88

Wer nur den lieben Gott   635   If thou but trust in God to guide thee

98. 98. D

Rendez à Dieu   301   Bread of the world, in mercy broken
    302   Father, we thank thee who hast planted
    413   New songs of celebration render

99. 99

Sheng En   342   O Bread of life, for sinners broken

9 10. 9 10. 10 10

Dir, dir, Jehovah   540   Awake, thou Spirit of the watchmen

10 6. 10 6

Evening Hymn   37   O brightness of the immortal Father's face

10 8. 88. 10

O heiliger Geist   505   O Spirit of Life, O Spirit of God

10. 10

Palmer Church   327   Draw nigh and take the Body of the Lord
Song 46   328   Draw nigh and take the Body of the Lord

10. 10 with Refrain

Crucifer   473   Lift high the cross
Let Us Break Bread   325   Let us break bread together

10 10. 7

Martins   619   Sing alleluia forth in duteous praise

10 10. 9 10

Slane   488   Be thou my vision, O Lord of my heart

10 10 10 with Alleluia

Engelberg   296   We know that Christ is raised and dies no more

| | 420 | When in our music God is glorified |
| | 477 | All praise to thee, for thou, O King divine |

10 10 10 with Alleluias

| Sine Nomine | 287 | For all the saints, who from their labors rest |

10. 10. 10. 6

| Faith | 689 | I sought the Lord, and afterward I knew |

10 10. 10 10

Birmingham	437	Tell out, my soul, the greatness of the Lord
Canticum refectionis	316	This is the hour of banquet and of song
Ellers	345	Savior, again to thy dear Name we raise
Eventide	662	Abide with me: fast falls the eventide
Flentge	698	Eternal Spirit of the living Christ
Litton	347	Go forth for God; go to the world in peace
Morestead	317	This is the hour of banquet and of song
National Hymn	718	God of our fathers, whose almighty hand
Nyack	318	Here, O my Lord, I see thee face to face
O quanta qualia	348	Lord, we have come at your own invitation
	623	O what their joy and their glory must be
Rosedale	305	Come, risen Lord, and deign to be our guest
Song 4	346	Completed, Lord, the Holy Mysteries
Song 22	703	Lead us, O Father, in the paths of peace
Sursum Corda	306	Come, risen Lord, and deign to be our guest
Toulon	359	God of the prophets, bless the prophets' heirs
Woodlands	438	Tell out, my soul, the greatness of the Lord

10 10. 10 10. 84

| Donne | 140 | Wilt thou forgive that sin, where I begun |
| So giebst du nun | 141 | Wilt thou forgive that sin, where I begun |

10 10. 10 10 10

| Old 124th | 149 | Eternal Lord of love, behold your Church |
| | 404 | We will extol you, ever-blessèd Lord |

10 10. 10 10. 10 10

Song 1	315	Thou, who at thy first Eucharist didst pray
	499	Lord God, you now have set your servant free
	617	Eternal Ruler of the ceaseless round
Unde et memores	337	And now, O Father, mindful of the love
Yorkshire	106	Christians, awake, salute the happy morn

10 10. 11 11

| Hanover | 388 | O worship the King, all glorious above |
| Laudate Dominum | 432 | O praise ye the Lord! Praise him in the height |

143

| West Park | 176 | Over the chaos of the empty waters |

11. 11. 11. 5

Christe, Lux mundi	33	Christ, mighty Savior, Light of all creation
Decatur Place	51	We the Lord's People, heart and voice uniting
Innisfree Farm	34	Christ, mighty Savior, Light of all creation
Mighty Savior	35	Christ, mighty Savior, Light of all creation

11 11. 11 11

Adoro devote	314	Humbly I adore thee, Verity unseen
	357	Jesus, Son of Mary, fount of life alone
Cradle Song	101	Away in a manger, no crib for his bed
Foundation	636	How firm a foundation, ye saints of the Lord
Lyons	637	How firm a foundation, ye saints of the Lord
St. Denio	423	Immortal, invisible, God only wise

11 11. 11 11. 11

| Fortunatus | 179 | "Welcome, happy morning!" age to age shall say |

11 11. 12 11

| Monk's Gate | 478 | Jesus, our mighty Lord, our strength in sadness |
| | 565 | He who would valiant be 'gainst all disaster |

11 12. 12 10

| Nicaea | 362 | Holy, holy, holy! Lord God Almighty |

12 9. 12. 12 9

| Wondrous Love | 439 | What wondrous love is this, O my soul |

12 10. 12 10

| Was lebet | 568 | Father all loving, who rulest in majesty |

12 11. 12 11

| Kremser | 433 | We gather together to ask the Lord's blessing |

12. 12. 12. 12 with Refrain

Mandatum	576	God is love, and where true love is
Ubi caritas	606	Where true charity and love dwell
Ubi caritas (Murray)	577	God is love, and where true love is

13. 11 7 with Alleluias

| Seek Ye First | 711 | Seek ye first the kingdom of God |

14 14. 478

14 14. 14 15

Irregular

Irregular with Refrain

Appendix III:

Check Lists for Planning Services

Daily Morning Prayer

Date and time: _____

Officiant: _____

Prelude: _____

Opening Sentence (yes or no): _____ Which? _____ Sung or said: _____

Confession of Sin (yes or no): _____

Opening Preces (sung or said): _____ Alleluia (yes or no): _____

Antiphon: _____

    Before Invitatory Psalm? _____ After Psalm? _____

    After each verse or section? _____

Invitatory Psalm (Venite or Jubilate) _____ or Christ our Passover _____

    or Psalm 95 _____

Psalm(s): _____ Sung or said: _____

Old Testament Lesson: _____

    Reader: _____

Silence (yes or no): _____ Duration: _____

Canticle: _____

New Testament Lesson: _____

    Reader: _____

Silence (yes or no): _____ Duration: _____

Sermon: _____

    Preacher: _____

Canticle: _____

*Gospel: _____

    Reader: _____

*Sermon: _____

    Preacher: _____

Apostles' Creed: _____ Sung or said: _____

The Lord's Prayer and the Suffrages: _____ Sung or said: _____

(Continued)

The Collect(s): _____ *Sung or said:* _____

Prayer for mission: _____ *Sung or said:* _____

Hymn or anthem: _____

Special intercessions: _____ *Sung or said:* _____

Special thanksgivings: _____ *Sung or said:* _____

The General Thanksgiving (yes or no): _____ *Sung or said:* _____

A Prayer of St. Chrysostom (yes or no): _____ *Sung or said:* _____

Concluding Versicle and Response (yes or no): _____ *Sung or said:* _____

The Grace (yes or no): _____ *Which?* _____ *Sung or said:* _____

Postlude: _____

---

*If three Lessons are used, Gospel and sermon come in this position.

Morning or Evening Prayer with the Holy Communion

Day or Occasion: _____ Morning or Evening Prayer: ____

Celebrant: _____

Prelude: _____

Opening Sentence (yes or no): _____ Which? _____ Sung or said: _____

Confession of Sin (yes or no): _____

Opening Preces (sung or said): _____ Alleluia (yes or no): _____

Antiphon: _____

    Before Invitatory Psalm? _____ After Psalm? _____

    After each verse or section? _____

Invitatory Psalm (Venite or Jubilate) _____ or Christ our Passover _____

    or Psalm 95 _____ or Phos hilaron _____

Psalm(s): _____ Sung or said: _____

First Reading: _____

    Reader: _____

Silence (yes or no): _____ Duration: _____

Canticle: _____

Second Reading: _____

    Reader: _____

Silence (yes or no): _____ Duration: _____

Canticle: _____

Gospel: _____

    Reader: _____

Sermon: _____

    Preacher: _____

Creed (yes or no): _____ Apostles'; _____ or Nicene: _____ Sung or said: _____

Salutation (sung or said): _____

Collect of the Day: _____ Sung or said: _____

(Continued)

Hymn or Anthem: _____

Prayers of the People (sung or said): _____

    Leader: _____

    Prayer for the Whole State of Christ's Church and the World: _____

    Form I _____; *Form II* _____; *Form III* _____; *Form IV* _____; *Form V* _____;

    Form VI _____

    Other forms: The Solemn Collects, page 277: _____

    Litany for Ordinations (Ember Days), page 548: _____

    Litany of Thanksgiving (Thanksgiving Day), page 836: _____

    Litany of Thanksgiving for a Church (Dedication festival), page 578: _____

    Prayers and Thanksgivings, pages 809–841, selected in conformity to directions on page 383:

    _____

    A form written for the occasion or gleaned from another source: _____

Special petitions to be included: _____

Collect after the Intercessions: _____ *Sung or said:* _____

Special rites: Thanksgiving for Birth or Adoption of a Child _____; *Commitment to Christian*

    Service _____; *Anointing of the Sick;* _____ *Other:* _____

The Peace (any special instructions): _____ *Sung or said:* _____

The Holy Communion

Offertory Sentence (yes or no): _____ *Which:* _____

Hymn, psalm, or anthem: _____

    Presenters: _____

    Preparation of the Table (deacon _____ *or assisting priest* _____ *)*

The Great Thanksgiving: _____ *Sung or said:* _____

    Proper Preface: _____

    Holy, holy, holy/Holy, holy, holy Lord (Sanctus): _____

    Memorial Acclamation (A, B, or D): _____

    Special Intercessions (D): _____

    Commemoration of a Saint (B or D): _____

    Continuation or conclusion of Prayer sung? _____ *Great Amen:* _____

The Lord's Prayer: _____

Duration of silence after Breaking of the Bread (and Pouring of the Wine): _____

Fraction Anthem (yes or no): _____ *Which:* _____ *Alleluia (yes or no):* _____

Rite One only—Prayer of Humble Access (yes or no): _____ *By priest* _____

    or by priest and people: _____

Invitation to Communion (longer or shorter form): _____ *Sung or said:* _____

    Ministers of Communion: _____

Hymn, psalm, or anthem during Communion: _____

Hymn during clearing of the Table: _____

Postcommunion Prayer: _____

Hymn: _____

Blessing: _____ *Which form:* _____ *Sung or said:* _____

Dismissal: _____ *Alleluia (yes or no):* ____ *Sung or said:* _____

    Deacon (or Celebrant): _____

Postlude: _____

An Order of Service for Noonday

Date and time: _____

Officiant: _____

Prelude: _____

Opening Preces (sung or said): _____ Alleluia (yes or no): _____

Hymn: _____

Psalm(s): _____ Sung or said: _____

Scripture: _____

Reader: _____

Meditation: _____

Leader: _____

Prayers: _____ Sung or said: _____

Dismissal (sung or said): _____

Postlude: _____

An Order of Worship for the Evening

Date and time: _____

Officiant: _____

Opening Acclamation: _____ Sung or said: _____

Lesson of Scripture (yes or no): _____ Which? _____ Sung or said: _____

    Reader: _____

Prayer for Light: _____ Sung or said: _____

Anthem, psalm, or silence: _____

O Gracious Light (Phos hilaron): _____

Psalm(s): _____ Sung or said: _____

Silence (yes or no): _____ Duration: _____

Psalter Collect (yes or no): _____ Which? _____

Lesson: _____

    Reader: _____

Sermon, homily, passage from Christian literature, or silence: _____

    Preacher: _____

Canticle or hymn of praise: _____

Prayers: _____ Sung or said: _____

The Lord's Prayer: _____ Sung or said: _____

Concluding Collect: _____ Sung or said: _____

Hymn: _____

Blessing: _____ Sung or said: _____

Dismissal: _____ Alleluia? _____ Sung or said: _____

Postlude: _____

An Order of Worship for the Evening with Daily Evening Prayer

Date and time: _____

Officiant: _____

Opening Acclamation: _____ Sung or said: _____

Lesson of Scripture (yes or no): _____ Which? _____ Sung or said: _____

    Reader: _____

Prayer for Light: _____ Sung or said: _____

Anthem, psalm, or silence: _____

O Gracious Light (Phos hilaron): _____

Psalm(s): _____ Sung or said: _____

Lesson: _____

    Reader: _____

Silence (yes or no): _____ Duration: _____

Sermon: _____

    Preacher: _____

Canticle: _____

Apostles' Creed: _____ Sung or said: _____

The Lord's Prayer and the Suffrages: _____ Sung or said: _____

The Collect(s): _____ Sung or said: _____

Prayer for mission: _____ Sung or said: _____

Hymn or anthem: _____

Special intercessions: _____ Sung or said: _____

Special thanksgivings: _____ Sung or said: _____

The General Thanksgiving (yes or no): _____

A Prayer of St. Chrysostom (yes or no): _____ Sung or said: _____

Concluding Versicle and Response (yes or no): _____ Sung or said: _____

The Grace (yes or no): _____ Which? _____ Sung or said: _____

Postlude: _____

Daily Evening Prayer

Date and time: _____

Officiant: _____

Prelude: _____

Opening Sentence (yes or no): _____ Which? _____ Sung or said: _____

Confession of Sin (yes or no): _____

Opening Preces (sung or said): _____ Alleluia (yes or no): _____

O Gracious Light (Phos hilaron), hymn, or Invitatory Psalm: _____

Psalm(s): _____ Sung or said: _____

Lesson: _____

    Reader: _____

Silence (yes or no): _____ Duration: _____

Sermon: _____

    Preacher: _____

Canticle: _____

Apostles' Creed: _____ Sung or said: _____

The Lord's Prayer and the Suffrages: _____ Sung or said: _____

The Collect(s): _____ Sung or said: _____

Prayer for mission: _____ Sung or said: _____

Hymn or anthem: _____

Special intercessions: _____ Sung or said: _____

Special thanksgivings: _____ Sung or said: _____

The General Thanksgiving (yes or no): _____

A Prayer of St. Chrysostom (yes or no): _____ Sung or said: _____

Concluding Versicle and Response (yes or no): _____ Sung or said: _____

The Grace (yes or no): _____ Which? _____ Sung or said: _____

Postlude: _____

An Order for Compline

Date and time: _____

Officiant: _____

Prelude: _____

Opening Preces (sung or said): _____

Confession of Sin (yes or no): _____

Preces (sung or said): _____ *Alleluia (yes or no):* _____

Psalm(s): _____ *Sung or said:* _____

Scripture: _____

Reader: _____

Hymn: _____

The Suffrages and The Lord's Prayer (sung or said): _____

Collects: _____ *Sung or said:* _____

Prayers: _____

Antiphon: _____ *Alleluias (yes or no):* _____

The Song of Simeon (Nunc dimittis): _____

Concluding Versicle and Response and Blessing (sung or said): _____

Postlude: _____

Ash Wednesday

Time: _____

Celebrant: _____

The silent entrance of the ministers: _____

Salutation and Collect of the Day (sung or said): _____

First Reading: Joel 2:1–2, 12–17 _____ or Isaiah 58:1–12 _____

    Reader: _____

Silence (yes or no): _____ Duration: _____

Gradual: Psalm 103 _____ or Psalm 103:8–14 _____

    Cantor: _____

Second Reading: 2 Corinthians 5:20b–6:10 _____

    Reader: _____

Silence (yes or no): _____ Duration: _____

Tract and/or Sequence: _____

Gospel: Matthew 6:1–6, 16–21 _____

    Reader: _____

Sermon: _____

    Preacher: _____

Exhortation: _____

Silence (duration): _____

Prayer over the ashes (yes or no): _____ Sung or said: _____

    Distributors of the ashes: _____

Psalm 51: _____

Litany of Penitence (sung or said): _____

The Peace (any special instructions): _____ Sung or said: _____

Offertory Sentence (yes or no): _____ Which? _____

Hymn, psalm, or anthem: _____

    Presenters: _____

    Preparation of the Table (deacon _____ or assisting priest _____)

(Continued)

The Great Thanksgiving: _____ *Sung or said:* _____

    Proper Preface: _____

    Holy, holy, holy/Holy, holy, holy Lord (Sanctus): _____

    Memorial Acclamation: _____

    Continuation or conclusion of Prayer sung? _____ *Great Amen:* _____

The Lord's Prayer: _____

Duration of silence after Breaking of the Bread (and Pouring of the Wine): _____

Fraction Anthem (yes or no): _____ *Which?* _____

Invitation to Communion: _____ *Longer or shorter form:* _____

    Sung or said: _____

    Ministers of Communion: _____

Hymn, psalm, or anthem during Communion: _____

Hymn during clearing of the Table: _____

Postcommunion Prayer: _____

Hymn: _____

Blessing or Prayer over the People: _____ *Sung or said:* _____

Dismissal: _____ *Sung or said:* _____

    Deacon (or Celebrant) _____

Postlude: _____

Palm Sunday

Time: _____

Gathering Place: _____

Celebrant: _____

Pre-service music: _____

Opening anthem: sung by choir _____; *said* _____ *or sung* _____ *as versicle and response;*

said _____*or sung* _____*by celebrant or cantor alone* _____

Collect (sung or said): _____

Lesson: **Year A** *Matthew 21:1–11* _____; **Year B** *Mark 11:1–11a* _____

   Year C *Luke 19:29–40* _____

   Reader: _____

Blessing of the Palms (sung or said): _____

Anthem: sung by choir _____; *said* _____ *or sung* _____ *as versicle and response;*

   said _____*or sung* _____ *by celebrant or cantor alone*

The Procession: "Let us go forth . . ." (sung or said): _____

   Deacon: _____

Hymns, psalms, or anthems: _____

Station Collect (yes or no): _____ *Sung or said:* _____

Entry into the church: _____

Salutation and Collect (sung or said): _____

First Reading: Isaiah 45:21–25 _____ *or Isaiah 52:13–53:12* _____

   Reader: _____

Silence (yes or no): _____ *Duration:* _____

Gradual: Psalm 22:1–21 _____ *or Psalm 221:1–11* _____

   Cantor: _____

Second Reading: Philippians 2:5–11 _____

   Reader: _____

Silence (yes or no): _____ *Duration:* _____

Tract and/or Sequence: _____

(Continued)

Passion Gospel: **Year A** *Matthew 26:36–27:54 (55–66)* ___ *or 27:1–54 (55–66)* _____

Year B *Mark 14:32–15:39 (40–47)* _____ *or 15:1–39 (40–47)* _____

Year C *Luke 22:39–23:49 (50–56)* _____ *or 23:1–49 (50–56)* _____

Readers or singers: _____

Congregation standing or seated: _____

Sermon: _____

Preacher: _____

Nicene Creed (yes or no): _____

Prayers of the People: _____ *Sung or said:* _____

Leader: _____

Concluding Collect: _____ *Sung or said:* _____

The Peace (any special instructions): _____ *Sung or said:* _____

Offertory Sentence (yes or no): _____ *Which?* _____

Hymn, psalm, or anthem: _____

Presenters: _____

Preparation of the Table (deacon _____ *or assisting priest* _____ *)*

The Great Thanksgiving: _____ *Sung or said:* _____

Proper Preface: _____

Holy, holy, holy/Holy, holy, holy Lord (Sanctus): _____

Memorial Acclamation: _____

Continuation or conclusion of Prayer sung? _____ *Great Amen:* _____

The Lord's Prayer: _____

Duration of silence after Breaking of the Bread (and Pouring of the Wine): _____

Fraction Anthem (yes or no): _____ *Which?* _____

Invitation to Communion: _____ *Longer or shorter form:* _____

Sung or said: _____

Ministers of Communion: _____

Hymn, psalm, or anthem during Communion: _____

Hymn during clearing of the Table: _____

Postcommunion Prayer: _____

Hymn: _____

(Continued)

164

Blessing or Prayer over the People: _____ *Sung or said:* _____

Dismissal: _____ *Sung or said:* _____

    Deacon (or Celebrant): _____

Postlude: _____

Maundy Thursday

Time: _____

Celebrant: _____

Prelude: _____

Entrance hymn, psalm, or anthem: _____

Opening Acclamation: _____ *Sung or said:* _____

Collect for Purity (yes or no): _____ *Sung or said:* _____

Kyrie _____ *Trisagion* _____ *or Song of Praise:* _____

Salutation and Collect (sung or said): _____

First Reading: Exodus 12:1–14a _____

    Reader: _____

Silence (yes or no): _____ *Duration:* _____

Gradual: Psalm 78:14–20, 23–24 _____

    Cantor: _____

Second Reading: 1 Corinthians 11:23–26 (27–32) _____

    Reader: _____

Silence (yes or no): _____ *Duration:* _____

Tract and/or Sequence: _____

Gospel: John 13:1–15 _____ *or Luke 22:14–30* _____

    Reader: _____

Sermon: _____

    Preacher: _____

Washing of Feet: _____

Anthems: _____

Prayers of the People: _____ *Sung or said:* _____

    Leader: _____

Concluding Collect: _____ *Sung or said:* _____

The Peace (any special instructions): _____ *Sung or said:* _____

Offertory Sentence (yes or no): _____ *Which?* _____

(Continued)

Hymn, psalm, or anthem: _____

    Presenters: _____

    Preparation of the Table (deacon _____ *or assisting priest* _____ *)*

The Great Thanksgiving: _____ *Sung or said:* _____

    Proper Preface: _____

    Holy, holy, holy/Holy, holy, holy Lord (Sanctus): _____

    Memorial Acclamation: _____

    Continuation or conclusion of Prayer sung? _____ *Great Amen:* _____

The Lord's Prayer: _____

Duration of silence after Breaking of the Bread (and Pouring of the Wine): _____

Fraction Anthem (yes or no): _____ *Which?* _____

Invitation to Communion: _____ *Longer or shorter form* _____

    Sung or said: _____

    Ministers of Communion: _____

Hymn, psalm, or anthem during Communion: _____

Hymn during clearing of the Table: _____

Postcommunion Prayer: _____

Hymn: _____ *Procession (yes or no):* _____

Stripping of the altar (yes or no): _____ *Psalm 22:* _____

Blessing or Prayer over the People: _____ *Sung or said:* _____

Dismissal: _____ *Sung or said:* _____

    Deacon (or Celebrant): _____

Postlude: _____ *Yes or No:* _____

Good Friday

Time: _____

Celebrant: _____

The silent entrance of the ministers: _____

Period of silent prayer (duration of silence): _____

Salutation (yes or no): _____ Sung or said: _____

Collect of the day (sung or said): _____

First Reading: Isaiah 52:13–53:12 _____ or Genesis 22:1–18 _____

    or Wisdom 2:1, 12–24 _____

    Reader: _____

Silence (yes or no): _____ Duration: _____

Gradual: Psalm 22:1–11 (12–21) _____ or 40:1–12 _____ or 69:1–23 _____

    Cantor _____

Second Reading: Hebrews 10:1–25 _____

    Reader: _____

Silence (yes or no): _____ Duration: _____

Tract and/or Sequence: _____

Passion Gospel: John 18:1–19:37 _____ or 19:1–37 _____

    Readers or singers: _____

    Congregation standing or seated: _____

Sermon: _____

    Preacher: _____

Hymn: _____

The Solemn Collects: _____ Sung or said: _____

    Deacon or other leader: _____

    Congregation standing or kneeling, or standing for biddings and kneeling for periods of silence:

    _____

    Duration of silences: _____

Bringing in of the Cross: _____

(Continued)

Anthems and/or hymns: _____

_____

Preparation of the Table and bringing in of the Sacrament: _____

A Confession of Sin (Rite One or Rite Two): _____

The Lord's Prayer: _____

The Communion: _____

    Ministers of Communion: _____

Concluding Prayer (p. 282), sung or said by Celebrant: _____

Holy Saturday

Time: _____

Celebrant: _____

The silent entrance of the ministers: _____

Collect of the Day (sung or said): _____

First Reading: Job 14:1–14 _____

    Reader: _____

Silence (yes or no): _____ Duration: _____

Gradual: Psalm 130 _____ or 31:1–5 _____

    Cantor: _____

Second Reading: I Peter 4:1–8 _____

    Reader: _____

Silence (yes or no): _____ Duration: _____

Tract and/or Sequence: _____

Gospel: Matthew 27:57–66 _____ or John 19:38–42 _____

    Reader: _____

Sermon: _____

    Preacher: _____

Anthem, "In the midst of life" (BCP, pp. 484 or 492): _____ Sung or said: _____

The Lord's Prayer: _____ Sung or said: _____

The Grace (BCP, page 59 or 102): _____ Sung or said: _____

The Great Vigil of Easter

Time: _____

Celebrant: _____

Lighting of the Paschal Candle—*Opening Address:* _____

Prayer (sung or said): _____

"The Light of Christ . . ." (sung or said): _____

The Exsultet (sung or said): _____

   Deacon or other person appointed: _____

The Liturgy of the Word—*Initial address:* _____

The story of Creation: Genesis 1:1–2:2: _____

   Reader: _____

Psalm 33:1–11 _____ *or 36:5–10:* _____

   Cantor: _____

Collect: _____ *Sung or said:* _____

The Flood: Genesis 7:1–5, 11–18; 8:6–18; 9:8–13: _____

   Reader: _____

Psalm 46: _____

   Cantor: _____

Collect: _____ *Sung or said:* _____

Abraham's sacrifice of Isaac: Genesis 22:1–18: _____

   Reader: _____

Psalm 33:12–22 _____ *or 16:* _____

   Cantor: _____

Collect: _____ *Sung or said:* _____

Israel's deliverance at the Red Sea (required): Exodus 14:10–15:1: _____

   Reader: _____

Canticle 8, **The Song of Moses***:* _____

   Cantor: _____

Collect: _____ *Sung or said:* _____

(Continued)

God's Presence in a renewed Israel: Isaiah 4:2–6: _____

    Reader: _____

Psalm 122: _____

    Cantor: _____

Collect: _____ *Sung or said:* _____

Salvation offered freely to all: Isaiah 55:1–11: _____

    Reader: _____

Canticle 9, **The First Song of Isaiah** *_ or Psalm 42:1–7:* _____

    Cantor: _____

Collect: _____ *Sung or said:* _____

A new heart and a new spirit: Ezekiel 36:24–28: _____

    Reader: _____

Psalm 42:1–7 _____ *or Canticle 9,* **The First Song of Isaiah:** _____

    Cantor: _____

Collect: _____ *Sung or said:* _____

The valley of dry bones: Ezekiel 37:1–14: _____

    Reader: _____

Psalm 30 _____ *or 143:* _____

    Cantor: _____

Collect: _____ *Sung or said:* _____

The gathering of God's people: Zephaniah 3:12–20: _____

    Reader: _____

Psalm 98 _____ *or 126:* _____

    Cantor: _____

Collect: _____ *Sung or said:* _____

Holy Baptism—(Here or after the Gospel and homily): _____

    Presentation and Examination and Baptismal Covenant (see p. 292 for address which precedes

      Baptismal Covenant): _____

    Procession to the Font: _____

    Prayers for the Candidates (sung or said): _____

      Leader: _____

(Continued)

Concluding Collect (sung or said): _____

Thanksgiving over the Water (sung or said): _____

Consecration of the Chrism (yes or no): _____ *Sung or said:* _____

The Baptism: _____

Procession: _____

Prayer (Sung or said): _____

The Signation and the Welcome: _____

At Confirmation, Reception, or Reaffirmation: Prayers _____

(Sung or said): _____

If there are no candidates for Baptism—The Renewal of Vows _____

(Here or after the Gospel and homily): _____

Prayer (Sung or said): _____

At the Eucharist—*Opening Acclamation (yes or no):* _____

Sung or said: _____

Canticle: _____

Salutation and Collect: _____ *Sung or said:* _____

Epistle: Romans 6:3–11 _____

Reader: _____

Silence (yes or no): _____ *Duration:* _____

Alleluia: _____

Psalm 114 _____ *or other psalm or hymn:* _____

Gospel: Matthew 28:1–10 _____

Reader: _____

Sermon: _____

Preacher: _____

Prayers of the People: _____ *Sung or said:* _____

Leader: _____

Concluding Collect: _____ *Sung or said:* _____

The Peace (any special instructions): _____ *Sung or said:* _____

Offertory Sentence (yes or no): _____ *Which?* _____

Hymn, psalm, or anthem: _____

(Continued)

Presenters: _____

Preparation of the Table (deacon _____ *or assisting priest* _____ *)*

The Great Thanksgiving: _____ *Sung or said:* _____

   Proper Preface: _____

   Holy, holy, holy/Holy, holy, holy Lord (Sanctus): _____

   Memorial Acclamation: _____

   Continuation or conclusion of Prayer sung? _____ *Great Amen:* _____

The Lord's Prayer: _____

Duration of silence after Breaking of the Bread (and Pouring of the Wine): _____

Fraction Anthem (yes or no): _____ *Which?* _____ *(Alleluia is used)* _____

Invitation to Communion: _____ *Longer or shorter form:* _____

   Sung or said: _____

   Ministers of Communion: _____

Hymn, psalm, or anthem during Communion: _____

Hymn during clearing of the Table: _____

Postcommunion Prayer: _____

Hymn: _____

Blessing: _____ *Sung or said:* _____

Dismissal (with "Alleluia, alleluia"): _____ *Sung or said:* _____

   Deacon (or Celebrant): _____

Postlude: _____

The Vigil of Pentecost

Time: _____

Celebrant: _____

The Service of Light—*Opening Acclamation:* _____ *Sung or said:* _____

Lesson of Scripture (yes or no): _____ *Which?* _____ *Sung or said* _____

Reader: _____

Prayer for Light: _____ *Sung or said:* _____

Anthem, psalm, or silence: _____

O Gracious Light (Phos hilaron) or other hymn: _____

At the Eucharist—*Salutation and Collect:* _____ *Sung or said:* _____

The Tower of Babel: Genesis 11:1–9: _____

Reader: _____

Silence (yes or no): _____ *Duration:* _____

Psalm 33:12–22 _____ *or another psalm, canticle, or hymn:* _____

Cantor: _____

The Covenant at Sinai: Exodus 19:1–9, 16–20a; 20:18–20: _____

Reader: _____

Silence (yes or no): _____ *Duration:* _____

Canticle 2 _____ *or 13* _____ *or another canticle, psalm or hymn:*

_____

Cantor: _____

The Dry Bones: Ezekiel 37:1–14: _____

Reader: _____

Silence (yes or no): _____ *Duration:* _____

Psalm 130 _____ *or another psalm, canticle, or hymn:* _____

Cantor: _____

The Outpouring of the Spirit: Joel 2:28–32: _____

Reader: _____

Silence (yes or no): _____ *Duration:* _____

(Continued)

Canticle 9 _____ *or another canticle, psalm or hymn:* _____

   Cantor: _____

Pentecost: Acts 2:1–11: _____

   Reader: _____

Silence (yes or no): _____ *Duration:* _____

Psalm 104:25–32 _____ *or another psalm, canticle, or hymn:* ____

   Cantor: _____

The Spirit you received: Romans 8:14–17, 22–27: _____

   Reader: _____

Silence (yes or no): _____ *Duration:* _____

Alleluia and/or Sequence: _____

Gospel: John 7:37–39a: _____

   Reader: _____

Sermon: _____

   Preacher: _____

Holy Baptism _____

   Presentation and Examination and Baptismal Covenant: _____

   Procession to the Font: _____

   Prayers for the Candidates (sung or said): _____

     Leader: _____

   Concluding Collect (sung or said): _____

   Thanksgiving over the Water (sung or said): _____

   Consecration of the Chrism (yes or no): _____ *Sung or said:* _____

   The Baptism: _____

   Procession: _____

   Prayer (sung or said): _____

   The Signation and the Welcome: _____

   At Confirmation, Reception, or Reaffirmation: Prayers _____

     (Sung or said): _____

   The Peace (any special instructions): _____ *Sung or said:* _____

If there are no candidates for Baptism—The Renewal of Vows (BCP, p. 292) ____

(Continued)

Prayer (Sung or said): _____

Prayers of the People: _____ *Sung or said:* _____

    Leader: _____

Concluding Collect: _____ *Sung or said:* _____

If there were no baptisms, the Peace (any special instructions): __ *Sung or said:* _____

Offertory Sentence (yes or no): _____ *Which?* _____

Hymn, psalm, or anthem: _____

    Presenters: _____

    Preparation of the Table (deacon _____ *or assisting priest* _____ *)*

The Great Thanksgiving: _____ *Sung or said:* _____

    Proper Preface: _____

    Holy, holy, holy/Holy, holy, holy Lord (Sanctus): _____

    Memorial Acclamation: _____

    Continuation or conclusion of Prayer sung? _____ *Great Amen:* _____

The Lord's Prayer: _____

Duration of silence after Breaking of the Bread (and Pouring of the Wine): _____

Fraction Anthem (yes or no): _____ *Which?* _____

    (Alleluia) _____

Invitation to Communion: _____ *Longer or shorter form:* _____

    Sung or said: _____

    Ministers of Communion: _____

Hymn, psalm, or anthem during Communion: _____

Hymn during clearing of the Table: _____

Postcommunion Prayer: _____

Hymn: _____

Blessing: _____ *Sung or said:* _____

Dismissal (with "Alleluia, alleluia"): _____ *Sung or said* _____

    Deacon (or celebrant): _____

Postlude: _____

Holy Baptism

Date and Time: _____

Celebrant: _____

Prelude: _____

Entrance hymn, psalm, or anthem: _____

Opening Acclamation: _____ Sung or said: _____

Versicles (sung or said): _____

Salutation and Collect: _____ Sung or said: _____

First Reading: _____

Reader: _____

Silence (yes or no): _____ Duration: _____

Gradual: Psalm _____

Cantor: _____

Second Reading: _____

Reader: _____

Silence (yes or no): _____ Duration: _____

Alleluia or Tract and/or Sequence: _____

Gospel: _____

Reader: _____

Sermon: _____

Preacher: _____

Presentation and Examination and Baptismal Covenant: _____

Procession to the Font: _____

Prayers for the Candidates (sung or said): _____

Leader: _____

Concluding Collect (sung or said): _____

Thanksgiving over the Water (sung or said): _____

(Continued)

Consecration of the Chrism (yes or no): _____ Sung or said: _____

The Baptism: _____

Procession: _____

Prayer (sung or said): _____

The Signation and the Welcome: _____

At Confirmation, Reception, or Reaffirmation: Prayers _____

    Sung or said: _____

The Peace (any special instructions): _____ Sung or said: _____

Prayers of the People: _____ Sung or said: _____

    Leader: _____

Concluding Collect: _____ Sung or said: _____

Offertory Sentence (yes or no): _____ Which? _____

Hymn, psalm, or anthem: _____

    Presenters: _____

    Preparation of the Table (deacon _____ or assisting priest _____)

The Great Thanksgiving: _____ Sung or said: _____

    Proper Preface: _____

    Holy, holy, holy/Holy, holy, holy Lord (Sanctus): _____

    Memorial Acclamation: _____

    Continuation or conclusion of Prayer sung? _____ Great Amen: _____

The Lord's Prayer: _____

Duration of silence after Breaking of the Bread (and Pouring of the Wine): _____

Fraction Anthem (yes or no): _____ Which? _____ Alleluia (yes or no): _____

Invitation to Communion: _____ Longer or shorter form: _____

    Sung or said: _____

    Ministers of Communion: _____

Hymn, psalm, or anthem during Communion: _____

Hymn during clearing of the Table: _____

Postcommunion Prayer: _____

Hymn: _____

Blessing (yes or no): _____ Which form: _____ Sung or said: _____

(Continued)

Dismissal: _____ Alleluia (yes or no): Sung or said: _____

Deacon (or Celebrant): _____

Postlude: _____

The Holy Eucharist: Rite One

Day or Occasion: _____

Celebrant: _____

The Entrance Rite

Special entrance rites for certain days or occasions: _____

Ash Wednesday, page 264_____   Confirmation, page 413 _____

Palm Sunday, page 270_____   Marriage, page 423 _____

Good Friday, page 276_____   Ministration to the Sick, page 453 _____

Holy Saturday, page 283_____   Burial of the Dead, page 469 _____

Easter Vigil, page 285_____   Ordinations, pages 512, 525, 537 _____

Pentecost Vigil, page 175_____   Celebration of a New Ministry, page 559 _____

Holy Baptism, page 299_____   Consecration of a Church, page 567 _____

Option 1: *Normal in festal seasons, permitted except in Advent and Lent:* _____

_____

   Prelude: _____

   Entrance hymn, psalm, or anthem: _____

   Opening Acclamation: _____ Sung or said: _____

   Collect for Purity (sung or said): _____

   Ten Commandments _____ or Summary of the Law_____ or neither: _____

   Lord, have mercy upon us (Kyrie), Kyrie eleison, or Holy God (Trisagion) (which, if any): __

    Music: _____

   Song of Praise: _____

Option II: *Normal in Advent and Lent, permitted except at certain festal times:* _____

   Prelude: _____

   Entrance hymn, psalm, or anthem: _____

   Opening Acclamation: _____ Sung or said: _____

   Collect for Purity (sung or said): _____

(Continued)

Ten Commandments _____ or Summary of the Law_____ or neither: _____

Lord, have mercy upon us (Kyrie), Kyrie eleison, or Holy God (Trisagion): _____

Music: _____

Option III: *A Penitential Order, page 319:* _____

Prelude: _____

Entrance hymn, psalm, or anthem: _____

Opening Acclamation: _____ Sung or said: _____

Decalogue (yes or no): _____ Sung or said: _____

Sentence of Scripture: _____

Confession of Sin (which form): _____

Lord, have mercy upon us (Kyrie), Kyrie eleison, or Holy God (Trisagion) (which, if any): ___

Music: _____

Option IV: *The Great Litany:* _____ Sung or said: _____

Lord, have mercy upon us or Kyrie eleison: _____

Litanist: _____

Option V: *An Order of Worship for the Evening:* _____

Opening Acclamation _____ Sung or said: _____

Lesson of Scripture (yes or no): _____ Which? _____ Sung or said: _____

Reader: _____

Prayer for Light: _____ Sung or said: _____

Anthem, psalm, or silence: _____

O Gracious Light (Phos hilaron): _____

The Ministry of the Word

Collect of the Day: _____ *Sung or said:* _____

First Reading: _____

   Reader: _____

Silence (yes or no): _____ *Duration:* _____

Gradual: Psalm _____

   Cantor: _____

Second Reading: _____

   Reader: _____

Silence (yes or no): _____ *Duration:* _____

Alleluia or Tract and/or Sequence: _____

Gospel: _____

   Reader: _____

Sermon: _____

   Preacher: _____

Reaffirmation of Vows, page 292 (Easter, Pentecost, Epiphany I, _____

   All Saints' Day or the Sunday after All Saints' Day); page 303 (Baptism); _____

   page 416 (Confirmation): _____

Nicene Creed (yes or no): _____ *Sung or said:* _____

Prayers of the People (sung or said): _____

   Leader: _____

   Prayer for the Whole State of Christ's Church and the World: _____

   Form I _____ *Form II* _____ *Form III* _____ *Form IV* _____ *Form V* _____

   Form VI _____

Other forms: The Solemn Collects, page 277: _____

   Litany for Ordinations (Ember Days), page 548: _____

   Litany of Thanksgiving (Thanksgiving Day), page 836: _____

   Litany of Thanksgiving for a Church (Dedication festival), page 578: _____

   A form written for the occasion or gleaned from another source: _____

   _____

(Continued)

Special petitions to be included: _____

_____

Collect after the Intercessions: _____ *Sung or said:*

Confession of Sin (yes or no): _____

   Bidding: _____

   Confession: _____

   Comfortable Words: _____

Special rites: Thanksgiving for Birth or Adoption of a Child: _____

   Commitment to Christian Service: _____

   Anointing of the Sick: _____ *Other:* _____

The Peace (any special instructions): _____ *Sung or said:* _____

The Holy Communion

Offertory Sentence (yes or no): _____ *Which?* _____

Hymn, psalm, or anthem: _____

   Presenters: _____

   Preparation of the Table (deacon _____ *or assisting priest* _____ *)*

The Great Thanksgiving (I or II): _____ *Sung or said:* _____

   Proper Preface: _____

   Holy, holy, holy (Sanctus): _____

   Blessed is he that cometh (Benedictus qui venit): _____

   Continuation or conclusion of Prayer sung? _____ *Great Amen:* _____

The Lord's Prayer: _____

Duration of silence after Breaking of the Bread (and Pouring of the Wine): _____

Fraction Anthem (yes or no): _____ *Which?* _____ *Alleluia (yes or no):* _____

Prayer of Humble Access (yes or no): _____ *By priest* _____ *,*

   or by priest and people: _____

Invitation to Communion (yes or no): _____ *Longer or shorter form:* _____

   Sung or said: _____

   Ministers of Communion: _____

Hymn, psalm, or anthem during Communion: _____

(Continued)

Hymn during clearing of the Table: _____

Postcommunion Prayer by priest _____ *or by priest and people:* _____

Hymn: _____

Blessing (longer or shorter form): _____ *Sung or said:* _____

Dismissal (yes or no): _____ *Which form?* _____ *Alleluia (yes or no):* _____

Sung or said: _____ *Deacon (or Celebrant):* _____

Postlude: _____

The Holy Eucharist: Rite Two

Day or Occasion: _____

Celebrant: _____

The Entrance Rite

Special entrance rites for certain days or occasions: _____

Ash Wednesday, page 264_____ Confirmation, page 413 _____

Palm Sunday, page 270_____ Marriage, page 423 _____

Good Friday, page 276_____ Ministration to the Sick, page 453 _____

Holy Saturday, page 283_____ Burial of the Dead, page 491 _____

Easter Vigil, page 285_____ Ordinations, pages 512, 525, 537 _____

Pentecost Vigil, page 227_____ Celebration of a New Ministry, page 559 _____

Holy Baptism, page 299_____ Consecration of a Church, page 567 _____

Option 1: *Normal in festal seasons, permitted except in Advent or Lent:* _____

    Prelude: _____

    _____

    Entrance hymn, psalm or anthem: _____

    Opening Acclamation: _____ Sung or said: _____

    Collect for Purity (yes or no): _____ Sung or said: _____

    Song of Praise: _____

Option II: *Normal in Advent and Lent, permitted except at certain festal times:* _____

    Prelude: _____

    _____

    Entrance hymn, psalm, or anthem: _____

    Opening Acclamation: _____ Sung or said: _____

    Collect for Purity (yes or no): _____ Sung or said: _____

    Lord, have mercy (Kyrie), Kyrie eleison, or Holy God (Trisagion): _____

    Music: _____

(Continued)

Option III: *A Penitential Order, page 351:* _____

    Prelude: _____

    Entrance hymn, psalm, or anthem: _____

    Opening Acclamation: _____ *Sung or said:* _____

    Decalogue (yes or no): _____ *Sung or said:* _____

    Sentence of Scripture: _____

    Song of Praise, Lord, have mercy (Kyrie), Kyrie eleison, or Holy God (Trisagion): _____

       Music: _____

Option IV: *The Great Litany:* _____ *Sung or said:* _____

    Lord, have mercy upon us or Kyrie eleison: _____

    The Kyrie: _____

    Litanist: _____

Option V: *An Order of Worship for the Evening:* _____

    Opening Acclamation: _____ *Sung or said:* _____

    Lesson of Scripture (yes or no): _____ *Which?* _____ *Sung or said:* _____

       Reader: _____

    Prayer for Light _____ *Sung or said:* _____

    Anthem, psalm, or silence: _____

    O Gracious Light (Phos hilaron): _____

The Ministry of the Word

Collect of the Day: _____ Sung or said: _____

First Reading: _____

Reader: _____

Silence (yes or no): _____ Duration: _____

Gradual: Psalm _____

Cantor: _____

Second Reading: _____

Reader: _____

Silence (yes or no): _____ Duration: _____

Alleluia or Tract and/or Sequence: _____

Gospel: _____

Reader: _____

Sermon: _____

Preacher: _____

Reaffirmation of Vows, page 292 (Easter, Pentecost, Epiphany I, All Saints' Day or the Sunday after

All Saints' Day); page 303 (Baptism); page 416 _____

(Confirmation) _____

Nicene Creed (yes or no): _____ Sung or said: _____

Prayers of the People (sung or said): _____

Leader: _____

Form I _____ Form II _____ Form III _____ Form IV _____ Form V _____

Form VI _____

Other forms: the Solemn Collects, page 277: _____

Litany for Ordinations (Ember Days), page 548: _____

Litany of Thanksgiving (Thanksgiving Day), page 836: _____

Litany of Thanksgiving for a Church (Dedication festival), page 578: _____

A form written for the occasion or gleaned from another source: _____

_____

(Continued)

Special petitions to be included: _____

_____

    Collect after the Intercessions: _____ *Sung or Said:* _____

Confession of Sin (yes or no): _____

Special rites: Thanksgiving for Birth or Adoption of a Child: _____

    Commitment to Christian Service: _____

    Anointing of the Sick: _____ *Other* _____

The Peace (any special instructions): _____ *Sung or said:* _____

The Holy Communion

Offertory Sentence (yes or no): _____ *Which?* _____

Hymn, psalm, or anthem: _____

    Presenters: _____

    Preparation of the Table (deacon _____ *or assisting priest* _____*)*

The Great Thanksgiving (A, B, C, or D): _____ *Sung or said:* _____

    Proper Preface: (A or B): _____

    Holy, holy, holy Lord (Sanctus): _____

    Memorial Acclamation: _____

    Special Intercessions (D): _____

    Commemoration of a Saint (B or D): _____

    Continuation or conclusion of Prayer sung? _____ *Great Amen:* _____

The Lord's Prayer: _____

Duration of silence after Breaking of the Bread (and Pouring of the Wine): _____

Fraction Anthem (yes or no): _____ *Which?* _____ *Alleluia (yes or no):* _____

Invitation to Communion (longer or shorter form): _____ *Sung or said:* _____

    Ministers of Communion: _____

Hymn, psalm, or anthem during Communion: _____

Hymn during clearing of the Table: _____

Postcommunion Prayer: _____

Hymn: _____

Blessing (yes or no): _____ *Which Form?* _____ *Sung or said:* _____

(Continued)

Dismissal: _____ *Alleluia (yes or no):* ____ *Sung or said:* _____

Deacon (or Celebrant): _____

Postlude: _____

An Order for Celebrating the Holy Eucharist ("Rite III")

Day or Occasion and time: _____

Celebrant: _____

The People and Priest

Gather in the Lord's Name: _____

_____

_____

_____

Proclaim and respond to the Word of God: _____

Readings and Readers: _____

_____

_____

_____

_____

Gospel: _____

   Reader: _____

Responses: _____

_____

_____

_____

Pray for the World and the Church: _____

_____

_____

Leader: _____

Exchange the Peace *(where in the service? any special instructions?):* _____

_____

_____

Prepare the Table: _____

(Continued)

By whom? _____

Presenters: _____

Music? _____

Any special instructions? _____

_____

Make Eucharist _____

Eucharistic Prayer: _____

  If Form 1 or Form 2 is used, how or by whom is it to be filled out? _____

  Music: _____

  The Lord's Prayer (yes or no): _____ *Which form?* _____

    Sung or said: _____ *Setting:* _____

Break the Bread _____

By whom? _____

Pour the Wine? _____ *By whom?* _____

Duration of silence: _____

Fraction Anthem? _____

Invitation to Communion? _____

Share the Gifts of God _____

Method of Ministration: _____

Ministers of Communion: _____

Music: _____

Ablutions (where and by whom?): _____

Postcommunion Prayer? _____

Music? _____

Blessing? _____

Dismissal? _____

Agape? _____

Confirmation, Reception, or Reaffirmation of Baptismal Vows

Date and Time: _____

Celebrant: _____

Prelude: _____

Entrance hymn, psalm, or anthem: _____

Opening Acclamation: _____ Sung or said: _____

Versicles: _____

Salutation and Collect: _____ Sung or said: _____

First Reading: _____

Reader: _____

Silence (yes or no): _____ Duration: _____

Gradual: Psalm _____

Cantor: _____

Second Reading: _____

Reader: _____

Silence (yes or no): _____ Duration: _____

Alleluia or Tract and or Sequence: _____

Gospel: _____

Reader: _____

Sermon: _____

Preacher: _____

Presentation and Examination: _____

Petitions for the Candidates (yes or no): _____ Sung or said: _____

Leader: _____

Prayer (sung or said): _____

The Laying on of Hands: _____

Prayer (sung or said): _____

The Peace (any special instructions): _____ Sung or said: _____

(Continued)

Prayers of the People: _____ *Sung or said:* _____

    Leader: _____

Concluding Collect: _____ *Sung or said:* _____

Offertory Sentence (yes or no): _____ *Which?* _____

Hymn, psalm, or anthem: _____

    Presenters: _____

    Preparation of the Table (deacon _____ *or assisting priest* _____)

The Great Thanksgiving: _____ *Sung or said:* _____

    Proper Preface: _____

    Holy, holy, holy/Holy, holy, holy Lord (Sanctus): _____

    Memorial Acclamation: _____

    Continuation or conclusion of Prayer sung? _____ *Great Amen:* _____

The Lord's Prayer: _____

Duration of silence after Breaking of the Bread (and Pouring of the Wine): _____

Fraction Anthem (yes or no): _____ *Which?* _____ *Alleluia (yes or no):* _____

Invitation to Communion: _____ *Longer or shorter form:* _____

    Sung or said: _____

    Ministers of Communion: _____

Hymn, psalm, or anthem during Communion: _____

Hymn during clearing of the Table: _____

Postcommunion Prayer: _____

Consecration of Chrism (BOS, pages 224–225): _____ *Sung or said:* _____

Hymn: _____

Blessing (yes or no): _____ *Which form?* _____ *Sung or said:* _____

Dismissal: _____ *Alleluia (yes or no): Sung or said:* _____

    Deacon (or Celebrant): _____

Postlude: _____

Celebration and Blessing of a Marriage

Names of the couple: _____

_____

Date and time of rite: _____

Celebrant: _____

Prelude: _____

_____

_____

Entrance hymn, psalm, anthem, or instrumental music: _____

_____

Order of procession: _____

_____

_____

Exhortation: _____

Charge, Declaration of Consent: _____

Presentation or Giving in Marriage: _____

Hymn, psalm, or anthem: _____

Salutation and Collect (sung or said): _____

First Reading: _____

    Reader: _____

Silence (yes or no): _____ Duration: _____

Gradual: Psalm _____

    Cantor: _____

Second Reading: _____

    Reader: _____

Silence (yes or no): _____ Duration: _____

Alleluia or Tract and/or Sequence: _____

(Continued)

Gospel: _____

    Reader: _____

Sermon: _____

    Preacher: _____

Apostles' Creed (yes or no): _____

Giving of the ring(s), single or double ring ceremony: _____

Blessing of the ring(s) (yes or no): _____ *Sung or said:* _____

Form to be used with giving of the ring(s): _____

The Prayers: _____ *Sung or said:* _____

    Leader: _____

The Blessing: _____ *Sung or said:* _____

The Peace (any special instructions): _____ *Sung or said:* _____

Offertory Sentence (yes or no): _____ *Which?* _____

Hymn, psalm, anthem, or instrumental music: _____

    Presenters: _____

    Preparation of the Table (deacon _____ *or assisting priest* _____ *)*

The Great Thanksgiving: _____ *Sung or said:* _____

    Proper Preface: _____

    Holy, holy, holy/Holy, holy, holy Lord (Sanctus): _____

    Memorial Acclamation: _____

    Continuation or conclusion of Prayer sung? _____ *Great Amen:* _____

The Lord's Prayer: _____

Duration of silence after Breaking of the Bread (and Pouring of the Wine): _____

Fraction Anthem (yes or no): _____ *Which?* _____ *Alleluia (yes or no):* _____

Invitation to Communion: _____ *Longer or shorter form:* _____

    Sung or said: _____

    Ministers of Communion: _____

Hymn, psalm, or anthem during Communion: _____

Hymn during clearing of the Table: _____

Postcommunion Prayer, page 432 (said or sung by celebrant): _____

Hymn: _____

(Continued)

Blessing and/or dismissal: _____

Hymn, psalm, anthem, or instrumental music: _____

_____

_____

An Order for Marriage

Names of the couple: _____

_____

Date and time of rite: _____

Celebrant: _____

Prelude: _____

_____

_____

Entrance hymn, psalm, anthem, or instrumental music: _____

_____

Order of procession: _____

_____

_____

Statement of the Church's teaching concerning Holy Matrimony: _____

_____

_____

Couple's statement of intention and consent: _____

_____

_____

Reading(s) and Reader(s): _____

_____

_____

_____

Gospel: _____

Reader: _____

Sermon? _____

Preacher: _____

(Continued)

Apostles' Creed (yes or no): _____

Vows (which form): _____

Blessing and giving of ring(s)? _____

_____

Declaration of the Marriage: _____

_____

Prayers: _____

_____

_____

    Leader: _____

Blessing of the Marriage: _____

_____

The Peace (any special instructions): _____

Offertory Sentence (yes or no): _____ *Which?* _____

Hymn, psalm, anthem, or instrumental music: _____

    Presenters: _____

    Preparation of the Table (deacon _____ *or assisting priest* _____)

The Great Thanksgiving: _____ *Sung or said:* _____

    Proper Preface: _____

    Holy, holy, holy/Holy, holy, holy Lord (Sanctus): _____

    Memorial Acclamation: _____

    Continuation or conclusion of Prayer sung? _____ *Great Amen:* _____

The Lord's Prayer: _____

Duration of silence after Breaking of the Bread (and Pouring of the Wine): _____

Fraction Anthem (yes or no): _____ *Which?* _____ *Sung or said:* _____

    Invitation to Communion: _____ *Longer or shorter form:* _____

    Sung or said: _____

    Ministers of Communion: _____

Hymn, psalm, or anthem during Communion: _____

Hymn during clearing of the Table: _____

Postcommunion Prayer: _____

(Continued)

Hymn: _____

Blessing and/or dismissal: _____

Hymn, psalm, anthem, or instrumental music: _____

Burial of the Dead:

Name of the deceased: _____

Date and time of the rite: _____

Celebrant: _____

Prelude: _____

Opening Anthems: _____ *Sung or said:* _____

Salutation and Collect: (sung or said) _____

First Reading: _____

    Reader: _____

Silence (yes or no): _____ *Duration:* _____

Gradual: Psalm _____

    Cantor: _____

Second Reading: _____

    Reader: _____

Silence (yes or no): _____ *Duration:* _____

Alleluia or Tract and/or Sequence: _____

Gospel: _____

    Reader: _____

Sermon: _____

    Preacher: _____

Apostles' Creed (yes or no): _____

The Prayers: _____ *Sung or said:* _____

    Leader: _____

Concluding Collect (Rite II): _____ *Sung or said:* _____

The Peace (any special instructions): _____ *Sung or said:* _____

Offertory Sentence (yes or no): _____ *Which?* _____

Hymn, psalm, or anthem: _____

    Presenters: _____

    Preparation of the Table (deacon _____ *or assisting priest* _____ *)*

(Continued)

The Great Thanksgiving: _____ *Sung or said:* _____

    Proper Preface: _____

    Holy, holy, holy/Holy, holy, holy Lord (Sanctus): _____

    Memorial Acclamation: _____

    Continuation or conclusion of Prayer sung? _____ *Great Amen:* _____

The Lord's Prayer: _____

Duration of silence after Breaking of the Bread (and Pouring of the Wine): _____

Fraction Anthem (yes or no): _____ *Which?* _____ *Alleluia (yes or no):* _____

Invitation to Communion: _____ *Longer or shorter form:* _____

    Sung or said: _____

    Ministers of Communion: _____

Hymn, psalm, or anthem during Communion: _____

Hymn during clearing of the Table: _____

Postcommunion Prayer (sung or said by Celebrant): _____

Anthem or hymn: _____

The Commendation (sung or said): _____

Blessing and/or Dismissal: _____ *Sung or said:* _____

Hymn, anthem(s), or canticle: _____

Postlude: _____

The Committal—Anthem(s): _____ *Sung or said:* _____

    The Committal: _____ *Sung or said:* _____

    Prayers: _____ *Sung or said:* _____

    Dismissal: _____ *Sung or said:* _____

    Deacon (or Celebrant): _____

An Order for Burial

Name of the deceased: _____

Date and time of the rite: _____

Celebrant: _____

Prelude: _____

Anthems, psalms, or hymn: _____

Prayer: _____

Reading(s) and Reader(s): _____

_____

_____

Psalms, hymns, or anthems following the readings: _____

_____

_____

Gospel: _____

Reader: _____

Homily: _____

Preacher: _____

Apostles' Creed (yes or no): _____

Prayers: _____

_____

_____

_____

Leader: _____

The Peace (any special instructions): _____

Offertory Sentence (yes or no): _____ *Which?* ___

Hymn, psalm, or anthem: _____

Presenters: _____

Preparation of the Table (deacon _____ *or assisting priest* _____ *)*

The Great Thanksgiving: _____ *Sung or said:* _____

(Continued)

Proper Preface: _____

Holy, holy, holy/Holy, holy, holy Lord (Sanctus): _____

Memorial Acclamation: _____

Continuation or conclusion of Prayer sung? _____ *Great Amen:* _____

The Lord's Prayer: _____

Duration of the Silence after the Breaking of the Bread (and the Pouring of the Wine): _____

_____

_____

Fraction Anthem (yes or no): _____ *Which?* _____ *Alleluia (yes or no):* _____

Invitation to Communion: _____ *Longer or shorter form:* _____

   Sung or said: _____

   Ministers of Communion: _____

Hymn, psalm, or anthem during Communion: _____

Hymn during clearing of the Table: _____

Postcommunion Prayer (sung or said by Celebrant): _____

Anthem or hymn: _____

The Commendation: _____

Blessing and/or Dismissal: _____

Hymn, anthem(s), or canticle: _____

Postlude: _____

The Committal—Anthem(s): _____

   The Committal: _____

   Prayers: _____

   Dismissal: _____

   Blessing: _____

An Ordination (Bishop, Priest, or Deacon)

The Ordinand: _____

Date and time of the rite: _____

Celebrant: _____

Prelude: _____

Entrance hymn, psalm, or anthem: _____

Opening Acclamation and Collect for Purity (sung or said): _____

Presenters—Priest(s): _____

Lay Person(s): _____

Litany for Ordinations (p. 548) _____ or other Litany: _____

Lord, have mercy: _____

Sung or said: _____

Litanist: _____

Collect(s): _____ Sung or said: _____

First Reading: _____

Reader: _____

Silence (yes or no): _____ Duration: _____

Gradual: Psalm _____

Cantor: _____

Second Reading: _____

Reader: _____

Silence (yes or no): _____ Duration: _____

Alleluia or Tract and/or Sequence: _____

Gospel: _____

Deacon: _____

Sermon: _____

Preacher: _____

Nicene Creed (at ordination of priest or deacon): _____

Examination and Consecration: _____

(Continued)

Veni Creator Spiritus or Veni Sancte Spiritus (see THE HYMNAL 1982, 500–504 or 226–228):

_____

The Prayer of Consecration: _____

The Peace (any special instructions): _____ *Sung or said:* _____

Offertory Sentence (yes or no): _____ *Which?* _____

Hymn, psalm, or anthem: _____

    Presenters: _____

    Preparation of the Table—Deacon: _____

The Great Thanksgiving: _____ *Sung or said:* _____

    Proper Preface: _____

    Holy, holy, holy/Holy, holy, holy Lord (Sanctus): _____

    Memorial Acclamation: _____

    Continuation or conclusion of Prayer sung? _____ *Great Amen:* _____

The Lord's Prayer: _____

Duration of silence after Breaking of the Bread (and Pouring of the Wine): _____

Fraction Anthem (yes or no): _____ *Which?* _____ *Alleluia (yes or no):* _____

Invitation to Communion: _____ *Longer or shorter form:* _____

    Sung or said: _____

    Ministers of Communion: _____

Hymn, psalm, or anthem during Communion: _____

Hymn during clearing of the Table: _____

Postcommunion Prayer: Celebrant at Ordination of a Priest or Deacon: _____

    Bishop and People at Ordination of a Bishop: _____ *Sung or said:* _____

Hymn: _____

Blessing: _____ *Sung or said:* _____

Dismissal: _____ *Alleluia (yes or no):* ____ *Sung or said:* _____

    Deacon: _____

Hymn of praise (ordination of a bishop only): _____

Postlude: _____

Celebration of a New Ministry

New Minister: _____

Date and time: _____

Celebrant: _____

Prelude: _____

Hymn, psalm, or anthem: _____

The Institution: _____

Presenters: _____

Litany for Ordinations (p. 548): _____ or other Litany: _____

Sung or said: _____

Lord, have mercy: _____

Litanist: _____

Salutation and Collect: _____ Sung or said: _____

First Reading: _____

Reader: _____

Silence (yes or no): _____ Duration: _____

Gradual: Psalm _____

Cantor: _____

Second Reading: _____

Reader: _____

Silence (yes or no): _____ Duration: _____

Alleluia or Tract and/or Sequence: _____

Gospel: _____

Deacon: _____

Sermon: _____

Preacher: _____

Response(s): _____

Hymn: _____

Induction: _____

(Continued)

Presenters of symbols— _____

    Bible: _____

    Stole: _____

    Book of Prayers: _____

    Olive oil: _____

    Keys (a warden): _____

    Constitution and Canons (diocesan clergy): _____

    Bread and wine: _____

    Other: _____

The Peace (any special instructions): _____ *Sung or said:* _____

Offertory Sentence (yes or no): _____ *Which?* _____

Hymn, psalm, or anthem: _____

    Presenters: _____

    Preparation of the Table (deacon _____ *or assisting priest* _____ *)*

The Great Thanksgiving: _____ *Sung or said:* _____

    Proper Preface: _____

    Holy, holy, holy/Holy, holy, holy Lord (Sanctus): _____

    Memorial Acclamation: _____

    Continuation or conclusion of Prayer sung? _____ *Great Amen:* _____

The Lord's Prayer: _____

Duration of silence after Breaking of the Bread (and Pouring of the Wine): _____

Fraction Anthem (yes or no): _____ *Which?* _____ *Alleluia (yes or no):* _____

Invitation to Communion: _____ *Longer or shorter form:* _____

    Sung or said: _____

    Ministers of Communion: _____

Hymn, psalm, or anthem during Communion: _____

Hymn during clearing of the Table: _____

Postcommunion Prayer: _____

Hymn: _____

(Continued)

Blessing: _____ *Sung or said:* _____

Dismissal: _____ *Alleluia (yes or no):* ____ *Sung or said:* _____

Deacon (or Celebrant): _____

Postlude: _____

Dedication and Consecration of a Church

Date and time: _____

Celebrant: _____

Prelude: _____

Exhortation and Prayer: _____ Sung or said: _____

Procession—hymns, psalms, anthems or instrumental music:

_____

Opening of the doors: _____

Signing of the threshold (sung or said): _____

Psalm: _____

Hymns or anthems: _____

Prayer for the Consecration: _____ Sung or said: _____

Processional psalm, hymn, or instrumental music: _____

Dedication of the Font: _____ Sung or said: _____

Processional psalm, hymn, or instrumental music: _____

Dedication of lectern-pulpit: _____ Sung or said: _____

First Reading: _____

    Reader: _____

Silence (yes or no): _____ Duration: _____

Gradual: Psalm _____

    Cantor: _____

Second Reading: _____

    Reader: _____

Silence (yes or no): _____ Duration: _____

Processional psalm, hymn, or instrumental music: _____

Dedication of instrument of music: _____ Sung or said: _____

Instrumental music, hymn or anthem: _____

(Continued)

Gospel: _____

    Deacon: _____

Sermon: _____

    Preacher: _____

Nicene Creed (yes or no): _____ *Sung or said:* _____

Prayers of the People: _____ *Sung or said:* _____

    Deacon or leader: _____

Concluding Prayers: _____ *Sung or said:* _____

Dedication of the Altar: _____ *Sung or said:* _____

Vesting of the Altar: _____

Bells or instrumental music: _____

The Peace (any special instructions): _____ *Sung or said:* _____

Offertory Sentence (yes or no): _____ *Which?* _____

Hymn, psalm, or anthem: _____

    Presenters: _____

    Preparation of the Table (deacon _____ *or assisting priest* _____ *)*

The Great Thanksgiving: _____ *Sung or said:* _____

    Proper Preface: _____

    Holy, holy, holy/Holy, holy, holy Lord (Sanctus): _____

    Memorial Acclamation: _____

    Continuation or conclusion of Prayer sung? _____ *Great Amen:* _____

The Lord's Prayer: _____

Duration of silence after Breaking of the Bread (and Pouring of the Wine): _____

Fraction Anthem (yes or no): _____ *Which?* _____ *Alleluia (yes or no):* _____

Invitation to Communion: _____ *Longer or shorter form:* _____

    Sung or said: _____

    Ministers of Communion: _____

Hymn, psalm, or anthem during Communion: _____

Hymn during clearing of the Table: _____

Postcommunion Prayer: _____

Hymn: _____

(Continued)

Blessing: _____ *Sung or said:* _____

Dismissal: _____ *Alleluia (yes or no):* ___ *Sung or said:* _____

   Deacon (or Celebrant): _____

Postlude: _____

Advent Festival of Lessons and Music

Date and time: _____

Officiant: _____

Opening Acclamation: _____ Sung or said: _____

Lesson of Scripture (yes or no): _____ Which? _____ Sung or said: _____

    Reader: _____

Prayer for Light: _____ Sung or said: _____

Anthem, psalm, or silence: _____

O Gracious Light (Phos hilaron) or hymn: _____

Bidding Prayer: _____

Genesis 2:4b-9, 15–25: _____

    Reader: _____

Silence (yes or no): _____ Duration: _____

Hymn, canticle, or anthem: _____

Genesis 3:1–22 or 3:1–15 (required): _____

    Reader: _____

Silence (yes or no): _____ Duration: _____

Hymn, canticle, or anthem: _____

Isaiah 40:1–11: _____

    Reader: _____

Silence (yes or no): _____ Duration: _____

Hymn, canticle, or anthem: _____

Jeremiah 31:31–34: _____

    Reader: _____

Silence (yes or no): _____ Duration: _____

Hymn, canticle, or anthem: _____

Isaiah 64:1–9a: _____

    Reader: _____

Silence (yes or no): _____ Duration: _____

(Continued)

Hymn, canticle, or anthem: _____

Isaiah 6:1–11: _____

    Reader: _____

Silence (yes or no): _____ *Duration:* _____

Hymn, canticle, or anthem: _____

Isaiah 35:1–10: _____

    Reader: _____

Silence (yes or no): _____ *Duration:* _____

Hymn, canticle, or anthem: _____

Baruch 4:36—5:9: _____

    Reader: _____

Silence (yes or no): _____ *Duration:* _____

Hymn, canticle, or anthem: _____

Isaiah 7:10–15: _____

    Reader: _____

Silence (yes or no): _____ *Duration:* _____

Hymn, canticle, or anthem: _____

Micah 5:2–4: _____

    Reader: _____

Silence (yes or no): _____ *Duration:* _____

Hymn, canticle, or anthem: _____

Isaiah 11:1–9: _____

    Reader: _____

Silence (yes or no): _____ *Duration:* _____

Hymn, canticle, or anthem: _____

Zephaniah 3:14–18: _____

    Reader: _____

Silence (yes or no): _____ *Duration:* _____

Hymn, canticle, or anthem: _____

Isaiah 65:17–25: _____

    Reader: _____

(Continued)

Silence (yes or no): _____ *Duration:* _____

Hymn, canticle, or anthem: _____

Luke 1:5–25 or Luke 1:26–38 or 1:26–56: _____

    Reader: _____

Silence (yes or no): _____ *Duration:* _____

Hymn, canticle, or anthem: _____

Collect: _____ *Sung or said:* _____

Advent Blessing: _____ *Sung or said:* _____

Postlude: _____

Vigil for Christmas Eve

Date and time: _____

Officiant: _____

Opening Acclamation: _____ Sung or said: _____

Lesson of Scripture (yes or no): _____ Which? _____ Sung or said: _____

    Reader: _____

Prayer for Light: Collect for the First Sunday after Christmas _____

    Sung or said: _____

Anthem, psalm, or silence: _____

The Song of Mary (Magnificat), hymn, or O Gracious Light (Phos hilaron): _____

Genesis 2:4b–9, 15–25: _____

    Reader: _____

Silence (yes or no): _____ Duration: _____

Anthem, canticle, hymn, carol, or instrumental music: _____

_____

Genesis 3:1–23 or 3:1–15: _____

    Reader: _____

Silence (yes or no): _____ Duration: _____

Anthem, canticle, hymn, carol, or instrumental music: _____

_____

Isaiah 40:1–11: _____

    Reader: _____

Silence (yes or no): _____ Duration: _____

Anthem, canticle, hymn, carol, or instrumental music: _____

_____

Isaiah 35:1–10: _____

    Reader: _____

Silence (yes or no): _____ Duration: _____

Anthem, canticle, hymn, carol, or instrumental music: _____

(Continued)

Isaiah 7:10–15: _____

    Reader: _____

Silence (yes or no): _____ *Duration:* _____

Anthem, canticle, hymn, carol, or instrumental music: _____

_____

Luke 1:5–25: _____

    Reader: _____

Silence (yes or no): _____ *Duration:* _____

Anthem, canticle, hymn, carol, or instrumental music: _____

_____

Luke 1:26–58: _____

    Reader: _____

Silence (yes or no): _____ *Duration:* _____

Anthem, canticle, hymn, carol, or instrumental music: _____

_____

Luke 1:39–46 or 1:39–56: _____

    Reader: _____

Silence (yes or no): _____ *Duration:* _____

Anthem, canticle, hymn, carol, or instrumental music: _____

_____

Luke 1:57–80: _____

    Reader: _____

Procession to the creche: _____

Versicle and Response (yes or no): _____ *Which?* _____ *Sung or said:* _____

Collect: _____ *Sung or said:* _____

The service proceeds with Entrance Hymn and Opening Acclamation of the Eucharist.

Christmas Festival of Lessons and Music

Date and time: _____

Officiant: _____

Opening Acclamation: _____ Sung or said: _____

Lesson of Scripture (yes or no): _____ Which? _____ Sung or said: _____

    Reader: _____

Prayer for Light: _____ Sung or said: _____

Anthem, psalm, or silence: _____

O Gracious Light (Phos hilaron) or hymn: _____

Bidding Prayer: _____

Genesis 2:4b–9, 15–25: _____

    Reader: _____

Carol, hymn, canticle, or anthem: _____

Genesis 3:1–23 or 3:1–15 (required): _____

    Reader: _____

Carol, hymn, canticle, or anthem: _____

Isaiah 40:1–11: _____

    Reader: _____

Carol, hymn, canticle, or anthem: _____

Isaiah 35:1–10: _____

    Reader: _____

Carol, hymn, canticle, or anthem: _____

Isaiah 7:10–15: _____

    Reader: _____

Carol, hymn, canticle, or anthem: _____

Luke 1:5–25: _____

    Reader: _____

Carol, hymn, canticle, or anthem: _____

Luke 1:26–58: _____

(Continued)

Reader: _____

Carol, hymn, canticle, or anthem: _____

Luke 1:39–46 or 1:39–56: _____

Reader: _____

Carol, hymn, canticle, or anthem: _____

Luke 1:57–80: _____

Reader: _____

Carol, hymn, canticle, or anthem: _____

Luke 2:1–20: _____

Reader: _____

Carol, hymn, canticle, or anthem: _____

Luke 2:21–36: _____

Reader: _____

Carol, hymn, canticle, or anthem: _____

Hebrews 1:1–12: _____

Reader: _____

Carol, hymn, canticle, or anthem: _____

John 1:1–18: _____

Reader: _____

Carol, hymn, canticle, or anthem: _____

Collect: _____ *Sung or said:* _____

Christmas Blessing: _____ *Sung or said:* _____

Postlude: _____

Service for New Year's Eve

Time: _____

Officiant: _____

Opening Acclamation: _____ Sung or said: _____

Lesson of Scripture (yes or no): _____ Which? _____ Sung or said: _____

    Reader: _____

Collect for the First Sunday after Christmas: _____ Sung or said: _____

Anthem, psalm, or silence: _____

O Gracious Light (Phos hilaron): _____

The Hebrew Year: Exodus 23:9–16, 20–21: _____

    Reader: _____

Psalm, canticle, or hymn: _____

Duration of silence: _____

Prayer sung or said: _____

The Promised Land: Deuteronomy 11:8–12, 26–28: _____

    Reader: _____

Psalm, canticle, or hymn: _____

Duration of silence: _____

Prayer sung or said: _____

A Season for all Things: Ecclesiastes 3:1–15: _____

    Reader: _____

Psalm, canticle, or hymn: _____

Duration of silence: _____

Prayer sung or said: _____

Remember your Creator: Ecclesiastes 12:1–8: _____

    Reader: _____

Psalm, canticle, or hymn: _____

Duration of silence: _____

Prayer sung or said: _____

(Continued)

Marking the Times, and Winter: Ecclesiasticus 43:1–22: _____

    Reader: _____

Psalm, canticle, or hymn: _____

Duration of silence: _____

Prayer sung or said: _____

The Acceptable Time: 2 Corinthians 5:17–6:2: _____

    Reader: _____

Psalm, canticle, or hymn: _____

Duration of silence: _____

Prayer sung or said: _____

While it is Called Today: Hebrews 3:1–15 (16–4:13): _____

    Reader: _____

Psalm, canticle, or hymn: _____

Duration of silence: _____

Prayer sung or said: _____

New Heavens and New Earth: Revelation 21:1–14, 22–24: _____

    Reader: _____

Psalm, canticle, or hymn: _____

Duration of silence: _____

Prayer sung or said: _____

Homily, sermon, or instruction: _____

Act of self-dedication: _____

Conclusion: _____

Option I: *The Great Litany or some other form of intercession:* _____

    Intercessor: _____ *Sung or said:* _____

    Postlude: _____

Option II: *We Praise Thee/You are God (Te Deum laudamus) or some other hymn of praise:* __

    Lord's Prayer: _____ *Sung or said:* _____

    Collect for Holy Name: _____ *Sung or said:* _____

(Continued)

Blessing and/or Dismissal: _____ *Sung or said:* _____

Postlude: _____

Option III: *Eucharist for the Feast of the Holy Name, beginning with Glory be to God/Glory to God*

(Gloria in excelsis) or some other song of praise: _____

Blessing in Homes at Epiphany

Place: _____

Date and time: _____

Officiant: _____

Greeting (sung or said): _____

The Song of Mary (Magnificat) (sung or said): _____

  Antiphon: _____ Setting: _____

  Setting of The Song of Mary (Magnificat) _____

  Glory to the Father (Gloria Patri) (yes or no): _____

  Sprinkling of baptismal water (yes or no): _____

Salutation and collect: _____ Sung or said: _____

Other Prayers: _____

Blessing (sung or said): _____

Peace (yes or no): _____ Sung or said: _____

Vigil for the Eve of the Baptism of Our Lord

Date and time: _____

Celebrant: _____

Opening Acclamation: _____ Sung or said: _____

Lesson of Scripture (yes or no): _____ Which? _____ Sung or said: _____

    Reader: _____

Prayer for Light: _____ Sung or said: _____

Anthem, psalm, or silence: _____

O Gracious Light (Phos hilaron) or other canticle or hymn: _____

Salutation and Collect of the Day: _____ Sung or said: _____

The Story of the Flood: Genesis (7:1–5, 11–18); 8:6–18; 9:8–13: _____

    Reader: _____

Silence (duration): _____

Psalm, canticle, or hymn: _____

The Lord who Makes a Way in the Sea: Isaiah 43:15–19: _____

    Reader: _____

Silence (duration): _____

Psalm, canticle, or hymn: _____

The Washing and Anointing of Aaron: Leviticus 8:1–12: _____

    Reader: _____

Silence (duration): _____

Psalm, canticle, or hymn: _____

The Anointing of David: I Samuel 16:1–13: _____

    Reader: _____

Silence (duration): _____

Psalm, canticle, or hymn: _____

The Cleansing of Naaman in the Jordan: 2 Kings 5:1–14: _____

    Reader: _____

Silence (duration): _____

(Continued)

Psalm, canticle, or hymn: _____

Salvation Offered Freely to All: Isaiah 55:1–11: _____

    Reader: _____

Silence (duration): _____

Psalm, canticle, or hymn: _____

A new Heart and a new Spirit: Ezekiel 36:24–28: _____

    Reader: _____

Silence (duration): _____

Psalm, canticle, or hymn: _____

The Spirit of the Lord is Upon Me: Isaiah 61:1–9: _____

    or *Behold my servant: Isaiah 42:1–9:* _____

    Reader: _____

Silence (duration): _____

Psalm, canticle, or hymn: _____

When God's Patience Waited in the Days of Noah: 1 Peter 3:15b–22: _____

    or *God Anointed Jesus with the Holy Spirit: Acts 10:34–38:* _____

    Reader: _____

Silence (duration): _____

Alleluia Verse, Psalm, canticle, or hymn: _____

The Baptism of Jesus: **Year A:** *Matthew 3:13–17:* _____

                Year B: *Mark 1:7–11:* _____

                Year C: *Luke 3:15–16, 21–22:* _____

or *The Resurrection and the Great Commission: Matthew 28:* _____

    1–10, 16–20: _____

    Reader: _____

Sermon: _____

    Preacher: _____

Holy Baptism _____

    Presentation and Examination and Baptismal Covenant: _____

    Procession to the Font: _____

    Prayers for the Candidates (sung or said): _____

(Continued)

Leader: _____

Concluding Collect (sung or said): _____

Thanksgiving over the Water (sung or said): _____

Consecration of the Chrism (yes or no): _____ Sung or said: _____

The Baptism: _____

Procession: _____

Prayer (sung or said): _____

The Signation and the Welcome: _____

At Confirmation, Reception, or Reaffirmation: _____

    Prayers (sung or said): _____

The Peace (any special instructions): _____ Sung or said: _____

If there are no candidates for Baptism—The Renewal of Vows (BCP, p. 292) _____

    Prayer (sung or said): _____

Prayers of the People: _____ Sung or said: _____

    Leader: _____

Concluding Collect: _____ Sung or said: _____

If no baptisms, the Peace (any special instructions): _____ Sung or said: _____

Offertory Sentence (yes or no): _____ Which? _____

Hymn, psalm, or anthem: _____

    Presenters: _____

    Preparation of the Table (deacon _____ or assisting priest _____)

The Great Thanksgiving: _____ Sung or said: _____

    Proper Preface: _____

    Holy, holy, holy/Holy, holy, holy Lord (Sanctus): _____

    Memorial Acclamation: _____

    Continuation or conclusion of Prayer sung? _____ Great Amen: _____

The Lord's Prayer: _____

Duration of silence after Breaking of the Bread (and Pouring of the Wine): _____

Fraction Anthem (yes or no): _____ Which? _____ Alleluia (yes or no): _____

Invitation to Communion (longer or shorter form): _____ Sung or said: _____

    Ministers of Communion: _____

(Continued)

Hymn, psalm, or anthem during Communion: _____

Hymn during clearing of the Table: _____

Postcommunion Prayer: _____

Hymn: _____

Blessing: _____ *Sung or said:* _____

Dismissal: _____ *Sung or said:* _____

    Deacon (or Celebrant): _____

Postlude: _____

Candlemas Procession

Date and time: _____

Celebrant: _____

Gathering Place: _____

Opening Acclamation: _____ Sung or said: _____

The Song of Simeon (Nunc dimittis): _____

Cantor: _____

Prayer (sung or said): _____

The Procession: _____

Deacon: _____

Psalms and/or hymns: _____

Station Collect: _____ Sung or said: _____

Psalm 48:1–2, 10–13: _____ Glory to the Father (Gloria Patri)? _____

Cantor: _____

The Eucharistic rite continues with the Gloria in excelsis or some other Song of Praise.

The Way of the Cross

Date and time: _____

Officiant: _____

Prelude: _____

Entrance Hymn: _____

Opening Devotions (sung or said): _____

Duration of Silence: _____

Collect (sung or said): _____

Hymn (yes or no): _____ Which? _____

The Stations (eight or fourteen): _____

Anthem (sung or said): _____ Setting: _____

Lessons (sung or said): _____

Readers: _____

_____

_____

Versicle and Response (sung or said): _____ Setting: _____

Duration of silences: _____

Collects (sung or said): _____

Holy God (Trisagion) (sung or said): _____ Setting: _____

Concluding Prayers before the Altar _____

Savior of the world (sung or said): _____ Setting: _____

Duration of silence: _____

Prayers (sung or said): _____

Postlude: _____

Tenebrae

Date and time: _____

Officiant: _____

First Nocturn:

Antiphon 1: _____

Psalm 69 or Psalm 69:1–23: _____

Antiphon 2: _____

Psalm 70: _____

Antiphon 3: _____

Psalm 74: _____

Versicle and Response: _____

Silent Prayer (duration): _____

Lesson 1: _____

Responsory 1 (omissible): _____

Lesson 2: _____

Responsory 2 (omissible): _____

Lesson 3: _____

Responsory 3: _____

Second Nocturn:

Antiphon 4: _____

Psalm 2: _____

Antiphon 5: _____

Psalm 22 or Psalm 22:1–21: _____

Antiphon 6: _____

Psalm 27: _____

Versicle and Response: _____

Silent Prayer (duration): _____

(Continued)

Lesson 4: _____

Responsory 4 (omissible): _____

Lesson 5: _____

Responsory 5 (omissible): _____

Lesson 6: _____

Responsory 6: _____

Third Nocturn:

Antiphon 7: _____

Psalm 54: _____

Antiphon 8: _____

Psalm 76: _____

Antiphon 9: _____

Psalm 88: _____

Versicle and Response: _____

Silent Prayer (duration): _____

Lesson 7: _____

Responsory 7 (omissible): _____

Lesson 8: _____

Responsory 8 (omissible): _____

Lesson 9: _____

Responsory 9: _____

Lauds:

Antiphon 10: _____

Psalm 63 or Psalm 63:1–8: _____

Antiphon 11: _____

Psalm 90 or Psalm 90:1–12: _____

Antiphon 12: _____

Psalm 143: _____

Antiphon 13: _____

(Continued)

The Song of Hezekiah: _____

Antiphon 14: _____

Psalm 150: _____

Versicle and Response: _____

Antiphon: _____

The Song of Zechariah (Benedictus Dominus Deus): _____

Christ for us became obedient unto death (Christus factus est): _____

Silence (duration): _____

Psalm 51: _____

Prayer: _____

Noise: _____

Blessing in Homes at Easter

Place: _____

Date and time: _____

Officiant: _____

Greeting (sung or said): _____

Psalm or canticle: _____ *Sung or said:* _____

Antiphon: _____ *Setting:* _____

Setting of Psalm or Canticle: _____

Glory to the Father (Gloria Patri) (yes or no): _____

Sprinkling of baptismal water (yes or no): _____

Salutation and Prayers: _____ *Sung or said:* _____

Blessing (sung or said): _____

Peace (yes or no): _____ *Sung or said:* _____

Rogation Procession

Date and time: _____

Celebrant: _____

Gathering Place: _____

Hymns, psalms, canticles, and anthems:

_____

_____

Bible Readings:

_____

_____

Readers:

_____

_____

Prayers: _____ Sung or said: _____

_____ Sung or said: _____

_____ Sung or said: _____

The Great Litany: _____ Sung or said: _____

Lord, have mercy upon us or Kyrie eleison: _____

Litanist: _____

The service continues:

Option I: The Eucharist, beginning with the Salutation and Collect _____

Option II: Prayer: _____ Sung or said: _____

Blessing: _____ Sung or said: _____

Vigil for the Eve of All Saints' Day or the Sunday After All Saints' Day

Date and time: _____

Celebrant: _____

Opening Acclamation: _____ Sung or said: _____

Lesson of Scripture (yes or no): _____ Which? _____ Sung or said: _____

    Reader: _____

Prayer for Light: _____ Sung or said: _____

Anthem, psalm, or silence: _____

O Gracious Light (Phos hilaron) or other canticle or hymn: _____

Salutation and Collect of the Day: _____ Sung or said: _____

The Call of Abraham: Genesis 12:1–8: _____

    Reader: _____

Silence (duration): _____

Psalm, canticle, or hymn: _____

Daniel Delivered from the Lions' Den: Daniel 6:(1–15) 16–23: _____

    Reader _____

Silence (duration): _____

Psalm, canticle, or hymn: _____

The Testament and Death of Mattathias: 1 Maccabees 2:49–64: _____

    Reader: _____

Silence (duration): _____

Psalm, canticle, or hymn: _____

The Martyrdom of the Seven Brothers: 2 Maccabees 6:1–2; 7:1–23: _____

    Reader: _____

Silence (duration): _____

Psalm, canticle, or hymn: _____

The Eulogy of the Ancestors: Ecclesiasticus 44:1–10, 13–14: _____

    Reader: _____

(Continued)

Silence (duration): _____

Psalm, canticle, or hymn: _____

Surrounded by a Great Cloud of Witnesses: Hebrews 11:32(33–38) 39—12:2: _____

    Reader: _____

Silence (duration): _____

Psalm, canticle, or hymn: _____

The Reward of the Saints: Revelation 7:2–4, 9–17: _____

    Reader: _____

Silence (duration): _____

Alleluia Verse, Psalm, canticle, or hymn: _____

The Gospel: The Beatitudes: Matthew 5:1–12: _____

    or *"I will give you rest": Matthew 11:27–30:* _____

    or *The Resurrection and the Great Commission: Matthew 28: 1–10, 16–20:* _____

    Reader: _____

Sermon: _____

    Preacher: _____

Holy Baptism _____

Presentation and Examination and Baptismal Covenant: _____

Procession to the Font: _____

Prayers for the Candidates (sung or said): _____

    Leader: _____

Concluding Collect (sung or said): _____

Thanksgiving over the Water (sung or said): _____

Consecration of the Chrism (yes or no): _____ *Sung or said:* _____

The Baptism: _____

Procession: _____

Prayer (sung or said): _____

The Signation and the Welcome: _____

At Confirmation, Reception, or Reaffirmation: _____

    Prayers (sung or said): _____

The Peace (any special instructions): _____ *Sung or said:* _____

(Continued)

If there are no candidates for Baptism—The Renewal of Vows *(BCP, p. 292)* _____

    Prayer (sung or said): _____

Prayers of the People: _____ *Sung or said:* _____

    Leader: _____

Concluding Collect: _____ *Sung or said:* _____

If no baptisms, the Peace (any special instructions): _____ *Sung or said:* _____

Offertory Sentence (yes or no): _____ *Which?* _____

Hymn, psalm, or anthem: _____

    Presenters: _____

    Preparation of the Table (deacon _____ *or assisting priest* _____ *)*

The Great Thanksgiving: _____ *Sung or said:* _____

    Proper Preface: _____

    Holy, holy, holy/Holy, holy, holy Lord (Sanctus): _____

    Memorial Acclamation: _____

    Continuation or conclusion of Prayer sung? _____ *Great Amen:* _____

The Lord's Prayer: _____

Duration of silence after Breaking of the Bread (and Pouring of the Wine): _____

Fraction Anthem (yes or no): _____ *Which?* _____ *Alleluia (yes or no):* _____

Invitation to Communion (longer or shorter form): _____ *Sung or said:* _____

    Ministers of Communion: _____

Hymn, psalm, or anthem during Communion: _____

Hymn during clearing of the Table: _____

Postcommunion Prayer: _____

Hymn: _____

Blessing: _____ *Sung or said:* _____

Dismissal: _____ *Sung or said:* _____

    Deacon (or Celebrant): _____

Postlude: _____

Service for All Hallows' Eve

Date and time: _____

Officiant: _____

Opening Acclamation: _____ Sung or said: _____

Lesson of Scripture (yes or no): _____ Which? _____ Sung or said: _____

Reader: _____

Prayer for Light (Festivals of Saints): _____ Sung or said: _____

Anthem, psalm, or silence: _____

O Gracious Light (Phos hilaron) or other canticle or hymn: _____

The Witch of Endor: 1 Samuel 28:3–25: _____

Reader(s): _____

Psalm, Canticle, or hymn: _____

Duration of silence: _____ Prayer sung or said: _____

The Vision of Eliphaz the Temanite: Job 4:12–21: _____

Reader: _____

Psalm, Canticle, or hymn: _____

Duration of silence: _____ Prayer sung or said: _____

The Valley of Dry Bones: Ezekiel 37:1–14: _____

Reader: _____

Psalm, Canticle, or hymn: _____

Duration of silence: _____ Prayer sung or said: _____

The War in Heaven: Revelation 12:(1–6)7–12: _____

Reader: _____

Psalm, Canticle, or hymn: _____

Duration of silence: _____ Prayer sung or said: _____

Homily, sermon, or instruction: _____

Preacher: _____

We Praise Thee/You are God (Te Deum laudamus) or other song of praise: _____

Lord's Prayer: _____ Sung or said: _____

(Continued)

Collect of All Saints' Day (sung or said): _____

Blessing: _____ *Sung or said:* _____

Dismissal: _____ *Sung or said:* _____

  Deacon (or Officiant): _____

Postlude: _____

A Vigil on the Eve of Baptism

Date and time: _____

Celebrant: _____

Opening Acclamation: _____ Sung or said: _____

Lesson of Scripture (yes or no): _____ Which? _____ Sung or said: _____

    Reader: _____

Prayer for Light: _____ Sung or said: _____

Anthem, psalm, or silence: _____

O Gracious Light (Phos hilaron) or other canticle or hymn: _____

Salutation and Collect: _____ Sung or said: _____

The Story of the Flood: Genesis (7:1–5, 11–18); 8:6–18; 9:8–13: _____

    Reader: _____

Silence (duration): _____

Psalm, canticle, or hymn: _____

The Story of the Covenant: Exodus 19:1–9a, 16–20a, 20:18–20: _____

    Reader: _____

Silence (duration): _____

Psalm, canticle, or hymn: _____

Salvation Offered Freely to All: Isaiah 55:1–11: _____

    Reader: _____

Silence (duration): _____

Psalm, canticle, or hymn: _____

A new Heart and a new Spirit: Ezekiel 36:24–28: _____

    Reader: _____

Silence (duration): _____

Psalm, canticle, or hymn: _____

The Valley of Dry Bones: Ezekiel 37:1–14: _____

    Reader: _____

Silence (duration): _____

(Continued)

Psalm, canticle, or hymn: _____

Baptized into his Death: Romans 6:3–5: _____

    or *We are Children of God: Romans 8:14–17:* _____

    or *Now is the Day of Salvation: 2 Corinthians 5:17–20:* _____

    Reader: _____

Silence (duration): _____

Alleluia Verse, Psalm, canticle, or hymn: _____

The Gospel: The Baptism of Jesus: Mark 1:1–6: _____

    or *You Must be Born Again: John 3:1–6:* _____

    or *The Resurrection and the Great Commission:* _____

    Matthew 18:1–10, 16–20: _____

Homily: _____

    Preacher: _____

Prayers (Form 1 or Form 2): _____ *Sung or said:* _____

Blessing: _____ *Sung or said:* _____

Dismissal: _____ *Sung or said:* _____

    Deacon (or Celebrant): _____

Postlude: _____

Celebration for a Home

Residence: _____

Date and time: _____

Celebrant: _____

Prelude: _____

Salutation and Collect: _____ Sung or said: _____

First Reading: _____

Reader: _____

Psalm: _____

Cantor: _____

Second Reading: _____

Reader: _____

Sequence: _____

Gospel: _____

Reader: _____

Homily or Address: _____

Preacher: _____

Invocation (yes or no): _____ Sung or said: _____

Procession: _____

_____

_____

_____

Hymns or Songs: _____

_____

_____

_____

The Blessing of the Home: _____

Antiphon (Sung or said): _____

Versicle and Response (Sung or said): _____

(Continued)

Duration of silence: _____

Blessing (Sung or said): _____

The Peace: _____ *Sung or said:* _____

Conclusion: _____

Option I: _____

Offertory Sentence (yes or no): _____ *Which?* _____

Hymn, psalm, or anthem: _____

   Presenters: _____

   Preparation of the Table (deacon _____ *or assisting priest* _____ *)*

The Great Thanksgiving: _____ *Sung or said:* _____

   Proper Preface: _____

   Holy, holy, holy/Holy, holy, holy Lord (Sanctus): _____

   Memorial Acclamation: _____

   Continuation or conclusion of Prayer sung? _____ *Great Amen:* _____

The Lord's Prayer: _____

Duration of the Silence after the Breaking of the Bread (and Pouring of the Wine): _____

Fraction Anthem (yes or no): _____ *Which?* _____ *Alleluia (yes or no):* _____

Invitation to Communion: _____ *Longer or shorter form:* _____

   Sung or said: _____

   Ministers of Communion: _____

Hymn, psalm, or anthem during Communion: _____

Hymn during clearing of the Table: _____

Postcommunion Prayer: _____

Hymn: _____

Dismissal: _____ *Sung or said:* _____

   Deacon (or Celebrant): _____

Option II: _____

The Lord's Prayer: _____

Blessing: _____ *Sung or said:* _____

Anniversary of a Marriage

Use the Check List for the Holy Eucharist

A Public Service of Healing

Use the Check List for the Holy Eucharist

Burial of One Who Does Not Profess the Christian Faith

Use the Check List for An Order for Burial

The Founding of a Church

Ground Breaking

Gathering Place: _____

Date and time: _____

Celebrant: _____

Prelude: _____

Litany for the Church (sung or said): _____

Leader: _____

Salutation and collect (sung or said): _____

Hymn: _____

Lesson (Genesis 28:10–17): _____

Reader: _____

Sermon or Address: _____

Preacher: _____

Psalm 132:1–9(10–19) with Antiphon: _____ *Sung or said:* _____

Cantor or choir: _____

Persons to stretch the cords: _____

Psalm 48:1–3, 7–13 with Antiphon: _____ *Sung or said:* _____

Cantor or choir: _____

Persons to stretch the cord: _____

The Ground Breaking: _____

Salutation and Lord's Prayer, Versicles and Responses, and Concluding _____

Prayer (sung or said): _____

Dismissal: _____ *Sung or said:* _____

Deacon (or Celebrant): _____

Laying of a Cornerstone

Date and time: _____

Celebrant: _____

Prelude: _____

Hymn or anthem: _____

Scripture Reading: _____

Reader: _____

Prayer: _____ Sung or said: _____

Leader: _____

Laying of the Cornerstone: _____

Prayer (sung or said): _____

Trumpets: _____

Celebrant's Acclamation (sung or said): _____

Alleluias: _____

Hymn: _____

Blessing: _____ Sung or said: _____

Dismissal: _____ Sung or said: _____

Deacon (or Celebrant): _____

Recognition and Investiture of a Diocesan Bishop

Date and time: _____

Celebrant: _____

Prelude: _____

Procession: _____

Opening of the door: _____

Warden: _____

Psalm or anthem: _____

The Recognition: _____

Litany: _____ Sung or said: _____

Leader: _____

Kyries: _____

Salutation and Collect: _____ Sung or said: _____

First Reading: _____

Reader: _____

Silence (yes or no): _____ Duration: _____

Gradual: Psalm _____

Cantor: _____

Second Reading: _____

Reader: _____

Silence (yes or no): _____ Duration: _____

Alleluia or Tract and/or Sequence: _____

Gospel: _____

Reader: _____

Sermon: _____

Preacher: _____

Nicene Creed (yes or no): _____ Sung or said: _____

Renewal of the commitments of ordination: _____

(Continued)

The Investiture: _____

_____

The Seating: _____

    Instrumental Music: _____

The Peace: _____ *Sung or said:* _____

Offertory Sentence (yes or no): _____ *Which?* _____

Hymn, psalm, or anthem: _____

    Presenters: _____

    Preparation of the Table (deacon _____ *or assisting priest* _____ *)*

The Great Thanksgiving: _____ *Sung or said:* _____

    Proper Preface: _____

    Holy, holy, holy/Holy, holy, holy Lord (Sanctus): _____

    Memorial Acclamation: _____

    Continuation or conclusion of Prayer sung? _____ *Great Amen:* _____

The Lord's Prayer: _____

Duration of the silence after the Breaking of the Bread and the Pouring of the Wine: _____

_____

Fraction Anthem (yes or no): _____ *Which?* _____ *Alleluia (yes or no):* _____

Invitation to Communion: _____ *Longer or shorter form:* _____

    Sung or said: _____

    Ministers of Communion: _____

Hymn, psalm, or anthem during Communion: _____

Hymn during clearing of the Table: _____

Postcommunion Prayer: _____

Hymn: _____

Blessing: _____ *Sung or said:* _____

Dismissal: _____ *Sung or said:* _____

    Deacon (or Celebrant): _____

Postlude: _____

Welcome and Seating of a Bishop in the Cathedral

Date and time: _____

Prelude: _____

Greeting: _____ *Sung or said:* _____

Psalm or anthem: _____

Welcome: _____

Instrumental Music: _____

Installation: _____

Instrumental Music: _____

We Praise Thee/You are God (Te Deum laudamus), Glory be to God/Glory to God (Gloria in excelsis),

or other song of praise: _____

The Eucharist continues, beginning with the Salutation and the Collect of the Day.

Setting Apart for a Special Vocation

Use the check list for a Daily Office (novitiate) or for the Holy Eucharist (temporary, annual, or life vows).

A Service for the Ending of a Pastoral Relationship and Leave-Taking from a Congregation

Use the check list for the Holy Eucharist.